BOOKMAN'S HOLIDAY

by
Holbrook Jackson

★

BOOKMAN'S HOLIDAY

A recreation for booklovers

designed by

HOLBROOK JACKSON

London 1946

READERS UNION / FABER & FABER

I like books about books.—CHARLES LAMB

The utmost which we can reasonably hope or fear, is
to fill a vacant hour with prattle, and be forgotten.
—DR. JOHNSON

The measure of choosing well is, whether a man likes
what he has chosen.—SIR WILLIAM TEMPLE

*This volume is produced in 1946 in complete conformity with the
authorized economy standards. First published in 1945 by Faber and
Faber Limited, it has been set in Bell 10 on 12 point and reprinted at
Bristol by Western Printing Services Limited. It is one of the books
produced for sale to its members only by Readers Union Limited, of
38 William IV Street, London, and of Letchworth, Hertfordshire.
Particulars of Readers Union are obtainable from either of these
addresses*

PREFACE

This anthology shows what writers of books think of their predecessors, their contemporaries, and themselves. It is not meant to be a collection of entertaining or elegant extracts but a mosaic made up of selected pieces, mostly, I hope, entertaining, and some even elegant. The glimpses I have given of many authors —what they looked like, where and how they lived, how they worked, played, talked, dined, loved, quarrelled, and died—are intended to make a composite portrait of a writer of books. A portrait thus devised should naturally reflect the vitality of its component parts which, being taken mainly from letters and diaries and similar personal documents, must have retained some of their original spontaneity and have thus perpetuated some of the liveliness of unpremeditated art. That, at least, is the effect which the anthologist would like to have created by the arrangement of so varied an assortment of exhibits taken from such a variety of sources.

But the fate of books is on the knees of the gods. You can never be certain what may happen to them. Books written for children, as we know, are often enjoyed mainly by adults, just as works of science may survive as entertainments, and theology as art. *Bookman's Holiday* began as a recreation, which accounts for the title, but there can be no guarantee that it will have the good fortune to continue in that way, for even during the process of selection and classification the compiler could not help feeling that such an assemblage of self-revelatory passages might serve also, not a more useful, but a more purposeful purpose: ethnological, perhaps, psychological, certainly.

It should not be necessary for me to say that the compilation

Preface

aims at being representative rather than exhaustive. My aim has been to make a portrait, not a directory, and anyone familiar with literary memoirs should be able to cap many of the quotations and even to make a portrait of his own. For the privilege of adopting and adapting is one of the numerous benefactions conferred by writers upon readers, and every competent reader is tempted to re-write the book he is reading. I have tried, however, to use the less familiar passages, sometimes deliberately avoiding, without regret, even better known examples, because they are sure to swim into the mind of the reader as he ponders over what is quoted. Now and then I have 'fallen for' an old favourite such as Ben Jonson's *De Shakespeare Nostrati*, or one of Dr. Johnson's evergreen *obiter dicta*; but such citations, generally of fine gold, need no excuse and a new context may even throw a new and pleasing light upon an old theme. On a closer inspection it will be found also that writers who have been written off by common opinion as unprofitable dullards have yielded some amusing material. Thus Hannah More and Mrs. Hemans and the Rev. James Beattie become sprightly contributors to my theme, and sententious Anna Seward refreshingly apposite.

The portrait of a writer as represented in such a mosaic is inevitably partial. I find that on the whole I have leaned without conscious effort towards the happier phases of the writer's craft, even when its practitioners are most acrimonious. I am aware that there is, as we are too often reminded, a tragic side to authorship as to most other activities, especially in connection with the struggles for life and love; but on the whole writing is a gratifying trade, otherwise such sacrifices would not be made by those who follow it, and I think there is justification for preferring the oblique ray of comedy to the more insistent records of those bludgeonings of chance so beloved of our fashionable debunkers. My drinkers have stopped this side of dipsomania, and my lovers have loved, so far as they have revealed themselves in these pages, without undue self-pity.

The quotations are documented so that readers who wish may trace them to their sources, and the list of books used in making

Preface

the selections will be a further aid to such pleasant researches. The table of Contents will serve as a Subject Index, the Index proper thus becoming free to cover authors quoted or referred to in the text. I have used paragraph headings only where they seemed essential to clarity for I have assumed that readers of this kind of book are so fit in their bookmanship that they prefer to find things out rather than to have their discoveries anticipated for them. Spelling has been modernized, but I have not tampered with a writer's punctuation or his use of capitals or italics, except to italicize all book-titles and quotations in foreign languages; omissions are indicated by the usual method of three stops.

I have to thank the following authors, publishers, and literary executors for permitting me to quote from copyright works under their control:

Messrs. George Allen & Unwin Ltd for *Some Winchester Letters* by Lionel Johnson, and the *Letters of Ruskin* and Cook's *Life of Ruskin*; Messrs. Edward Arnold & Co. for the *Letters of George Birkbeck Hill*; The Society of Authors for the *Letters of Robert Louis Stevenson* and the *Letters of Katherine Mansfield*; Messrs. G. Bell & Sons Ltd for their editions of the *Correspondence of Jonathan Swift, The Journal to Stella*, the *Letters of P. B. Shelley*, the *Memoirs and Correspondence of Coventry Patmore*, and the *Diary of Fanny Burney*; Messrs. Ernest Benn Ltd for the *Letters of Edward Lear*; Messrs. A. & C. Black Ltd for the *Letters of Dr. John Brown*, and *Kate Greenaway* by Spielman and Lazard; The Syndics of the Cambridge University Press for the *Collected Letters of Oliver Goldsmith*; Messrs. Jonathan Cape Ltd for *Arnold Bennett* by Dorothy Cheston Bennett, and *A.E.H.* by Laurence Housman; Miss Dorothy Carleton for *My Diaries*, by Wilfrid Scawen Blunt; The Delegates of the Clarendon Press for the *Early Letters of William and Dorothy Wordsworth*, ed. E. de Selincourt, the *Supplement to the Letters of Horace Walpole*, ed. by Paget Toynbee, the *Life of F. York Powell* by Oliver Elton, and the *Letters of Robert Burns,* ed. by J. D. Ferguson; The Delegates of the Clarendon Press and the Yale University Press for the *American Notebooks* of Nathaniel Hawthorne; Messrs. Constable & Co. Ltd and Mr. A. C. Gissing for the *Letters of George Gissing to His Family*; Messrs. Constable & Co. Ltd and Messrs. Houghton Mifflin Co., Boston, U.S.A., for the *Journals of Emerson* and the *Letters of Charles Eliot Norton*; Messrs. Peter Davies Ltd for *Self-Portrait of Charles Ricketts R.A.*, by T. Sturge Moore and Cecil Lewis; Miss Violet Dickinson and Messrs. Macmillan & Co. Ltd for *Miss Eden's Letters*; Professor E. R. Dodds and Messrs. Constable & Co. Ltd for the *Journal and Letters of Stephen MacKenna*; Messrs. Gerald Duckworth & Co. Ltd for *Letters of Walter Savage Landor*, ed. Stephen Wheeler; Miss Eva Dugdale and Messrs. Macmillan & Co. Ltd for *The Later Years of Thomas Hardy* by Florence Emily Hardy; The Epworth Press for John Wesley's *Journal*; Viscount Esher for *Ionicus* by Reginald, Viscount Esher; Messrs. Faber & Faber Ltd for *A FitzGerald Friendship*; Messrs. Fisher, Dowson & Wasbrough and Messrs. Macmillan & Co. Ltd for *Tennyson: A Memoir by His Son*; Mr. E. M. Forster for *Goldsworthy Lowes Dickinson*; Messrs. Victor Gollancz Ltd for the *Life of George Moore*, by Joseph Hone, and *Bernard Shaw* by Frank Harris; Messrs. William Heinemann Ltd for *The Summing-Up* by W. Somerset Maugham, and *Life and Letters of Edward Thomas* by John Moore, *Arnold Bennett's Letters to His Nephew*, the *Letters of Algernon Charles Swinburne*; Messrs. Hutchinson & Co. Ltd for the *Life and Letters of George Wyndham*, J. W. Mackail and Guy Wyndham; Mr Geoffrey Keynes and Messrs. Jonathan Cape Ltd for *Letters between Samuel Butler and Miss E. M. A. Savage*; Messrs. John Lane, The Bodley Head Ltd for *New Letters of Jane WelshCarlyle, New Lettersof Thomas Carlyle*, the *Letters of Thomas Carlyle*, the *Letters of Miss Mitford*, and *Travels in England* by Richard le Gallienne; The Rt. Hon. Godfrey Locker-Lampson for Frederick Locker-Lampson's *My Confidences*; Messrs. Longmans Green & Co. Ltd for *Aubrey de Vere: A Memoir* by Wilfrid Ward; Messrs. Sampson Low Marston & Co. Ltd for the *Life and Letters*

Preface

of *Oliver Wendell Holmes*, ed. J. T. Morse; Messrs. Macmillan & Co. Ltd for the *Memoirs of Edward Burne-Jones* by Georgiana, Lady Burne-Jones; Messrs. Macmillan & Co. Ltd for the *Letters of William Cowper*, edited by Sir James G. Frazer, the *Journals of Dorothy Wordsworth*; Messrs. Methuen & Co. Ltd for *W. B. Donne and His Friends*; Mr. Louis Marlowe and Messrs. Chapman & Hall Ltd for *Welsh Ambassadors*; Mr. C. D. Medley for extracts from George Moore; Messrs. Methuen & Co. Ltd for the *Letters of Sir Walter Raleigh*; Sir Humphrey Milford and the Oxford University Press for the *Letters of Hartley Coleridge* and the *Groombridge Diary* by Dorothy Hale White; Mr. Guy Morley and Messrs. Macmillan & Co. Ltd for *Recollections by John, Viscount Morley*; Messrs. John Murray for the *Letters of Jane Welsh Carlyle to Her Family*, the *Biography of John Addington Symonds*, *The Letters of Benjamin Jowett*, and *Lord Byron's Letters and Diaries*, ed. by R. E. Prothero, and the *Letters and Diaries of John Bailey*; Messrs. Pearn, Pollinger & Higham Ltd and Messrs. William Heinemann Ltd for *Studies in Classic American Literature* and the *Letters of D. H. Lawrence*; Mr. Hesketh Pearson for the *Life of Frank Harris*; Mr. Michael Sadleir for *Trollope: A Commentary*; Mr. Bernard Shaw for *Man and Superman*, *The Irrational Knot*, and *Ellen Terry and Bernard Shaw: A Correspondence*; Sir Osbert Sitwell and Messrs. Macmillan & Co. Ltd for *Penny Foolish: A Book of Tirades and Panegyrics*; Mr. R. J. Stopford and Messrs. Macmillan & Co. Ltd for *Letters of John Richard Green*; the executrix of the late Mr. G. K. Chesterton and Messrs. Hutchinson & Co. Ltd for *Autobiography of G. K. Chesterton*; Mr. H. G. Wells for *Experiment in Autobiography*; and Messrs. Williams & Norgate for *New Letters of Edward FitzGerald*.

Finally, there are a few small or single quotations which I have ventured to use without formal acknowledgement, but the books from which they have been taken are included in the bibliography at the end of this volume. I trust that owners of copyrights will accept this general acknowledgement of my indebtedness, which also applies to a few instances of failure to trace the owners of

Preface

copyright. Should these be discovered, formal acknowledgement will be made in any further edition of this book which may be published.

I have also to thank Mr. Daniel George for the loan of books and for verifying references.

CONTENTS

11

Contents

OVERTURE

It is so pleasant to talk of oneself that one had almost rather talk of one's faults than not talk of oneself at all. HANNAH MORE to HORACE WALPOLE, 14 September 1793: *Memoirs* (1835), ii, 376.

Conceit is just as natural a thing to human minds as a centre is to a circle. Oliver Wendell Holmes, *Autocrat of the Breakfast Table* (1858), 9.

I desire you and all my friends will take a special care that my Disaffection to the world may not be imputed to my Age, for I have credible witnesses ready to depose, that it hath never varied from the twenty-first to the f—ty-eighth year of my life (pray fill that blank charitably)! I do not hate mankind, it is *vous autres* who hate them, because you have them reasonable Animals, and are angry at being disappointed: I have always rejected that definition, and made another of my own. I am no more angry with —— than I was with the Kite that last week flew away with one of my chickens; and yet I was pleased when one of my Servants shot him two days after. This, I say, because you are so hardy as to tell me of your intentions to write Maxims in opposition to Rochefoucault, who is my favourite, because I found my whole character in him; however, I will read him again, because it is possible that I may have since undergone some alterations. JONATHAN SWIFT to ALEXANDER POPE, 26 November 1725: *Works of Pope* (1753), ix, 45-6.

I am afraid to be popular. I see so many who write to the living, and deserve not to live, that I content myself with a resurrection when dead. AARON HILL to SAMUEL RICHARDSON, 1 April 1730: *Correspondence of Richardson* (1804), i, 3.

Those who know me at all, know that I have always been actuated by different principles from the rest of Mankind, and while none regarded the interests of his friends more, no man on earth regarded his own less. I have often affected bluntness to avoid the imputation of flattery, have frequently seem'd to overlook those merits too obvious to escape notice, and pretended disregard to those instances of good nature and good sense which I could not fail tacitly to applaud; and all this lest I should be rank'd among the grinning tribe who say very true to all that is said, who fill a vacant chair at a tea table whose narrow souls never moved in a wider circle than the circumference of a guinea, and who had rather be reckoning the money in your pocket than the virtue in your breast; all this, I say, I have done and a thousand other very silly, though disinterested things in my time, and for all which no soul cares a farthing about me. OLIVER GOLDSMITH to MRS. JANE LAWDER, 15 August 1758: *Collected Letters* (1928), 43–4.

About a fortnight ago the hurry of my winter business began; and, at the same time, my malady recurred with more violence than ever, rendering me at once incapable of reading, writing, and thinking. Luckily I am now a little better. . . . My hopes and my spirits begin to revive once more. I flatter myself I shall soon get rid of this infirmity; nay, that I shall ere long be in the way of becoming a *great man*. For have I not headaches, like Pope? vertigo, like Swift? grey hairs, like Homer? Do I not wear large shoes (for fear of corns), like Virgil? and sometimes complain of sore eyes (though not of *lippitude*), like Horace? Am I not at this present writing invested with a garment not less ragged than that of Socrates? Like Joseph the patriarch, I am a mighty dreamer of dreams; like Nimrod the hunter, I am an eminent builder of castles (in the air). I procrastinate, like Julius Caesar; and very lately, in imitation of Don Quixote, I rode a horse, lean, old, and lazy, like Rozinante. Sometimes, like Cicero, I write bad verses; and sometimes bad prose, like Virgil. This last instance I have on the authority of Seneca. I am of small stature, like Alexander the Great; I am somewhat inclined to fatness, like Dr. Arbuthnot and Aristotle; and I drink brandy and water, like Mr. Boyd. I might compare myself, in relation to many other infirmities, to many other *great men*; but if fortune is not influenced in my favour by the particulars already enumerated I shall despair of ever recommending myself to her good graces. JAMES BEATTIE to the HON. CHARLES BOYD, 16 November 1766: SIR WILLIAM FORBES, *Life* (1824), i, 82–3.

I am in a fair way of becoming as eminent as Thomas à Kempis or John Bunyan; and you may expect henceforth to see my birthday inserted among the wonderful events in the *Poor Robin's* and *Aberdeen Almanacks*, along with the black Monday and the battle of Bothwell Bridge. My Lord Glencairn and the Dean of Faculty, Mr. H. Erskine, have taken me under their wing; and by all probability I shall soon be the tenth worthy, and the eighth Wise man of the world. ROBERT BURNS to GAVIN HAMILTON, 7 December, 1786: *Letters* (1931), i, 55.

I am a compositor of an infinite variety of ingredients. I have been formed by a vast number of scenes of the most different natures, and I question if any uniform education could have produced a character so agreeable. JAMES BOSWELL, *Boswelliana* (1874), 233.

I am more famed in heaven for my works than I could well conceive. In my brain are studies and chambers filled with books and pictures of old, which I wrote and painted in ages of eternity before my mortal life; and those works are the delight and study of archangels. Why then should I be anxious about the riches and fame or mortality? The Lord our Father will do for us and with us according to His divine will. WILLIAM BLAKE to JOHN FLAXMAN, 21 September 1800: *Life* (1863), ii 21.

In morality, I prefer Confucius to the Ten Commandments, and Socrates to St. Paul (though the two latter agree in their opinion of marriage). In religion, I favour the Catholic emancipation, but do not acknowledge the Pope; and I have refused to take the sacrament, because I do not think eating bread or drinking wine from the hand of an earthly vicar will make me an inheritor of heaven. I hold virtue, in general, or the virtues severally, to be only in the disposition, each a *feeling*, not a principle. I believe truth the prime attribute of the Deity, and death an eternal sleep, at least of the body. You have here a brief compendium of the sentiments of the *wicked* George, Lord Byron. LORD BYRON to ROBERT CHARLES DALLAS, 21 January 1808: *Letters* (Everyman Ed. 1936), 11.

I feel every confidence that, if I choose, I may be a popular writer. That I will never be; but for all that I will get a livelihood. I equally dislike the favour of the public with the love of a woman. They are both a cloying treacle to the wings of Independence. I shall ever consider them . . . as debtors to me for verses not myself to them for admiration—which I can do without. I have of late been indulging my spleen by composing a preface AT them: after all resolving never to write a preface at all. 'There are so many verses', would I have said to them, 'give so much means for me to buy pleasure with, as a relief to my hours of labour.' You will observe at the end of this, if you put down the letter, 'How a solitary life engenders pride and egotism!' True—I know it does: but this pride and egotism will enable me to write finer things than anything else could—so I will indulge it. Just so much as I am humbled by the genius above my grasp am I exalted and look with hate and contempt upon the literary world. JOHN KEATS at Winchester to JOHN TAYLOR, 23 August 1819: *Works* (1901), v, 84.

I know there is within me something *different* from the vulgar herd of mortals; I think it is something *superior*; and if once I had overpassed those bogs and brakes and quagmires, that lie between me and the free arena, I shall make some fellows stand to the right and left—or I mistake me greatly. THOMAS CARLYLE to his brother ALEXANDER, 19 February 1821: *Early Letters* (1886), 155.

Overture

One day at a large party Wordsworth leaned forward to Sir Humphry Davy at a moment of silence, and said, 'Davy, do you know the reason I published my *White Doe* in quarto?' 'No,' said Davy, slightly blushing at the attention this awakened. 'To express my own opinion of it', replied Wordsworth. BENJAMIN ROBERT HAYDON, 23 March 1824: *Autobiography* (1853), ii, 82.

I have put an end to my ride of August, September, and October, 1826, during which I have travelled five hundred and sixty-eight miles, and have slept in thirty different beds, having written three monthly pamphlets, called the *Poor Man's Friend*, and have also written (including the present one) eleven *Registers*. I have been in three cities, in about twenty market towns, in perhaps five hundred villages; and I have seen the people nowhere so well off as in the neighbourhood of Weston Grove, and nowhere so badly off as in the dominions of the Select Vestry of Hurstbourn Tarrant, commonly called Uphusband. During the whole of this ride I have rarely been abed after daylight; I have drunk neither wine nor spirits. I have eaten no vegetables, and only a very moderate quantity of meat; and it may be useful to my readers to know that the riding of twenty miles was not so fatiguing to me at the end of my tour, as the riding of ten miles was at the beginning of it. Some ill-natured fools will call this 'egotism'. Why is it egotism? Getting upon a good strong horse and riding about the country has no merit in it; there is no conjuration in it; it requires neither talents nor virtues of any sort; but *health* is a very valuable thing; and when a man has had the experience which I have had, in this instance, it is his duty to state to the world, and to his own countrymen, and neighbours in particular, the happy effects of early rising, sobriety, abstinence, and a resolution to be active. WILLIAM COBBETT, 26 October 1826: *Rural Rides* (1912), ii, 204.

I am annoyed sometimes at being misconceived by meaner men —not as a poet, but as a man. My sorrows are not literary ones, but those of daily life. I pass through the world and meet with scarcely a response to the affectionateness of my nature . . . I go

out sometimes with my heart so full of yearning towards my
fellows that the indifferent look with which even entire strangers
pass me brings tears into my eyes. And then to be looked upon
by those who *do* know me (externally), as 'Lowell the poet'—it
makes me sick. Why not Lowell the man—the boy rather—as
Jemmy Lowell, as I was at school? JAMES RUSSELL LOWELL to
C. F. BRIGGS, 21 August 1845: *Letters* (1894), i, 111.

My actual life is a fact, in view of which I have no occasion to
congratulate myself; but for my faith and aspiration I have
respect. It is from these that I speak. Everyman's position is in
fact too simple to be described. I have sworn no oath. I have no
designs on society, or nature, or God. I am simply what I am, or
I begin to be that. I *live* in the *present*. I only remember the past,
and anticipate the future. I love to live. I love reform better than
its modes. There is no history of how bad became better. I believe something, and there is nothing else but that. I know that
I am. I know that another is who knows more than I, who takes
interest in me, whose creature, and yet whose kindred, in one
sense, am I. I know that the enterprise is worthy. I know that
things work well. I have heard no bad news. H. D. THOREAU,
27 March 1848: *Familiar Letters* (1894), 196.

One thing is certain . . . I shall have as many readers as I desire
to have in other times than ours. I shall dine late; but the dining-
room will be well-lighted, the guests few and select. I neither
am, nor ever shall be, popular. Such never was my ambition.
WALTER SAVAGE LANDOR to JOHN FORSTER, 1850: *Life* (1876),
500.

I wish critics would judge me as an *author*, not as a woman.
CHARLOTTE BRONTË to GEORGE HENRY LEWES, 19 January
1850: *Life* (1857), ii, 143.

My literary reputation is tabooed as worse than libertine in certain virtuous Societies . . . there have been meetings to banish
me from book-clubs. . . . And . . . Pater Familias has given Mr.
Mudie a very large bit of his petticoated mind concerning me.

Overture

George Meredith to the Rev. Augustus Jessopp, 20 December 1861: *Letters* (1912), i, 59.

I was born, I live, I shall die a peculiar man. . . . I wrote the first serious novels in English. I invented adultery, which didn't exist in the English novel till I began writing. . . . George Moore, *Life* (1936), 150, 373.

I

PORTRAITS

Ah, did you once see Shelley plain,
And did he stop and speak to you?
And did you speak to him again?
How strange it seems, and new!
      Robert Browning, 'Memorabilia',
            Men and Women (1855), xxvii.

THOMAS FULLER, D.D. He was of middle stature; strong set; curled hair; a very working head, in so much that, walking and meditating before dinner, he would eat up a penny loaf, not knowing that he did it. His natural memory was very great . . . he would repeat to you forwards and backwards all the signs from Ludgate to Charing Cross. JOHN AUBREY, 1680, *Brief Lives* (1898), i, 257.

EDMUND WALLER. Somewhat above a middle stature, thin body, not at all robust: fine thin skin, his face somewhat of an olivaster, his hair frizzed, of a brownish colour; full eye popping out and working; oval faced, his forehead high and full of wrinkles; his head but small, brain very hot and apt to be choleric. *Quanto doctior, eo iracundio.* Cicero. He is something majesterial, graceful elocution, and exceeding ready. JOHN AUBREY, *Ib.* ii, 277.

ALEXANDER POPE. Sir Joshua Reynolds once saw Pope. It was about the year 1740, at an auction of books or pictures. He remembers that there was a lane formed to let him pass freely through the assemblage, and he proceeded along bowing to those who were on each side. He was, according to Sir Joshua's account, about four feet six high; very humpbacked and deformed; he wore a black coat; and according to the fashion of that time, had on a little sword. Sir Joshua adds that he had a large and very fine eye, and a long handsome nose; his mouth had those peculiar marks which always are found in the mouths of crooked persons; and the muscles which run across the cheek were so strongly marked as to appear like small cords. EDWARD MALONE, 1791: *Life of Malone*, Prior (1860), 428–9.

DR. JOHNSON. That the most minute singularities which belonged to him, and made very observable parts of his appearance and manner, may not be omitted, it is requisite to mention, that while talking or even musing as he sat in his chair, he commonly held his head to one side towards his right shoulder, and shook it in a tremulous manner, moving his body backwards and forwards, and rubbing his left knee in the same direction, with the palm of his hand. In the intervals of articulating he made various sounds with his mouth, sometimes as if ruminating, or what is called chewing the cud, sometimes giving a half whistle, sometimes making his tongue play backwards from the roof of his mouth, as if clucking like a hen, and sometimes protruding it against his upper gums in front, as if pronouncing quickly under his breath, *too, too, too*: all this accompanied sometimes with a thoughtful look, but more frequently with a smile. Generally when he had concluded a period, in the course of a dispute, by which time he was a good deal exhausted by violence and vociferation, he used to blow out his breath like a Whale. This I suppose was a relief to his lungs; and seemed in him to be a contemptuous mode of expression, as if he had made the arguments of his opponent fly like chaff before the wind. JAMES BOSWELL, 1791: *Life of Johnson*, (1887), 485–6.

Mrs. & Miss Thrale, Miss Owen, and Mr. Seward came. . . . My sister Burney was invited to meet and play to them. The conversation was supported with a good deal of vivacity . . . for about half an hour, and then Hetty and *Sukey*, for the first time *in public*, played a duet; and in the midst of this performance Dr. Johnson was announced. He is, indeed, very ill-favoured; is tall and stout; but stoops terribly; he is almost bent double. His mouth is almost (constantly opening and shutting), as if he were chewing. He has a strange method of frequently twirling his fingers, and twisting his hands. His body is in continual agitation, *see-sawing* up and down; his feet are never a moment quiet; and, in short, his whole person is in *perpetual motion.* His dress, too, considering the times, and that he had meant to put on his *best becomes*, being engaged to dine in a large company, was as much out of the common road as his figure; he had a large wig, snuff-coloured coat, and gold buttons, but no ruffles to his shirt, (doughy fists, and black worsted stockings). He is shockingly near-sighted and did not, till she held out her hand to him, even know Mrs. Thrale. He *poked his nose* over the keys of the harpsichord, till the duet was finished, and then my father introduced Hetty to him as an old acquaintance, and he (cordially) kissed her! When she was a little girl, he had made her a present of *The Idler*. His attention, however, was not to be diverted five minutes from the books, as we were in the library; he pored over them, (shelf by shelf) almost touching the backs of them with his eyelashes, as he read their titles. At last, having fixed up one, he began, without further ceremony, to read (to himself,) all the time standing at a distance from the company. We were (all) very much provoked, as we perfectly languished to hear him talk; but it seems he is the most silent creature, when not particularly drawn out, in the world. FANNY BURNEY, 27 March 1777: *Diary* (1913), ii, 152.

WILLIAM WORDSWORTH. Mr. Wordsworth, in his person, is above the middle size, with marked features and an air somewhat stately and Quixotic. He reminds one of some of Holbein's heads: grave, saturnine, with a slight indication of sly humour, kept under by the manners of the age or by the pretensions of the person. He has a peculiar sweetness in his smile, and great depth and manliness and a rugged harmony in the tones of his voice. His manner of reading his own poetry is particularly imposing; and in his favourite passages his eye beams with preternatural lustre, and the meaning labours slowly up from his swelling breast. No one who has seen him at these moments could go away with an impression that he was a 'man of no mark or likelihood'. Perhaps the comment of his face and voice is necessary to convey a full idea of his poetry. His language may not be intelligible; but his manner is not to be mistaken. It is clear that he is either mad or inspired. WILLIAM HAZLITT, *The Spirit of the Age* (1825). *Works* (1932), xi, 91.

Wordsworth may be bordering on sixty; hard-featured, brown, wrinkled, with prominent teeth and a few scattered gray hairs, but nevertheless not a disagreeable countenance; and very cheerful, merry, courteous, and talkative, much more so than I should have expected from the grave and didactic character of his writing. CHARLES GREVILLE, *The Greville Memoirs* (1875), ii, 120.

S. T. COLERIDGE. At first I thought him very plain, that is, for about three minutes: he is pale and thin, has a wide mouth, thick lips, and not very good teeth, longish loose-growing half-curling rough black hair. But if you hear him speak for five minutes you think no more of them. His eye is large and full, not dark but grey; such an eye as would receive from a heavy soul the dullest expression; but it speaks every emotion of his animated mind; it has more of the 'poet's eye in a fine frenzy rolling' than I ever witnessed. He has fine dark eyebrows, and an overhanging forehead. DOROTHY WORDSWORTH, June 1797: *Early Letters of William and Dorothy Wordsworth* (1935), 168–9.

His forehead was broad and high, light as if built of ivory, with large projecting eyebrows, and his eyes rolling beneath them like a sea with darkened lustre. 'A certain tender bloom his face o'erspread,' a purple tinge as we see it in the pale thoughtful complexions of the Spanish portrait-painters, Murillo and Velazquez. His mouth was gross, voluptuous, open, eloquent; his chin good-humoured and round; but his nose, the rudder of the face, the index of the will, was small, feeble, nothing—like what he has done. It might seem that the genius of his face as from a height surveyed and projected him . . . into the world unknown of thought and imagination, with nothing to support or guide his veering purpose, as if Columbus had launched his adventurous course for the New World in a scallop, without oars or compass. . . . His person was rather above the common size, inclining to the corpulent, or like Lord Hamlet, 'somewhat fat and pursy'. WILLIAM HAZLITT, *The Liberal*, April 1823.

The good man, he was now getting old, towards sixty perhaps; and gave you the idea of a life that had been full of sufferings; a life heavy-laden, half-vanquished, still swimming painfully in seas of manifold physical and other bewilderment. Brow and head were round, and of massive weight, but the face was flabby and irresolute. The deep eyes, of a light hazel, were as full of sorrow as of inspiration; confused pain looked mildly from them, as in a kind of mild astonishment. The whole figure and air, good and amiable otherwise, might be called flabby and irresolute; expressive of weakness under possibility of strength. He hung loosely on his limbs, with knees bent, in stooping attitude; in walking, he rather shuffled than decisively stept; and a lady once remarked, he never could fix which side of the garden-walk would suit him best, but continually shifted, in corkscrew fashion, and kept trying both. A heavy-laden, high-aspiring and surely much-suffering man. His voice, naturally soft and good, had contracted itself into a plaintive snuffle and singsong; he spoke as if preaching—you would have said, preaching earnestly and also hopelessly the weightiest things. I still recollect his 'object' and 'subject', terms of continual recurrence in the Kantean province; and how he sung and snuffled them into 'om-m-mject' and 'sum-m-mject', with a kind of solemn shake or quaver, as he rolled along. No talk, in his century or any other, could be more surprising. THOMAS CARLYLE, *John Sterling* (1851), 71.

LEIGH HUNT. My first sight of Leigh Hunt . . . was in this wise. I, being at 17 or 18 years of age, or perhaps younger, an admirer of the *Indicator* and *Rimini*, set off with a letter from my Father, an old friend of the Poet, informing him of my ambition to see him. Arriving at his house, a very small one in a small square somewhere in the extreme west, after a walk of some five or six miles, I was informed that the poet was at home, and asked me to sit down until he came to me. This he did after I had waited in the little parlour at least two hours, when the door was opened and a most picturesque gentleman, with hair flowing nearly or quite to his shoulders, a beautiful velvet coat and a Vandyck collar of lace about a foot deep, appeared, rubbing his hands and smiling ethereally, and saying without a word of preface or notice of my having waited so long, 'This is a beautiful world, Mr. Patmore!' I was so struck by this remark that it has eclipsed all memory of what occurred during the remainder of my visit. COVENTRY PATMORE to EDMUND GOSSE, 6 February 1899: *Memoirs* (1900), i, 32–3.

SHELLEY. His figure was slight and fragile, and yet his bones and joints were large and strong. He was tall, but he stooped so much that he seemed of a low stature. His clothes were expensive, and made according to the most approved mode of the day; but they were tumbled, rumpled, unbrushed. His gestures were abrupt, and sometimes violent, occasionally even awkward, yet more frequently gentle and graceful. His complexion was delicate and almost feminine, of the purest red and white; yet he was tanned and freckled by exposure to the sun, having passed the autumn, as he said, in shooting. His features, his whole face, and particularly his head, were, in fact, unusually small; yet the last *appeared* of a remarkable bulk, for his hair was long and bushy, and in fits of absence, and in the agonies (if I may use the word) of anxious thought, he often rubbed it fiercely with his hands, or passed his fingers quickly through his locks unconsciously, so that it was singularly wild and rough. . . . His features were not symmetrical (the mouth, perhaps, excepted), yet was the effect of the whole extremely powerful. They breathed an animation, a fire, an enthusiasm, a vivid and preternatural intelligence, that I never met with in any other countenance. THOMAS JEFFERSON HOGG, 1858, *Life of Shelley* (1906), 46.

Portraits

JOHN KEATS. A loose, slack, not well-dressed youth met Mr. (Green) and myself in a lane near Highgate. (Mr. Green) knew him, and spoke. It was Keats. He was introduced to me and stayed a minute or so. After he had left us a little way, he came back and said: 'Let me carry away the memory, Coleridge, of having pressed your hand!'—'There is death in that hand,' I said to (Mr. Green), when Keats was gone; yet this was, I believe, before the consumption showed itself distinctly. S. T. COLERIDGE, *Table-Talk* (1874), 195.

GEORGE ELIOT. Her countenance was equine—she was rather like a horse; and her head had been intended for a much longer body—she was not a tall woman. She wore her hair in not pleasing, out-of-fashion loops, coming down on either side of her face, so hiding her ears; and her garments concealed her outline—they gave her a waist like a milestone. FREDERICK LOCKER-LAMPSON, 1869: *My Confidences* (1896), 307.

G. H. LEWES. His appearance is very peculiar, and indicates physical delicacy. He is very slightly built, his hands full of nervous expression as well as his face, and constantly used in gesticulation. His face is very plain, pitted with small-pox—dark, handsome, feeling eyes, but worn, and with a sadness and waywardness of expression that at times takes the place of the more than common sentiment. His nose and mouth are exceedingly irregular, and straggly, thin moustaches and beard, combined with long, ragged hair, guiltless of a brush, quite serve to de-Anglicize his appearance. A collar which, though white, was crumpled, was nearly hidden by a loose, slovenly black scarf, tied loosely and slipping round to one side. CHARLES ELIOT NORTON, 1868. *Letters* (1913), i, 308.

GEORGE BORROW. A tall, ungainly, uncouth man, with great physical strength, a quick penetrating eye, a confident manner, and a disagreeable tone and pronunciation. He was sitting on one side of the fire, and his old mother on the other. His spirits always sink in wet weather, and to-day was very rainy, but he was most courteous and not displeased to be a little lionized, for his delicacy is not of the most susceptible. CAROLINE FOX, 21 October 1843: *Memories of Old Friends* (1882), 184.

ALFRED TENNYSON. I think he must be under forty, not much under it. One of the finest looking men in the world. A great shock of rough dusky dark hair; bright, laughing, hazel eyes; massive aquiline face, most massive yet most delicate; of sallow brown complexion, almost Indian looking, clothes cynically loose, free-and-easy, smokes infinite tobacco. His voice is musical, metallic, fit for loud laughter and piercing wail, and all that may lie between; speech and speculation free and plenteous; I do not meet in these late decades such company over a pipe! THOMAS CARLYLE to RALPH WALDO EMERSON, *Correspondence* (1883).

AUBREY DE VERE. He entered the room swiftly and gracefully, the front of his body thrown a little forward, as is frequently the case with tall and active old men. His countenance bore a singular resemblance to the portraits of Wordsworth, although the type was softer and less vigorous. His forehead, which sloped a little, and was very high and domed, was much observed in the open air from a trick he had of tilting his tall hat back. . . . There was something extraordinarily delicate and elevated in his address. He was, in fact, conversation made visible. EDMUND GOSSE 1902, *Aubrey de Vere: a Memoir*, Ward (1904), 390.

THOMAS CARLYLE. A hearty laugher with discoloured teeth—very broad Scotch—talks not unlike his writing—unreserved—unaffected, of course—a leetle shy and awkward—but very likeable. W. H. BROOKFIELD to MISS ELTON (afterwards Mrs. Brookfield), 2 April 1841: *Mrs. Brookfield and her Circle* (1905), i, 88.

JOHN RUSKIN. John Ruskin, the Oxford Graduate, is a very elegant and distinguished-looking young man, tall, fair, and slender—too slender, for there is a consumptive look, and I fear a consumptive tendency—the only cause of grief that he has ever given to his parents. He must be, I suppose, twenty-six or twenty-seven, but he looks much younger, and has a gentle playfulness —a sort of pretty waywardness, that is quite charming. Miss Mitford to Charles Boner, September 1848, *Letters* (1925), 209–10.

Cardinal Newman. The most interesting part of my visit to Birmingham was a call I made by appointment on Cardinal Newman. He was benignly courteous, and we excellencied and eminenced each other by turns. A more gracious senescence I never saw. There was no 'monumental pomp', but a serene decay, like that of some ruined abbey in a woodland dell, consolingly forlorn. I was surprised to find his head and features smaller than I expected—modelled on lines of great vigour, but reduced and softened by a certain weakness, as if a powerfully masculine face had been painted in miniature by Malbone. He was very kindly and sympathetic—his benignity as well as his lineaments reminding me of the old age of Emerson. James Russell Lowell to C. E. Norton, 17 October 1884: *Letters* (1894), ii, 315–16.

Walt Whitman. He is apparently the greatest democrat the world has seen. Kings and Aristocracy go by the board at once, as they have long deserved to. A remarkably strong though coarse, nature, of a sweet disposition, and much prized by his friends. Though peculiar and rough in his exterior, his skin—all over—red, he is essentially a gentleman. I am still somewhat in a quandary about him,—feel that he is essentially strange to me, at any rate; but I am surprised by the sight of him. He is very broad, but, as I have said, not fine. He said that I misapprehended him. I am not quite sure that I do. He told us that he loved to ride up and down Broadway all day on an omnibus, sitting beside the driver, listening to the roar of the carts, and sometimes gesticulating and declaiming Homer at the top of his voice. H. D. Thoreau, 19 November 1856: *Essays and Other Writings* (Scott Library Ed.), 229.

Walt Whitman is a large man, six feet in height, broad of build, symmetrical, with an ineffable freedom evident even in these days of his broken physical fortunes. In years of health he weighed fully two hundred pounds. His head and face betray power and fortitude in high degree. . . . His complexion, while still fine, is nowadays somewhat paled; and yet it has the same marvellous purity and transparency which of old showed its unpolluted origin. The rosy pink tint of the skin, of body as of face, and the skin's peculiar softness and richness of texture, are unlike similar features of any man I have known. His eye is dull—one realizes how dull when he is seen sitting face to face with his friend Dr. Bucke, who has an eagle's orb. Twenty years, with their history of physical disaster, have dimmed and troubled his sight, and not infrequently, through painful symptoms, aroused a suspicion of impending eclipse. HORACE L. TRAUBEL, 1883: *In re Walt Whitman* (1893), 116.

MRS. BROWNING. Her physique was peculiar: curls like the pendent ears of a water-spaniel, and poor little hands—so thin that when she welcomed you she gave you something like the foot of a young bird; the Hand that made her great had not made her fair. But she had striking eyes, and we forgot any physical shortcomings—they were entirely lost sight of in what I may call her incomparable sweetness, I might almost say affectionateness; just as, while we are reading it, we lose sight of the incompleteness of her poetry—its lack of artistic control. She vanquishes by her genius and her charm. FREDERICK LOCKER-LAMPSON, *My Confidences* (1896), 157–8.

LONGFELLOW. I have been seeing a great deal of Longfellow, almost always between twelve and one at night, after his return from his parties, and while he was smoking his pipe before going to bed. He is a very fine-looking man, a little like H. Taylor in face, though with not as much either of beauty or of dignity. . . . It is not saying much for him to say that he has remained wholly unaffected by the great stir which people have made about him. AUBREY DE VERE to CHARLES SPRING RICE, 11 July 1868: *Memoir* (1904), 275.

MACAULAY. His general appearance is singularly commonplace. I cannot describe him better than by saying he has exactly that kind of face and figure which by no possibility would be selected, out of even a very small number of persons, as those of a remarkable personage. He is of middle height, neither above nor below it. The outline of his face in profile is rather good. The nose, very slightly aquiline, is well cut, and the expression of the mouth and chin agreeable. His hair is thick and silvery, and he looks a good deal older than many men of his years. . . . The face . . . seen in front, is blank, and as it were badly lighted. There is nothing luminous in the eye, nothing impressive in the brow. The forehead is spacious, but it is scooped entirely away in the region where benevolence ought to be, while beyond rise reverence, firmness, and self-esteem, like Alps on Alps. The under eyelids are so swollen as almost to close the eyes, and it would be quite impossible to tell the colour of those orbs, and equally so, from the neutral tint of his hair and face, to say of what complexion he had originally been. His voice is agreeable, and its intonations delightful, although that is so common a gift with Englishmen as to be almost a national characteristic. JOHN LOTHROP MOTLEY to his Wife, 30 May 1858: *Correspondence* (1889), i, 236–7.

THACKERAY. He has the appearance of a colossal infant, smooth, white, shiny, ringlety hair, flaxen, alas, with advancing years, a roundish face, with a little dab of a nose upon which it is a perpetual wonder how he keeps his spectacles, a sweet but rather piping voice, with something of the childish treble about it, and a very tall, slightly stooping figure—such are the characteristics of the great 'snob' of England. His manner is like that of everybody else in England,—nothing original, all planed down into perfect uniformity with that of his fellow-creatures. There was not much more distinction in his talk than in his white choker or black coat and waistcoat. JOHN LOTHROP MOTLEY to his Wife, 28 May 1858: *Correspondence* (1889), i, 229.

CHARLES DICKENS. He looks about the age of Longfellow. His hair is not much grizzled and is thick, although the crown of his head is getting bald. His features are good, the nose rather high, the eyes largish, greyish and very expressive. He wears a moustache and beard, and dresses at dinner in exactly the same uniform which every man in London or the civilized world is bound to wear, as much as the inmates of a penitentiary are restricted to theirs. I mention this because I had heard that he was odd and extravagant in his costume. I liked him exceedingly. We sat next each other at table, and I found him genial, sympathetic, agreeable, unaffected, with plenty of light easy talk and touch-and-go fun without any effort or humbug of any kind. JOHN LOTHROP MOTLEY to his Mother, 15 March 1861: *Correspondence* (1889), i, 365.

ANTHONY TROLLOPE. Hirsute and taurine of aspect, he would glare at you from behind two fierce spectacles. His ordinary tones had the penetrative capacity of two people quarrelling, and his voice would ring through and through you, and shake the windows in their frames, while all the time he was most amiably disposed towards you under his waistcoat. To me his *viso sciolto* and bluff geniality were very attractive, and so were his gusty denunciations, but most attractive of all was his unselfish nature. Literary men might make him their exemplar, as I make him my theme; for he may quite well have been the most generous man of letters, of mark, since Walter Scott. FREDERICK LOCKER-LAMPSON, *My Confidences* (1896), 332.

SWINBURNE. His appearance was very unusual and in some ways beautiful, for his hair was glorious in abundance and colour and his eyes indescribably fine. When repeating poetry he had a perfectly natural way of lifting them in a rapt, unconscious gaze, and their clear green colour softened by thick brown eyelashes was unforgettable: 'Looks commercing with the skies' expresses it without exaggeration. He was restless beyond words, scarcely standing still at all and almost dancing as he walked, while even in sitting he moved continually, seeming to keep time, by a swift movement of the hands at the wrists, and sometimes of the feet also, with some inner rhythm of excitement. He was courteous and affectionate and unsuspicious, and faithful beyond most people to those he really loved. The biting wit which filled his talk so as at times to leave his hearers dumb with amazement always spared one thing, that was an absent friend. GEORGIANA, LADY BURNE-JONES, 1860: *Memoirs of Edward Burne-Jones* (1904), i, 215.

HENRY JAMES. H. J. has shaved off his beard and is now clean-shaved, a rather stout, middle-aged man, with a large, regular, pale face, cold yet kind grey eyes, and something the look of a clever French priest in secular dress. He has a very hesitating yet decisive way of speaking—I mean the thought is decisive and the search for its expression gives one an impression of fastidious choice. ANNE DOUGLAS SEDGWICK, 23 May 1900: *Anne Douglas Sedgwick* (1936), 17.

G. K. CHESTERTON. I first beheld him on a Yorkshire moor far from his natural element, which is London. . . . He was staying at the house of a Bradford merchant adjoining the moor, and I was to meet him there. It was April, and raining. I trudged through the damp furze and heather up to the house only to find that the object of my pilgrimage had disappeared without leaving a trace behind him. No alarm was felt, as this was one of his habits. . . . Therefore I adjourned with the lady of the house and Mrs. Chesterton to an upper hall, where a noble latticed window commanded a wide vista of the moor. I peered into the wild, half hoping that I should first behold the great form of Gilbert Chesterton looming over the bare brown of the wold, silhouetted against the grey sky like the symbol of a new large faith. But G. K. C. did not fill the high horizon on the far wold, he did not burst upon our ken like a titan growing bigger as he came nearer. His coming was not melodramatic; it was, on the contrary, quite simple and quite characteristic. In fact, he did not come at all, rather was it that our eyes, and later our herald, went to him. For quite near to the house we espied him, hatless and negligently clad in a Norfolk suit of homespun, leaning in the rain against a budding tree, absorbed in the pages of a little red book. . . . He came into the house shortly afterwards and consumed tea

Portraits

and cake like any mortal and talked the talk of Olympus with the abandonment and irresistibility of a child. I found his largeness wonderfully proportionate, even, as is so rarely the case with massive men, to his head. He wears a tangled mass of light brown hair prematurely streaked with grey, and a slight moustache. His grey-blue eyes laugh happily as his full lips unload themselves of a constant flow of self-amused and piquant words. Like Dr. Johnson, whom he resembles so much in form, he is a great talker. But while I looked at him I was not reminded of the lexicographer, but of Balzac. And as his monologue rolled on and we laughed and wondered, I found myself carried away to a studio in France, where the head of Chesterton became one with the head of Rodin's conception of France's greatest literary genius. HOLBROOK JACKSON, *Romance and Reality* (1911), 140–2.

WILLIAM MORRIS. He is unlike any fancy picture which the imagination might draw of him. He is broad-shouldered, ruddy, wears blue shirt with no neck-tie and talks with great vehemence; oftentimes with a kind of put-on roughness I think —as if he meant to say, 'If you think that I am an Earthly-Paradisical creature with wings you are egregiously mistaken.' Nevertheless he was very interesting and humorous. MARK RUTHERFORD to MRS. COLENUTT, 21 April 1884: *Letters to Three Friends* (1924), 24.

CHARLOTTE BRONTË. Dark when I got to Windermere station; a drive along the level road to Low-wood; then a stoppage at a pretty house, and then a pretty drawing-room, in which were Sir James and Lady Kay Shuttleworth, and a little lady in a black-silk gown, whom I could not see at first for the dazzle in the room; she came up and shook hands with me at once. I went up to unbonnet, etc.; came down to tea; the little lady worked away and hardly spoke, but I had time for a good look at her. She is (as she calls herself) *undeveloped*, thin, and more than half a head shorter than I am; soft brown hair, not very dark; eyes (very good and expressive, looking straight and open at you) of the same colour as her hair; a large mouth, the forehead square,

33

broad and rather overhanging. She has a very sweet voice; rather hesitates in choosing her expressions, but when chosen they seem without an effort admirable, and just befitting the occasion; there is nothing overstrained, but perfectly simple. MRS. GASKELL, 1850: *Life of Charlotte Brontë* (1857), ii, 171.

D. H. LAWRENCE. I only met Lawrence once, when he and his wife were living in Tuscany. I was staying nearby and they asked my sister and myself to have tea with them; so we drove through the blossoming countryside—for it was high May—to his farmhouse. This square blue-painted house stood among gentle hills, with rather Japanese pines, springing from rocks and brown earth in the distance, and with the foreground sprinkled with bushes of cistus, flowering in huge yellow, white and purple paper roses. A few cypresses, the most slender of exclamation-marks—not robust, as they are further south—orchestrated the landscape. Lawrence opened the door to us, and it was the first time I had ever realised what a fragile and goatish little saint he was: a Pan and a Messiah: for in his flattish face, with its hollow, wan cheeks, and rather red beard, was to be discerned a curious but happy mingling of satyr and ascetic: qualities, too, which must really have belonged to him, since they are continually to be found in his work. It was, certainly, a remarkable appearance. Unlike the faces of most geniuses, it was the face of a genius. SIR OSBERT SITWELL, *Penny Foolish: a Book of Tirades and Panegyrics* (1935), 295–6.

II

SELF-PORTRAITS

I do not love great folks till they have pulled off their buskins and put on their slippers, because I do not care sixpence for what they would be thought, but for what they are. HORACE WALPOLE, 1764: *Letters* (1891), iv, 277.

SAMUEL RICHARDSON. I go thro' the Park once or twice a week to my little retirement; but I will for a week together be in it every day for three or four hours, at your command, till you tell me you have seen a person who answers to this description, namely, Short; rather plump than emaciated, notwithstanding his complaints: about five foot five inches: fair wig; lightish cloth coat, all black besides: one hand generally in his bosom, the other a cane in it, which he leans upon under the skirts of his coat usually, that it may imperceptibly serve him as a support, when attacked by sudden tremors or startings, and dizziness, which too frequently attack him, but, thank God, not so often as formerly: looking directly foreright, as passers-by would imagine, but observing all that stirs on either hand of him without moving his short neck; hardly ever turning back: of a light-brown complexion; teeth not yet failing him; smoothish faced, and ruddy cheeked; at sometimes looking to be about sixty-five, at other times much younger: a regular even pace, stealing away ground, rather than seeming to rid it: a gray eye, too often over-clouded by mistinesses from the head: by chance lively; very lively it will be, if he have hope of seeing a lady whom he loves and honours: his eye always on the ladies; if they have very large hoops, he looks down and supercilious, and as if he would be thought wise, but perhaps the sillier for that: as he approaches a lady, his eye is never fixed first upon her face, but upon her feet, and thence he raises it up, pretty quickly for a dull eye; and one would think (if we thought him at all worthy of observation) that from her air and (the last beheld) her face, he sets her down in his mind as *so* or *so*, and then passes on to the next object he meets; only then looking back, if he greatly likes or dislikes, as if he would see if the lady appear to be all of a piece, in the one light or in the other . . . from this odd, this grotesque figure, think you, Madam, that you have anything to apprehend? Any thing that will not rather promote than check your mirth? I dare be bold to say (and allow it too) that you would rather see this figure than any other you ever saw, whenever you should find yourself graver than you wish to be. SAMUEL RICHARDSON to LADY BRADSHAIGH, 1749: *Correspondence* (1804), iv, 290–2.

JAMES BOSWELL. I have given a little sketch of Dr. Johnson: my readers may wish to know a little of his fellow traveller. Think then, of a gentleman of ancient blood, the pride of which was his dominant passion. He was then in his thirty-third year, and had been about four years happily married. His inclination was to be a soldier; but his father, a respectable Judge, had pressed him into the profession of the law. He had travelled a good deal, and seen many varieties of human life. He had thought more than anybody supposed, and had a pretty good stock of learning and knowledge. He had all Dr. Johnson's principles, with some degree of relaxation. He had rather too little, than too much prudence; and, his imagination being lively, he often said things of which the effect was very different from the intention. He resembled sometimes

The best good man, with the worst natur'd muse.

He cannot deny himself the vanity of finishing with the encomium of Dr. Johnson, whose friendly partiality to the companion of his Tour represents him as one 'whose acuteness would help my enquiry, and whose gaiety of conversation, and civility of manner, are sufficient to counteract the inconvenience of travel, in countries less hospitable than we have passed'. JAMES BOSWELL,

Self-Portraits

18 August 1773: 'Tour to the Hebrides', *Boswell's Life of Johnson* (1887), v, 51–2.

JANE AUSTEN. I think I may boast myself to be, with all possible vanity, the most unlearned and uninformed female who ever dared to be an authoress. JANE AUSTEN, *Memoir*, J. E. Austen-Leigh (1871), 122.

CHARLES LAMB. Charles Lamb was born in the Inner Temple, 10 February 1775, educated in Christ's Hospital afterwards a clerk in the Accountants office East India House pensioned off from that service 1825 after 33 years service, is now a Gentleman at large, can remember a few specialities in his life worth noting except that he once caught a swallow flying (*testa sua manu*); below the middle stature, cast of face slightly Jewish, with no Judaic tinge in his complexional religion; stammers abominably and is therefore more apt to discharge his occasional conversation in a quaint aphorism or a poor quibble than in set and edifying speeches; has consequently been libelled as a person always aiming at wit, which, as he told a dull fellow that charged him with it, is at least as good as aiming at dullness; a small eater but not drinker; confesses a partiality for the production of the juniper berry, was a fierce smoker of Tobacco, but may be resembled to a volcano burnt out, emitting only now and then a casual puff. Has been guilty of obtruding upon the Public a Tale in Prose, called Rosamund Gray, a Dramatic Sketch named John Woodvil, a Farewell Ode to Tobacco, with sundry other Poems and light prose matter, collected in Two slight crown Octavos and pompously christened his Works, tho' in fact they were his Recreations and his true works may be found on the shelves of Leadenhall Street, filling some hundred Folios. He is also the true Elia whose Essays are extant in a little volume published a year or two since; and rather better known from that name without a meaning, than from anything he has done or can hope to do in his own. He also was the first to draw the Public attention to the old English Dramatists in a work called 'Specimens of English Dramatic Writers who lived about the time of Shakespeare', published about 15 years since. In short all his merits and demerits to set forth would take to the end of Mr. Upcott's book and then not be told truly. He died much lamented. Witness his hand, CHARLES LAMB. 10th April 1827. *Miscellaneous Prose* (1912), 375–6.

JOHN RUSKIN. They've been doing photographs of me again, and I'm an orang outang as usual, and am in despair. I thought with my beard I was beginning to be just the least bit nice to look at. I would give up half my books for a new profile. JOHN RUSKIN, *Hortus Inclusus* (1887), 112–13.

WALT WHITMAN. An American bard. . . . One of the roughs, large, proud, affectionate, eating, drinking, and breeding, his costume manly and free, his face sunburnt and bearded, his posture strong and erect, his voice bringing hope and prophecy to the generous races of young and old. WALT WHITMAN, 'Walt Whitman and His Poems', 1856: *In re Walt Whitman* (1893), 13.

GEORGE BERNARD SHAW. Some day, when you have two hours to spare, you must let me read *Candida* to you. You will find me a disagreeably cruel-looking middle-aged Irishman with a red beard; but that cannot be helped. GEORGE BERNARD SHAW to ELLEN TERRY, 6 April 1896: *Ellen Terry and Bernard Shaw: A Correspondence* (1931), 29.

ARNOLD BENNETT. As a *man*, I should be disgusted if I could not earn plenty of money and the praise of the discriminating. ARNOLD BENNETT, *Journals* (1932), 30.

D. H. LAWRENCE. I live in pyjamas, barefoot, all day: lovely hot days of bright sun and sea, but a cool wind through the straits. We do our own work—I prefer it, can't stand people about: so when the floors must be washed (gently washed merely) or when I must put my suit of pyjamas in the tub, behold me, *in puris naturalibus*, performing the menial labours of the day. It is very nice to shed so much. D. H. LAWRENCE in Taormina to DOUGLAS GOLDRING, 20 July 1920: *Letters* (1932), 508–9.

III

MINIATURES

SHAKESPEARE. A handsome, well-shaped man: very good company, and of a ready and pleasant and smoothe wit. JOHN AUBREY, 1680: *Brief Lives* (1898), ii, 225.

FRANCIS BACON. He had a delicate, lively, hazel eye . . . like the eye of a viper. JOHN AUBREY, *Ib.* i, 72.

JOHN SELDEN. He was very tall, I guess about 6 foot high; sharp oval face; head not very big; long nose inclining to one side; full popping eye (gray). JOHN AUBREY, *Ib.* ii, 223.

SIR JOHN SUCKLING. He was of middle stature and slight strength, brisk round eye, reddish face and red nose (ill liver), his head not very big, his hair a kind of sand colour, his beard turned-up naturally, so that he had [a] brisk and graceful look. JOHN AUBREY, *Ib.* ii, 242.

RICHARD LOVELACE. A most beautiful gentleman. . . . One of the handsomest men in England. . . . He was an extraordinary handsome man, but proud. JOHN AUBREY, *Ib.* ii, 37.

THOMAS GRAY. A little man of very ungainly appearance. HORACE WALPOLE, *Walpoliana* (1800), 68.

MARTIN TUPPER. A happy, little, blue-eyed man, who evidently enjoys talking, but does not approach the dignity of his didactic poem. CAROLINE FOX, 20 June 1856: *Memories of Old Friends* (1882), 307.

LEIGH HUNT. A pretty man . . . with the airiest kindly style of sparkling talk wanting only wisdom of a sound kind, and true insight into fact. Thomas Carlyle, *Reminiscences* (1881), ii, 174.

Henry David Thoreau. He is as ugly as sin, long-nosed, queer-mouthed, and with uncouth and somewhat rustic, although courteous manners, corresponding very well with such an exterior. But his ugliness is of an honest and agreeable fashion, and becomes him much better than beauty. Nathaniel Hawthorne, September 1842: *American Notebooks* (1932), 166.

James Anthony Froude. His face exhibits the cynical insincerity of his disposition. Charles Eliot Norton, 1873: *Letters* (1913), 461.

Edward Gibbon. An ugly, affected, disgusting fellow, and poisons our literary Club to me. James Boswell to Rev. W. J. Temple, 8 May 1779: *Letters* (1857), 242.

Matthew Arnold. A Detroit newspaper compared me, as I stooped now and then to look at my manuscript on a music stool, to 'an elderly bird pecking at grapes on a trellis'. Matthew Arnold to his younger daughter, 21 January 1884: *Letters* (1895), ii, 254.

Richard Monckton Milnes (Lord Houghton). Fat, easy, affable, and obliging. Ralph Waldo Emerson, *Journals* (1914), vii, 483

Wilkie Collins. A little man, with black hair, large white forehead, large spectacles, and small features. He is very unaffected, vivacious, and agreeable. J. L. Motley, *Correspondence* (1889), i, 302.

IV

CARICATURES

The London Literati *appear to me to be very much like little potatoes, that is . . . a compost of nullity and dullity.* S. T. Coleridge to Robert Southey, 1797: *Letters* (1895), i, 224.

DR. JOHNSON. Johnson gives you a forcible hug, and shakes laughter out of you, whether you will or no. DAVID GARRICK, 1773: *Boswell's Life of Johnson* (1887), ii, 231.

JAMES BOSWELL. An ungrateful impudent man . . . capable of insulting any person who cannot inflict the punishment of corporal correction. Defenceless against such a being is every woman, who has neither father nor brother to awe the assailant. ANNA SEWARD, *Letters* (1811), iii, 353.

REV. JAMES GRANGER. The dog is a Whig. I do not like much to see a Whig in any dress; but I hate to see a Whig in a parson's gown. BOSWELL, 25 September 1773: 'Tour to the Hebrides', *Boswell's Life of Johnson* (1887), v, 255.

RICHARD BRINSLEY SHERIDAN. He had a Bardolph countenance, with heavy features, but his eye possessed the most distinguished brilliancy. SIR WALTER SCOTT, 13 January 1826: *Journal* (1890), i, 81.

ROBERT SOUTHEY. Southey was what you call a cold man. He was never happy except when reading a book or making one. Coleridge once said to me, 'I can't *think* of Southey, without seeing him either mending or using a pen.' SAMUEL ROGERS, *Table Talk* (1856), 206.

S. T. COLERIDGE. A puffy, anxious, obstructed-looking, fattish old man, hobbled about with us, talking with a kind of solemn emphasis on matters which were of no interest (and even *reading* pieces in *proof* of his opinions thereon). THOMAS CARLYLE, *Reminiscences* (1881), ii, 131.

SAMUEL ROGERS. An ugly little man, a wrinkled Maecenas. FREDERICK LOCKER-LAMPSON, *My Confidences* (1896), 98.

MATTHEW ARNOLD. The great Matthew looks at the Universe —and for that part at God—*through an eye-glass*, one eye shut, and a supreme air. DR. JOHN BROWN to SIR THEODORE MARTIN, 6 January 1882: *Letters* (1907), 277.

CHARLES LAMB. Not genius, but diluted insanity. THOMAS CARLYLE. *New Letters and Memorials of Jane Welsh Carlyle* (1903), i, 35.

LORD HOUGHTON. I had a pleasant journey out, (to Montreal) travelling with some rather nice people; also with old Lord Houghton from whom I won 26s. at whist on various nights. We had service on board on Sunday. I accompanied the chants and hymns on the piano, and old Lord Houghton warbled 'Rock of Ages' in a very edifying manner. Mrs. Eustace Smith who was also on board with her husband, the member for N. Shields (I think) assured me that Lord H. is the most 'horrid old reprobate—oh, *horrid, horrid,* I assure you' so I liked hearing him sing 'Rock of Ages'. SAMUEL BUTLER, 1875: *Letters between Samuel Butler and Miss E. M. A. Savage* (1935), 107–8.

JOHN STUART MILL. Disraeli, when Mill made an early speech in Parliament, raised his eyeglass, and murmured to a neighbour on the bench, 'Ah, the Finishing Governess'. JOHN, VISCOUNT MORLEY, *Recollections* (1917), i, 55.

EDWARD BULWER-LYTTON. A woman of genius enclosed . . . in a man's form. HARRIET MARTINEAU, *Autobiography* (1877), i, 353.

MACAULAY. A tumid even a flatulent man . . . not one of the

immortals. Dr. John Brown to Coventry Dick, 1849: *Letters* (1907), 74.

Macaulay. A book in breeches. . . . He has occasional flashes of silence, that makes his conversation perfectly delightful. Sydney Smith, *Memoir,* (1865), 363.

Mr. and Mrs. Carlyle. It was very good of God to let Carlyle and Mrs. Carlyle marry one another and so make only two people miserable instead of four, besides being very amusing. Samuel Butler, 1884: *Letters between Samuel Butler and Miss E. M. A. Savage* (1935), 349–50.

Walter Pater. I always think of him as a soft, kind cat; he purred so persuasively that I lost the sense of what he was saying. Jane Harrison, *Reminiscences* (1925), 46.

George Meredith. A queer voluble creature, with a play-acting voice, and his conversation like one dictating to a secretary, a constant search for epigrams. Wilfrid Scawen Blunt, 1894: *My Diaries* (1910), i, 143.

George Moore. Very tall and very blond, with a long colourless face that looked like a codfish crossed by a satyr. Gertrude Atherton, *Life of George Moore,* Hone (1936), 158.

V

CHARACTERS

What is character but the determination of incident? What is incident but the illustration of character? Henry James, 'The Art of Fiction', *Partial Portraits* (1888), 392.

DE SHAKESPEARE NOSTRATI. I remember the players have often mentioned it as an honour to Shakespeare, that in his writing (whatsoever he penn'd), he never blotted out a Line. My answer hath been, 'Would he had blotted out a thousand', which they thought a malevolent speech. I had not told posterity this but for their ignorance, who chose that circumstance to commend their friend by, wherein he most faulted. And to justify mine own candour, for I loved the man, and do honour his memory on this side idolatry as much as any. He was, indeed, honest, and of an open and free nature; had an excellent phantasy, brave Notions, and gentle Expressions, wherein he flow'd with that facility that sometimes it was necessary it should be stopped. *Sufflaminandus erat*, as Augustus said of Haterius. His Wit was in his own Power; would the rule of it had been so, too. Many times he fell into those things, could not escape laughter, as when he said in the person of Caesar, one speaking to him, *Caesar, thou dost me wrong*. He replied, *Caesar did never wrong, but with just cause*; and such like, which were ridiculous. But he redeemed his vices with his virtues. There was ever more in him to be praised than to be pardoned. BEN JONSON, *Timber* (1641).

SAMUEL PEPYS. A very worthy, industrious and curious person, none in England exceeding him in knowledge of the navy, in which he had passed through all the most considerable offices,

Clerk of the Acts and Secretary of the Admiralty, all which he performed with great integrity. When King James II went out of England, he laid down his office, and would serve no more; but withdrawing himself from all public affairs, he lived in Clapham with his partner, Mr. Hewer, formerly his clerk, in a very noble house and sweet place, where he enjoyed the fruit of his labours in great prosperity. He was universally beloved, hospitable, generous, learned in many things, skilled in music, a very great cherisher of learned men of whom he had the conversation. His library and collection of other curiosities were of the most considerable, the models of ships especially. Besides what he published of an account of the navy, as he found and left it, he had for divers years under his hand the History of the Navy, or *Navalia*, as he called it; but how far advanced, and what will follow of his, if left, I suppose, to his sister's son, Mr Jackson, a young gentleman, whom Mr. Pepys educated in all sorts of useful learning, sending him to travel abroad, from whence he returned with extraordinary accomplishments, and worthy to be heir. Mr. Pepys had been for near forty years so much my particular friend, that Mr. Jackson sent me complete mourning, desiring me to be one to hold up the pall at his magnificent obsequies; but my indisposition hindered me from doing him this last office. JOHN EVELYN, 26 May 1703: *Diary* (1908), 456–7.

HENRY FIELDING. I am sorry for H. Fielding's death, not only as I shall read no more of his writings, but I believe he lost more than others, as no man enjoyed life more than he did, though few had less reason to do so, the highest of his preferment being raking in the lowest sinks of vice and misery. I should think it a nobler and less nauseous employment to be one of the staff-officers than conduct the nocturnal weddings. His happy constitution (even when he had, with great pains, half demolished it) made him forget everything when he was before a venison pasty, or over a flask of champagne, and I am persuaded he has known more happy moments than any prince upon the earth. His natural spirits gave him rapture with his cook-maid, and cheerfulness when he was fluxing in a garret. There was a great similitude between his character and that of Sir Richard Steele. He had the advantage both in learning and, in my opinion, genius; they both agreed in wanting money in spite of all their friends, and would have wanted it, if their hereditary lands had been as extensive as their imaginations; yet each of them was so formed for happiness, it is a pity he was not immortal. LADY MARY WORTLEY MONTAGU to the COUNTESS OF BUTE, 22 September 1755: *Letters and Works* (1837), iii, 120–1, 459.

OLIVER GOLDSMITH. A poor fretful creature, eaten up with affectation and envy. He was the only person I ever knew who acknowledged himself to be envious. In Johnson's presence he was quiet enough; but in his absence expressed great uneasiness in hearing him praised. He envied even the dead; he could not bear that Shakespeare should be so much admired as he is. There might, however, be something like magnanimity in envying Shakespeare and Dr. Johnson; as in Julius Caesar's weeping to think that at an age at which he had done so little, Alexander should have done so much. But surely Goldsmith had no occasion to envy me; which, however, he certainly did, for he owned it (though, when we met, he was always very civil); and I received undoubted information that he seldom missed an opportunity of speaking ill of me behind my back. Goldsmith's common conversation was a strange mixture of absurdity and silliness; of silliness so great, as to make me sometimes think that he affected it. Yet he was a genius of no mean rank: somebody, who knew him well, called him *an inspired idiot*. DR. BEATTIE to SIR WILLIAM FORBES, 10 July 1788: *Life and Writings*, (1824), ii, 220.

JAMES BOSWELL. From his open, communicative, good-humoured variety, which leads him to display events and feelings that other men, of more frequent, though slighter pretensions, would have studiously concealed, he depressed himself below his just level in public estimation. His information is extensive; his talents far from despicable, and he seems so exactly *adapted*, even by his very foibles, that we might almost suppose him purposely created to be the chronicler of Johnson. THOMAS GREEN, 29 September 1796: *Extracts from the Diary of a Lover of Literature* (1810), 6.

TOM MOORE. A delightful, gay, voluptuous, refined, natural creature; infinitely more unaffected than Wordsworth; not blunt and uncultivated like Chantrey, or bilious and shivering like Campbell. No affectation, but a true, refined, delicate, frank poet, with sufficient air of the world to prove his fashion, and sufficient honesty of manner to show fashion has not corrupted his native tastes; making allowance for prejudices instead of condemning them, by which he seemed to have none himself; never talking of his own works, from intense consciousness that everybody else did, while Wordsworth is always talking of his own productions from apprehension that they are not enough matter of conversation. Men must not be judged too hardly; success or failure will either destroy or better the finest natural parts. BENJAMIN ROBERT HAYDON, *Autobiography* (1853), ii, 81–2.

WALTER SAVAGE LANDOR. One of the most extraordinary men that it has ever been my fortune to fall in with, and one who would be one of the greatest, if it were possible to tame him. ROBERT SOUTHEY to JOHN RICKMAN, 18 January 1809: *Letters* (1856), ii, 119.

JOHN KEATS. In fireside conversation he was weak and inconsistent, but he was in his glory in the fields. The humming of a bee, the sight of a flower, the glitter of the sun, seemed to make his nature tremble; then his eyes flashed, his cheek glowed, his mouth quivered. He was the most unselfish of human creatures; unadapted to this world, he cared not for himself, and put himself to any inconvenience for the sake of his friends. He was haughty, and had a fierce hatred of rank; but he had a kind gentle heart, and would have shared his fortune with any man who wanted it. His classical knowledge was inconsiderable, but he could feel the beauties of the classical writers. He had an exquisite sense of humour, and too refined a notion of female purity to bear the little sweet arts of love with patience. He had no decision of character, and having no object upon which to direct his great powers, was at the mercy of every petty theory ———'s ingenuity might start. BENJAMIN ROBERT HAYDON, 29 March 1821: *Autobiography* (1853), iii, 9–11.

SIR WALTER SCOTT. There is one part of your observations in the pamphlet which I shall venture to remark upon;—it regards Walter Scott. You say that 'his character is little worthy of enthusiasm', at the same time you mention his productions in the manner they deserve. I have known Walter Scott long and well, and in occasional situations which call forth the *real* character— and I can assure you that his character *is* worthy of admiration— that of all men he is the most *open*, the most *honourable*, and most amiable. With his politics I have nothing to do: they differ from mine, which renders it difficult for me to speak of them. But he is *perfectly sincere* in them; and Sincerity may be humble, but she cannot be servile. I pray you, therefore, to correct or soften that passage. You may, perhaps, attribute this officiousness of mine to a false affectation of *candour*, as I happen to be a writer also. Attribute it to what motive you please, but *believe* the *truth*. I say that Walter Scott is as nearly a thorough good man as man can be, because I *know* it by experience to be the case. LORD BYRON to HENRI BEYLE (Stendhal), 29 May 1823: *Letters* (1901), vi, 220.

BYRON. In talents he was unequalled, and his faults were those rather of a bizarre temper arising from an eager and irritable nervous habit, than any depravity of disposition. He was devoid of selfishness, which I take to be the basest ingredient in the human composition. He was generous, humane, and noble-minded, when passion did not blind him. The worst I ever saw about him was that he rather liked indifferent company, than that of those with whom he must from character and talent have necessarily conversed more upon an equality. I believe much of his affected misanthropy, for I never thought it real, was founded upon instances of ingratitude and selfishness experienced at the hands of those from whom better could not have been expected. SIR WALTER SCOTT to LADY ABERCORN, 4 June 1824: *Letters* (1894), ii, 205–6.

WORDSWORTH AND SOUTHEY. I am just come from breakfasting
with Henry Taylor to meet Wordsworth; the same party as
when he had Southey—Mill, Elliot, Charles Villiers. Wordsworth may be bordering on sixty; hard-featured, brown,
wrinkled, with prominent teeth and a few scattered grey hairs,
but nevertheless not a disagreeable countenance; and very cheerful, merry, courteous, and talkative, much more so than I should
have expected from the grave and didactic character of his writings. He held forth on poetry, painting, politics, and metaphysics, and with a great deal of eloquence; he is more conversible
and with a greater flow of animal spirits than Southey. He mentioned that he never wrote down as he composed, but composed
walking, riding, or in bed, and wrote down after; that Southey
always composes at his desk. CHARLES C. F. GREVILLE, 25 February 1831: *The Greville Memoirs* (1875), ii, 120.

COLERIDGE. When I heard of the death of Coleridge, it was
without grief. It seemed to me that he long had been on the con-
fines of the next world,—that he had a hunger for eternity. I
grieved then that I could not grieve. But since, I feel how great
a part he was of me. His great and dear spirit haunts me. I cannot think a thought, I cannot make a criticism on men or books,
without an ineffectual turning and reference to him. He was the
proof and touchstone of all my cogitations. He was a Grecian (or
in the first form) at Christ's Hospital, where I was deputy
Grecian; and the same subordination and deference to him I have
preserved through a life-long acquaintance. Great in his writings,
he was greatest in his conversation. In him was disproved that
old maxim, that we should allow every one his share of talk. He
would talk from morn to dewy eve, nor cease till far midnight,
yet who ever would interrupt him,—who would obstruct that
continuous flow of converse, fetched from Helicon or Zion? He
had the tact of making the unintelligible seem plain. Many who
read the abstruser parts of his *Friend* would complain that his
works did not answer to his spoken wisdom. They were identical.
But he had a tone in oral delivery, which seemed to convey sense

to those who were otherwise imperfect recipients. He was my fifty-years old friend without a dissension. Never saw I his likeness, nor probably the world can see again. I seem to love the house he died at more passionately than when he lived. I love the faithful Gilmans more than while they exercised their virtues towards him living. What was his mansion is consecrated to me a chapel. CHARLES LAMB, 21 October 1834: *Miscellaneous Prose* (1912), 406–7.

EDWARD FITZGERALD. His life and conversation are the most perfectly philosophic of any I know. They approach in grand quiescence to some of the marvels of contentment in *Plutarch*. He is Diogenes without his dirt. He confesses to so much ease, as to make it a question whether since he cannot find, he should not create for himself some salutary trouble, and consults me if he should marry, or open a Banker's Book. I advise him however to let well alone. W. B. DONNE to R. C. TRENCH, 16 December 1836: *W. B. Donne and his Friends* (1905), 24.

TENNYSON. Carlyle went to dine at Mr. Chadwick's the other day and I not being yet equal to a dinner altho' I was asked to 'come in a blanket and stay all night'! had made up my mind for a nice long quiet evening of *looking into the fire*, when I heard a carriage drive up, and men's voices asking questions, and then the carriage was sent away! and the men proved to be Alfred Tennyson of all people and his friend Mr. Moxon—Alfred lives in the country and only comes to London rarely and for a few days so that I was overwhelmed with the sense of Carlyle's misfortune in having missed the man he likes best, for stupid Chadwicks, especially as he had gone against his will at *my* earnest persuasion. Alfred is dreadfully embarrassed with women alone —for he entertains at one and the same moment a feeling of almost adoration for them and an ineffable contempt! adoration I suppose for what they *might be*—contempt for what they *are*! The only chance of my getting any right good of him was to make him forget my womanness—so I did just as Carlyle would have done, had he been there; got out *pipes* and *tobacco*—and *brandy and water*—with a deluge of *tea* over and above.—The effect of these accessories was miraculous—he *professed* to be *ashamed* of polluting my room, 'felt', he said, 'as if he were stealing cups and sacred vessels in the Temple'—but he smoked on all the same—for *three* mortal hours!—talking like an angel— only exactly as if he were talking with a clever *man*—which— being a thing I am not used to—men always *adapting* their conversation to what they *take to be* a woman's taste—strained me to a terrible pitch of intellectuality. JANE WELSH CARLYLE to HELEN WELSH, 31 January 1845: *Letters to her Family*, 1839–1863 (1924), 230.

EMERSON. He came to Oxford just at the end of Lent term, and stayed three days. Everybody liked him, and as the orthodox mostly had never heard of him, they did not suspect him; he is the quietest, plainest, unobtrusivest man possible; will talk, but will rarely *discourse* to more than a single person, and wholly declines 'roaring'. He is very Yankee to look at, lank and sallow, and not quite without the twang; but his looks and voice are pleasing nevertheless, and give you the impression of perfect intellectual cultivation, as completely as would any great scientific man in England—Faraday or Owen for instance, more in their way perhaps than in that of Wordsworth or Carlyle. I have been with him a great deal; for he came over to Paris and was there a month, during which we dined together daily; and since that I have seen him often in London, and finally here. One thing that struck everybody is that he is much less Emersonian than his Essays. There is no dogmatism or arbitrariness or positiveness about him. ARTHUR HUGH CLOUGH to T. ARNOLD, 16 July 1848: *Letters and Remains* (1865), i, 116.

BENJAMIN ROBERT HAYDON. The vulgar idea of a man of genius. He had all the morbid peculiarities which are supposed by fools to belong to intellectual superiority—eccentricity, jealousy, caprice, infinite disdain for other men; and yet he was as poor, commonplace a creature as any in the world. He painted signs, and gave himself more airs than if he had painted the Cartoons.

. . . Whether you struck him or stroked him, starved him or fed him, snapped at your hand in just the same way. He would beg you in piteous accents to buy an acre and a half of canvas that he had spoiled. Some good-natured lord asks the price. Haydon demands a hundred guineas. His lordship gives the money out of mere charity, and is rewarded by some such entry as this in *Haydon's Journal*: 'A hundred guineas, and for such a work! I expected that, for very shame, he would have made it a thousand. But he is a mean and sordid wretch.' In the meantime the purchaser is looking out for the most retired spot in his house to hide the huge daub which he has bought, for ten times its value, out of mere compassion. T. B. MACAULAY, 11 July 1853: *Life*, Trevelyan (1876), ii, 355–6.

SAMUEL ROGERS. I suppose no man ever was so much attended to and thought of, who had so slender a fortune and such calm abilities. I am sure you will know what I mean: no man ever seemed so important, who did so little, aye, and said so little, (in spite of table-talk) for his fellowmen. His God was Harmony; and over his life Harmony presided, sitting on a lukewarm cloud. He was *not* 'the poet, sage, and philosopher' people expect to find he was, but a man in whom the tastes (rare fact!) preponderated over the passions; who defrayed the expenses of his tastes as other men make outlay for the gratification of their passions; all within limit of reason, he did not squander more than won the affection of his seraglio, the Nine Muses, nor bet upon Pegasus, though he entered him for the races when he had a fair chance of winning. He did nothing rash. I am sure Rogers as a baby never fell down, *unless he was pushed*; but walked from chair to chair of the drawing-room furniture steadily and quietly till he reached the place where the sunbeam fell on the carpet. He must always have preferred a lullaby to the merriest game of romps; and if he could have spoken would have begged his long-clothes might be made of fine *Mull* muslin instead of cambric or jacquenet, the first fabric being of incomparable softness, and the two latter capable of that which he loathed, *starch*. He was the very embodiment of quiet, from his voice to the last harmonious little picture that hung in his lulled room, and a curious figure he seemed—an elegant, pale watch-tower, showing for ever what a quiet port literature and the fine arts might offer, in an age of 'progress', when every one is tossing, struggling, wrecking, and foundering on a sea of commercial speculation or political adventure. MRS. NORTON to ABRAHAM HAYWARD, 8 May 1856: *Mr. Hayward's Letters* (1886), i, 286–7.

ELIZABETH BARRETT BROWNING. Of your liking Miss Barrett's marvellous work I am still more certain . . . and recollect that they are the production of a lovely graceful girl, timid as a fawn, whose hands tremble in yours, and whose beautiful eyes fill with tears as you speak to her, seems to me to bring together two things which seem incompatible—youth and maturity. Her history, too, is as interesting as her character, and her position, living in profound seclusion, in the midst of London, occupied in teaching her little brothers Greek, is almost as singular as her genius and her character. MISS MITFORD to LADY DACRE, 6 June 1836.

MISS MITFORD. She is in fact a sort of prose Crabbe in the sun, but with more grace and less strength; and also with a more steadfast look upon scenic nature—never going higher than the earth to look for the beautiful, but always finding it as surely as if we went higher. . . . In my own mind . . . she herself is better and stronger than any of her books; and her letters and conversation show more grasp of intellect and general power than would be inferable from her finished compositions. ELIZABETH BARRETT BROWNING to RICHARD HENGIST HORNE, 2 October 1843: *Letters of Elizabeth Barrett Browning to Richard Hengist Horne* (1877), i, 150–1–2.

SWINBURNE. Yesterday I was in Swinburne's rooms. I wish you knew the little fellow; he is the most enthusiastic fellow I ever met, and one of the cleverest. He wanted to read me some poems he had written. . . . They are really very good, and he read them with such earnestness, so truly feeling everything he had written, that I for the first time in my life enjoyed hearing the poetry of an amateur. GEORGE BIRKBECK HILL at Oxford to MISS ANNE SCOTT, 4 March 1857: *Letters* (1906), 65.

NATHANIEL HAWTHORNE. The most bashful man that ever lived, certainly the most bashful American, *mauvaise honte* not being one of our national traits, but he is a very sincere, unsophisticated, kind-hearted person, and looks the man of genius he undoubtedly is. JOHN LOTHROP MOTLEY, 29 December 1859: *Correspondence* (1889), i, 332.

J. S. MILL. An utterly shallow and wretched segment of a human creature, incapable of understanding *Anything* in the ultimate conditions of it, and countenancing with an unhappy fortune, whatever is fatallest in the popular error of English mind. JOHN RUSKIN, 12 September 1869: *Letters of Ruskin to C. E. Norton* (1905), i, 245–6.

THOREAU. A keen and delicate observer of nature—a genuine observer—which, I suspect, is almost as rare a character as even an original poet; and Nature, in return for his love, seems to adopt him as her especial child, and shows him secrets which few others are allowed to witness. He is familiar with beast, fish, fowl, and reptile, and has strange stories to tell of adventures and friendly passages with these lower brethren of mortality. Herb and flower, likewise, wherever they grow, whether in garden or wild wood, are his familiar friends. He is also on intimate terms with the clouds, and can tell the portents of storms. It is a characteristic trait, that he has a great regard for the memory of the Indian tribes, whose wild life would have suited him so well. . . . With all this he has more than a tincture of literature—a deep and true taste for poetry . . . and he is a good writer—at least, he has written a good article, a rambling disquisition on Natural History, in the last *Dial*, which, he says, was chiefly made up from journals of his own observations. Methinks this article gives a very fair image of his mind and character—so true, innate, and literal in observation, yet giving the spirit as well as letter of what he sees, even as a lake reflects its wooded banks, showing every leaf, yet giving the wild beauty of the whole scene. Then there are in the article passages of cloudy and dreamy metaphysics, and also passages where his thoughts seem to measure and attune themselves into spontaneous verse, as they rightfully may, since there is real poetry in them. There is a basis of good sense and of moral truth, too, throughout the article, which also is a reflection of his character; for he is not unwise to think and feel, and I find him a healthy and wholesome man to know. NATHANIEL HAWTHORNE at Concord, 1 September 1842: *Note-Books* (1869), 189–90.

TRELAWNEY. The most splendid old man I have seen since Landor and my own grandfather. . . . He was most cordial and friendly in his reception of me, whom he affirmed to be the last of the poets, having apparently no faith in the capacity of this country to produce more of our breed; while I lament to add that he (metaphorically) spits and stamps on the bare suggestion that it did produce any between Shelley and Byron and myself. Of the excellence of his principles I will say but this: that I did think, by the grace of Laban (unto whom, and not unto me, be glory and thanksgiving. Amen: Selah), I was a good atheist, and a good republican; but in the company of this magnificent old rebel, a lifelong incarnation of the divine right of insurrection, I feel myself, by comparison, a Theist and a Royalist. A. C. SWINBURNE to EDWIN HARRISON, 27 August 1876: *Letters, A. C. Swinburne* (1918), 67–8.

JOHN RUSKIN. I was knocked up yesterday in a good cause. We went to see Mr. Ruskin at Herne Hill. I find him *far* more *personally* lovable than I had expected. Of course he lives in the incense of an adoring circle, but he is absolutely unaffected himself, and with a GREAT charm. So much gentler and more refined than I had expected, and such clear Scotch turquoise eyes. He had been out to buy buns and grapes for *me*(!), carrying the buns himself very carefully that they might not be crushed!! JOANNA HORATIA EWING to her husband MAJOR ALEXANDER

Characters

EWING, 11 October 1879: *J. H. Ewing: Her Books and Letters* (1896), 214.

MATTHEW ARNOLD. No one ever united so much kindness and light-heartedness with so much strength. He was the most sensible man of genius whom I have ever known and the most free from personality, and his mind was very far from being exhausted. BENJAMIN JOWETT to SIR R. B. D. MORIER, 11 May 1888: *Letters* (1899).

ROBERT BRIDGES. He is delightfully grumpy. He mentions thing after thing which is commonly believed and says that of course it's not so. He's always right. His intellect has been so completely self-indulged that it now can't understand rubbish. He has never obeyed anyone or adapted himself to anyone, so he's as clear as crystal, and can't do with fogs. SIR WALTER RALEIGH, 30 November 1912: *Letters* (1926), ii, 390–1.

G. LOWES DICKINSON. Charm, in most men and nearly all women, is a decoration. It genuinely belongs to them as a good complexion may, but it lies on the surface and can vanish. Charm in Dickinson was structural. It penetrated and upheld everything he did, it remained into old age. E. M. FORSTER, *Goldsworthy Lowes Dickinson* (1934), 100–1.

BERNARD SHAW. One of his hostesses said Shaw was a most dangerous man, and, on being asked how and why (in the hope of eliciting some scandal), explained, 'You invite him down to your place because you think he will entertain your guests with his brilliant conversation; and before you know where you are he has chosen a school for your son, made your will for you, regulated your diet, and assumed all the privileges of your family solicitor, your housekeeper, your clergyman, your doctor, your dressmaker, your hairdresser, and your estate agent. When he has finished with everybody else, he incites the children to rebellion. And when he can find nothing more to do, he goes away and forgets all about you.' FRANK HARRIS, *Bernard Shaw* (1931), 277.

VI

SPECIMEN DAYS

I suppose that most persons would rather know what Shakespeare was doing on any one day from dawn to sunset . . . than be instructed as to the history of the congress of Vienna. Mark Rutherford, *Last Pages from a Journal* (1915), 232–3.

JOHN MILTON'S STUDIOUS DAY. He was an early riser (scil. at 4 a clock *manè*); yea, after he lost his sight. He had a man to read to him. The first thing he read was the Hebrew Bible, and that was at 4 h. *manè*, ½ h. +. Then he contemplated. At 7 his man came to him again, and then read to him again, and wrote till dinner: the writing was as much as the reading. His daughter, Deborah, could read to him Latin, Italian and French, and Greek. . . . After dinner he used to walk three or four hours at a time (he always had a garden where he lived); went to bed about 9. JOHN AUBREY, 1680: *Brief Lives* (1898), ii, 68.

SWIFT SPENDS A DAY IN THE CITY. Sir Andrew Fountaine came this morning, and caught me writing in bed. I went into the city with him; and we dined at the chophouse with Will Pate, the learned woollen-draper: then we sauntered at china-shops and booksellers; went to the tavern, drank two pints of white wine, and never parted till ten: and now I am come home, and must copy out some papers I intend for Mr. Hartley, whom I am to see as I told you, to-morrow afternoon: so that this night I shall say little to MD, but that I heartily wish myself with them, and will come as soon as I either fail, or compass my business. JONATHAN SWIFT, 6 October 1710: *Journal to Stella*: (Bohn Lib. 1924), 22.

Specimen Days

HORACE WALPOLE GIVES AN ACCOUNT OF HIMSELF. You bid me give you some account of myself: I can in a very few words: I am quite alone; in the morning I view a new pond I am making for gold fish, and stick in a few shrubs or trees, wherever I can find a space, which is very rare: in the evening I scribble a little; all this mixed with reading; that is, I can't say I read much, but I pick up a good deal of reading. The only thing I have done that can compose a paragraph, and which I think you are whig enough to forgive me, is, that on each side of my bed I have hung Magna Charta, and the Warrant for King Charles's execution, on which I have written Major Charta; as I believe, without the latter, the former by this time would be of very little importance. HORACE WALPOLE, Letter to GEORGE MONTAGU, 14 October 1756: *Letters* (1891), iii, 35.

THE WORDSWORTHS AND COLERIDGE AT GRASMERE. We walked in the wood by the lake. W. read *Joanna*, and the *Firgrove*, to Coleridge. They bathed. The morning was delightful, with somewhat of an autumnal freshness. After dinner, Coleridge discovered a rock-seat in the orchard. Cleared away brambles. Coleridge went to bed after tea. John and I followed Wm. up the hill, and then returned to go to Mr. Simpson's. We borrowed some bottles for bottling rum. The evening somewhat frosty and grey, but very pleasant. I broiled Coleridge a mutton chop, which he ate in bed. Wm. was gone to bed. I chatted with John and Coleridge till near 12. DOROTHY WORDSWORTH, 1 September 1800: *Journal* (1924), 47–8.

SIR WALTER SPENDS A DELICIOUS DAY AT ABBOTSFORD. A most delicious day, in the course of which I have not done

'The least right thing'.

Before breakfast I employed myself in airing my old bibliomaniacal hobby, entering all the books lately acquired into a temporary catalogue, so as to have them shelved and marked. After breakfast I went out, the day being delightful—warm, yet cooled with a gentle breeze, all around delicious; the rich luxuriant green refreshing to the eye, soft to the tread, and perfume to the smell. Wandered about and looked at my plantations. Came home, and received a visit from Sir Adam. Loitered in the library till dinner-time. If there is anything to be done at all to-day, it must be in the evening. But I fear there will be nothing. One can't work always *nowther*.

'Neque semper arcum tendit Apollo'.

There's warrant for it. SIR WALTER SCOTT, *Journal* (1890), ii, 1.

A DAY IN THE LIFE OF JANE CARLYLE. For my part I am very content. I have everything here my heart desires, that I could have anywhere else, except society, and even that deprivation is not to be considered wholly an evil: if people we like and take pleasure in do not come about us here as in London, it is thankfully to be remembered that here 'the wicked cease from troubling, and the weary are at rest'. If the knocker make no sound for weeks together, it is so much the better for my nerves. My Husband is as good company as reasonable mortal could desire. Every fair morning we ride on horse-back for an hour before breakfast (my previous horse knew me again and neighed loud and long when he found himself in his old place). Then we eat such a surprising breakfast of home-baked bread, and eggs, etc. etc., as might incite anyone that had breakfasted so long in London to write a pastoral. Then Carlyle takes to his writing, while I, like Eve, 'studious of household good', inspect my house, my garden, my live-stock, gather flowers for my drawing-room, and lapfuls of eggs; and finally betake myself also to writing, or reading, or making, or mending, or whatever work seems fittest. After dinner, and only then, I lie on the sofa and (to my shame be it spoken) sometimes *sleep*, but oftenest dream waking. In the evening I walk on the moor (how different from Holborn and the Strand!) and read anything that does not exact much attention. Such is my life,—agreeable as yet from its novelty, if for nothing else. JANE WELSH CARLYLE at Craigenputtock to MISS ELIZA MILES, 16 June 1832: *New Letters* (1903), i, 43–4.

Specimen Days

THOMAS CARLYLE ON HOLIDAY AT KIRKCALDY. Healthy limitation, that is the rule of things here; dashed pretty well considerably with the virtuous-insipid: all right and well. My bedroom is the back bedroom; . . . I awake generally about an hour too early, but put off the time in some tolerable way; this morning, for example, at half-past seven, I sallied out in blustering wind, and plunged myself into the sea, an adventurous, but rather successful step, which perhaps when there is not rain I shall repeat. Shaving and deliberate dressing carries one on to nine o'clock, when some kind of a thing (a gong I think) gives a huge low growl somewhere in the lower premises and indicates that breakfast is on the table. A most plenteous breakfast, in the many good things of which, except tea and coffee (with some eminent ham), I must hesitate to partake. Slowly with some loose conversation we breakfast; a certain old surgeon, one Johnson (the Edinburg Bailie's brother) stalks in daily, with hardly any speech at all, to look at the newspaper, and stalks out again: they say he has done it daily these fifteen years! Our breakfast done, the ladies leave us for the drawing-room; and after a due space, we remaining two do also withdraw, John to his counting-house or to his farms till five in the afternoon, I to my own premises or to the drawing-room, or whither I list. Hitherto almost every morning there has been a hurried letter to write, for the South Post at twelve; London letters not *arriving* (which is unlucky) till after one. After one, however, the post has arrived too, and the Newspaper; after which there is clearly nothing to be looked for from the world; you are then clearly 'left to your own intrepidity and force of purpose'. . . . I smoke, I have books, I have the sea and the highways. These two last especially; I have bathed hitherto every day (except yesterday when John had me riding out far and wide among his farms); I have also ridden two hours or more every day—putting on bad clothes if it rain; in bright days, with the fresh woods, clear hill-tops, with the blue everlasting deep and the Bass and Lothian ever and anon in sight, and a swift beast to carry you, it is as pleasant riding as could be contrived. The people here are all grown utter strangers to me;

but yonder is the old Bass Rock, yonder is my poor Jeannie's birthland, and twenty years of fateful time are written on them for me. O my dear bairn, if I had thee here, I feel as if I should be quite happy for a while. We are to come next year when the *great* house is done building: we actually will, I think; shall we not? It is a tolerably good sign of me, when I long to have loved ones near me, especially sharptempered wives; accordingly I do incline to say that I have made considerable improvement this week, though the hours do not suit me altogether. But to proceed: the gong growls again at half-past five, and luncheoned, or unluncheoned as I, but all in full dress of solemn black with what of silk is fit, we solemnly descend to dinner. There is free allowance of good things a-many; of good wines among others, in which latter I think I shall cease or nearly so to partake: two glasses, one glass, four glasses, a glass of whisky punch, all seem to do me mischief alike. A walk ensues, executed by John and me about the doors, I smoking as I walk; then, near eight I suppose, is found limited supply of excellent tea, and talk in which I have to do more than I want, till on the stroke of ten enter *garçon* again with a tray of bottles, with two biscuits, and the promise (soon fulfilled) to me of a plate of tolerable porridge. . . . At half-past ten, 'candles' are ordered, but not brought to us; they are stuck in our rooms, fine wax-lights, and we are all sent marching thither at that early hour. Indeed a certain solemnity is throughout visible here; a great dressing and washing; manifold creatures carrying off your clothes to ever new brushings etc. etc.: but all is right at bottom, and you do find yourself served, that a hospitable spirit, better everyway than common, encircles you. THOMAS CARLYLE TO HIS WIFE, 26 August 1838: *New Letters* (1904), i, 136–9.

EDWARD FITZGERALD SPENDS A HAPPY DAY AT GELDERSTONE HALL, BECCLES. Here I live with tolerable content: perhaps with as much as most people arrive at, and what if one were properly grateful one would perhaps call perfect happiness. Here is a glorious sunshiny day; all the morning I read about Nero in

Specimen Days

Tacitus lying at full length on a bench in the garden: a nightingale singing and some red anemones eyeing the sun manfully not far off. A funny mixture all this: Nero, and the delicacy of the Spring: all very human however. Then at half-past one lunch on Cambridge cream cheese: then a ride over hill and dale: then spudding up some weeds from the grass: and then coming in, I sit down and write to you, my sister winding red worsted from the back of a chair, and the most delightful little girl in the world chattering incessantly. So runs the world away. You think I live in Epicurean ease: but this happens to be a jolly day: one isn't always well, or tolerably good, the weather is not always clear, nor nightingales singing, nor *Tacitus* full of pleasant atrocity. But such as life is, I believe I have got hold of a good end of it. . . . EDWARD FITZGERALD to JOHN ALLEN, 28 April 1839: *Letters* (1889), 50.

MACAULAY ENJOYS HIMSELF AT VENTNOR. I shall be at Ryde to meet you next Saturday. I only hope that the weather may continue to be just what it is. The evenings are a little chilly out-of-doors; but the days are glorious. I rise before seven; breakfast at nine; write a page; ramble five or six hours over rocks and through copse-wood, with *Plutarch* in my hand; come home; write another page; take Fra Paolo, and sit in the garden reading till the sun sinks behind the Undercliff. Then it begins to be cold; so I carry my Fra Paolo into the house and read on till dinner. While I am at dinner *The Times* comes in, and is a good accompaniment to a delicious dessert of peaches, which are abundant here. I have also a novel of Theodore Hook by my side, to relish my wine. I then take a short stroll by starlight, and go to bed at ten. I am perfectly solitary; almost as much so as Robinson Crusoe before he caught Friday. I have not opened my lips, that I remember, these six weeks, except to say 'Bread, if you please', or, 'Bring a bottle of soda water'; yet I have not had a moment of ennui. Nevertheless I am heartily glad that you can give me nine days. I wish it were eighteen. T. B. MACAULAY to T. F. ELLIS, 8 September 1850: *Life*, Trevelyan (1876), ii, 281.

Specimen Days

TOM MOORE READS AND SINGS AT DONNINGTON PARK. My time here by no means hangs heavily on me, notwithstanding that I am so little accustomed to solitude. I rise rather early, breakfast heartily, employ the day in walking or *hunting*—among old books, dine off two courses, no less; in the evening sing down the sun like a true Pythagorean, and then seasonably take to my pillow, where I sleep sweetly, nor dream of ambition though beneath the roof of an earl. THOMAS MOORE to his Mother, 5 May 1801: *Memoirs* (1853), i, 115.

JOHN RICHARD GREEN FILLS HIS TIME. In the country there is no excuse for remissness *in re literaria*—it is the only charm against the devil. Excuse there might be for me—breakfasting at 8 and snatching half an hour of Stanley's book over my bread and butter,—then hurrying from morning prayer at St. Matthew's to open the school and confer with my vicar; letter and lecture-writing, visiting and the etceteras of the day till 12; then, after luncheon, a walk to the British Museum and grind there till 4.30; dinner and a trot home; tea at the parsonage; a chat with Mrs. W.; a romp with the children till the parish again claims me from 7 to 9 for lectures, Bible classes, music do., confirmation do., committee meetings, and the like. A good two hours' reading or sermon-writing send me to bed at 12. J. R. GREEN, 1861: *Letters* (1901), 75-6.

EDWARD LEAR GRUMBLES AT ST. LEONARD'S-ON-SEA. My own life is—I rise at six or 6.30—& work a short hour before breakfast at 8. Bkft as slight as possible—2 cups of tea, 2 bits of dry toast, 2 ditto bacon, work till 11—: newspaper. Work again till 2. small bit of cake.—work till 4. Dine. simple sole & beneficial beer; work again till 7. wash brushes and swear till 7.30. Prowl in the dark along the melancholy sea till 8.45. Bed at 9.30. For I am too sad and tired by that time to work again. Bed extremely uncomfortable—like a plum pie turned into stone. Lie awake and have the cramp & the side-ache till morning. Then the 'break, break, break', of the sea gets me to sleep. I have a piano, but seldom play. Housemaid vexatious & a goose,—wears crino-

lines. EDWARD LEAR to CHICHESTER FORTESCUE (Lord Car-
lingford), 29 August 1861: *Letters* (1907), 192.

A TENNYSONIAN DAY. His hours were quite regular: he breakfasted at 8, lunched at 2, dined at 7. At dessert, if alone, he would
read to himself, or if friends were in the house, he would sit with
them for an hour or so, and entertain them with varied talk. He
worked chiefly in the morning over his pipe, or in the evening
after his pint of port, also over his pipe. . . . His afternoons he
generally spent on one of our smaller lawns, surrounded by birch
and different sorts of pine and fir and cypress, after the fashion
of separate green parlours. Here he would read the daily papers
or some book to my mother lying out in her sofa-chair, or would
receive friends from the neighbourhood, or would talk to guests
staying in the house. HALLAM, LORD TENNYSON, *Memoir*
(1897), ii, 210–11.

WILLIAM CORY RECORDS A DAY IN A COUNTRY HOUSE. This is
our day:—We are called at eight, shutters unbarred (this is a
detestable practice, shuttering, I rebel against it). Gong at nine.
We meet in the library. My Lord reads Job, chapter vii, without
a word of comment. Job tells us we are not to rise from the
grave, which is a doctrine decidedly out of harmony with the
prayer which follows. We talk a few minutes; then to breakfast,
where the girl, aged fifteen, makes coffee, and the servants hand
round delicate morsels of hot meat; not at all a coarse meal. Then
we all rise together. I find myself soon in the library. I rummage.
Two ladies come in and *cause* over photographs, leaving me alone.
When I calculate the housemaid has done her worst in my room,
I go to it. Then, with an open lattice, letting in the bird-voices and
tempting me to look at a beloved cedar, I sit and scribble. Meanwhile all the males are shooting—females writing letters, I hope.
I stroll. I find the shrubbery and glades empty. I can look at
every tree at leisure, squeeze the fragrant juniper berries, and
count the acorns on a spray. Then I go with F. to see the shoot-
ing-people, and share their very solid luncheon under a rick of
sainfoin. The luncheon is plain but excellent. I eat more than I

should eat indoors with the ladies, and our talk is more lively. I come back sooner than they, and read again: but at six I go to the schoolroom and join the ladies at tea. My host comes too, and calls me off for a grave private talk in the adjoining small morning room, which is the meeting-place before dinner. Then I go back and get a feast of music. At eight, very punctually, gong and dinner: this punctuality is delightful, and has a moral effect. . . . When we returned to the library, we had too many things offered to us: after coffee, liqueur, then tea, then seltzer water, finally tobacco. Two ladies and two males played whist, the rest talked. No music, no general conversation. This is liberty, but not mutual improvement. All my host says about politics is genuine partisanship, but sound liberalism, considerate patriotism, public spirit, prudence, generosity. WILLIAM CORY at Lord Northbrook's, Stratton, Hampshire, 1868: *Letters and Journals* (1897), 253–4.

RUSKIN IN ROME. I've never told you—though I've meant to twenty times—how I spend my Roman day. I rise at six, dress quietly, looking out now and then to see the blue sky through the pines beyond the Piazza del Popolo. Coffee at seven, and then I write and correct press till nine. Breakfast, and half-an-hour of *Virgil*, or lives of saints, or other pathetic or improving work. General review of colour-box and apparatus, start about ten for Sistine Chapel, nice little jingling drive in open one-horse carriage. Arrive at chapel, sauntering a little about the fountains first. Public are turned out at eleven, and then I have absolute peace with two other artists—each on a separate platform—till two, when public are let in again. I strike work; pack up with dignity; get away about three; take the first little carriage at the door again, drive to Capitol, saunter a little about Forum, or the like, or into the Lateran, or San Clemente, and so home to dinner at five. Dine very leisurely; read a little French novel at dessert; then out to Pincian—sit among the roses and hear band play. Saunter down Trinita steps as it gets dark; tea; and a little more French novel; a little review of day's work; plans for tomorrow; and to bed. JOHN RUSKIN to ——, 4 June 1874: *Life*, Cook (1911), ii, 248–9.

RUSKIN WORKS AND READS A VICIOUS BOOK AT VENICE. I wake as a matter of course, about half past five, and get up and go out on my balcony in my nightgown to see if there's going to be a nice dawn. . . . Generally there is a good dawn. . . . At six I get up, and dress, with occasionally balcony interludes—but always get to my writing table at seven, where, by scolding and paying, I secure my punctual cup of coffee, and do a bit of the *Laws of Plato* to build the day on. I find Jowett's translation is good for nothing and shall do one myself, as I've intended these fifteen years. At half past seven the gondola is waiting and takes me to the bridge before St. John and Paul, where I give an hour of my very best day's work to painting the school of Mark and vista of Canal to Murano. It's a great Canaletto view, and I'm painting it against him.

I am rowed back to breakfast at nine, and, till half past ten, think over and write what little I can of my new fourth vol. of *Stones of Venice*. At half past ten, I go to the Academy, where I find Moore at work; and we sit down to our picture together. They have been very good to me in the Academy, and have taken down St. Ursula and given her to me all to myself in a locked room and perfect light. I'm painting a small carefully toned general copy of it for Oxford, and shall make a little note of it for you, and am drawing various parts larger. Moore is making a study of the head, which promises to be excellent.

He sits beside me till twelve, then goes to early dinner with Mrs. Moore and Bessie—I have a couple of hours *tête-à-tête* with St. Ursula, very good for me. I strike work at two or a little after—go home, read letters, and dine at three. Lie on sofa and read any vicious book I can find to amuse me—to prevent St. Ursula having it all her own way. Am greatly amused with the life of Casanova at present. At half-past four, gondola again,— I am floated, half asleep, to Murano—or the Armenians—or the San Giorgio in Alga—wake up, and make some little evening sketch, by way of diary. Then take oar myself, and row into the dark or moonlight. Home at seven, well heated—quiet tea—after that, give audiences, if people want me; otherwise read Venetian history—if no imperative letters—and to bed at ten. JOHN RUSKIN to CHARLES ELIOT NORTON, 5 October 1876: *Letters of John Ruskin to Charles Eliot Norton* (1905), ii, 138.

WALT WHITMAN SUN-BATHES. Another day quite free from mark'd prostration and pain. It seems indeed as if peace and nutriment from heaven subtly filter into me as I slowly hobble down these country lanes and across fields, in the good air—as I sit here in solitude with Nature—open, voiceless, mystic, far removed, yet palpable, eloquent Nature. I merge myself in the scene, in the perfect day. . . . An hour or so after breakfast I wended my way down to the recesses of the dell, which I and certain thrushes, cat-birds, &c., had all to ourselves. A light south-west wind was blowing through the tree-tops. It was just the place and time for my Adamic air-bath and flesh-brushing from head to foot. So hanging clothes on a rail near by, keeping old broadbrim straw on head and easy shoes on feet, havn't I had a good time the last two hours! First with the stiff-elastic bristles rasping arms, breast, sides, till they turn'd scarlet—then partially bathing in the clear waters of the running brook—taking everything very leisurely, with many rests and pauses—stepping about barefooted every few minutes now and then in some neighbouring black ooze, for unctuous mud-bath to my feet—a brief second and third rinsing in the crystal running waters—rubbing with a fragrant towel—slow negligent promenades on the turf up and down in the sun, varied with occasional rests, and further friction of the thistle-brush—sometimes carrying my portable chair with me from place to place, as my range is quite extensive here, nearly a hundred rods, feeling quite secure from intrusion, (and that indeed I am not at all nervous about, if it accidentally happens). . . . Some good people may think it a feeble or half-crack'd way of spending one's time. . . . May-be it is. WALT WHITMAN, 27 August 1877: *Specimen Days* (1882).

Specimen Days

GEORGE GISSING HAS A BAD DAY. A terrible day, got up with a headache, from 9.30 to 2 wrote—or rather struggled to write —achieving not quite two pages. Suffered anguish worse than any I remember in the effort to compose. Ate nothing at 2, but started and walked to Hampstead and back. Head a little better. Dined at a café extravagantly spending 1s. 9d. At 7 tried to write again, and by 9.30 finished one page. GEORGE GISSING, 25 January 1888: *Letters* (1926), 207.

LOWELL WOULD SHARE A PERFECT DAY WITH TOM HUGHES. I wish you could share my day with me. It is simply what a day should be that has a good conscience—nothing left in it but a well-mannered sunshine and the mere pleasure of being. I can't bear to think that our politicians should have any share in it. It was meant for better men. JAMES RUSSELL LOWELL to THOMAS HUGHES, 1 October 1890: *Letters* (1894), ii, 468

A DAY IN PARIS WITH ARNOLD BENNETT—To-day I spent such a day as ought to satisfy a man of letters. Having done my correspondence, I went out at 10.15 for a walk, and to consider the plot of my story. I strolled about the Quartier de l'Europe till 11.30, and then lunched at my usual restaurant where I am expected, and where my maternal waitress advised me in the selection of my lunch. During lunch I read *Le Journal*, read *Don Quixote*, and fell asleep. Then at 1.30, I amused myself on the piano. At 2 I began, in my Bouges chair, to ponder further on my story, and the plot seemed to be coming. At 3.30 I made my afternoon tea, and then read more *Don Quixote*, and fell asleep for about a minute. The plot was now coming, faster and faster, and at 5 I decided that I would, at any rate, begin to sketch the story. At 6.45 I had done a complete rough draft of the whole story.

Then I dressed and went out to dine at my other restaurant in the Place Blanche, where the food and wine are good, and the waiters perfect models, and the chasseur charming, where men bring their mistresses, and where occasionally a 'mistress' dines alone, and where the atmosphere is a curious mixture of discretion and *sans gêne* (the whole place seems to say: 'You should see what fun we have here between midnight and 3 a.m. with our Hungarian music and our improvised dancing, and so on and so on'). I *dined* slowly and well, while reading *Le Temps* and the *Pilot*, and while watching the human life of the place. Then I took coffee and a cigar. I returned home at 8.30, and played the piano. The idea of writing my *chronique* for *T. P's Weekly* a day earlier than usual came into my head, the scheme of the article presented itself, and at 9.30 I suddenly began to write it, finishing it at 11.35. I then went to bed and read *Don Quixote* till 12.15. ARNOLD BENNETT, 8 November 1905: *Journals* (1932), 125.

AND ANOTHER IN LONDON. In bed at 11.30. I woke up about six times; but I slept $6\frac{1}{2}$ hours in all. At 8 a.m. I am up and making notes and doing oddments. At 8.45 breakfast. At 9.15 Miss Nerney, for urgencies. At 9.20 Fjillstedt. Dressed at 10.30. Walk for half an hour. In the interstices I have done all my business and some other letters. At 11 Knoblock. We toil for 2 hours ensemble. Lunch at 1. In bed at 2. Slept till 2.30. I shall shortly go out for another walk, and shall work from 4 to 6 on *Prohack*. At 6.15 Mrs. L. is coming to see me about A.'s proposed marriage. (Why?) I may do a bit more work after her departure. I shall dine at Countess Russell's, but the dinner isn't till 8.30. I shall leave early, so as to be in bed early. ARNOLD BENNETT to DOROTHY CHESTON BENNETT, 20 January 1925: *Arnold Bennett*, Dorothy Cheston Bennett (1935), 258–9.

YEATS AT COOLE PARK. I have got into my routine here—always my place of industry. After breakfast Chaucer—garden for 20 minutes—then work from 11 to 2 then lunch then I fish from 3 till 5, then I read and then work again at lighter tasks till dinner—after dinner walk. To this I have added sandow exercises twice daily. Today I break the routine sufficiently to bicycle over to Edward Martyn's and dine there—I have therefore given up my fishing hour to writing. W. B. YEATS to MRS. EMERY (Florence Farr), *Florence Farr, Bernard Shaw and W. B. Yeats* (1941), 53.

Specimen Days

FRANK HARRIS KEEPS BUSY. I wake about eight in the morning, get a grape-fruit and a couple of cups of tea and write or dictate till twelve-thirty; then I get up and dress. I try to go out for five or ten minutes' walk or run before my lunch at one-thirty; from two-thirty to three-thirty I snoozel; at three-thirty I go to the office to see people, deal with correspondence, calls, etc.; from six to seven-thirty I take a walk if I can; then I come in and have a cup of soup, no bread; afterwards I either read or correct manuscript till one o'clock. Then I am supposed to go to bed; but if I have taken any coffee during the day, and it is a perpetual temptation to me, I probably do not sleep till three or four and pay for it by feeling tired and worn out next morning. . . . FRANK HARRIS to HESKETH PEARSON, 30 April 1918: *Modern Men and Mummers*, Hesketh Pearson (1921), 129.

VII

THIS LOVE

This love is that salt that seasoneth our harsh and dull labours, and gives a pleasant relish to our other unsavoury proceedings. Robert Burton, *Anatomy of Melancholy* (1638), II, ii, 3.

In the afternoon to Henry the Seventh's chapel, where I heard a sermon and spent (God forgive me) most of my time in looking upon Mrs. Butler. SAMUEL PEPYS, 15 July 1660: *Diary* (1893), i, 202.

Being weary last night, I slept till almost seven o'clock, a thing I have not done many a day. So up and to my office (being come to some angry words with my wife about neglecting the keeping of the house clean, I calling her a beggar, and she me a pricklouse, which vexed me) and there all the morning. SAMUEL PEPYS, 2 May 1663: *Diary* (1893), iii, 108.

Looked over Godwin's *Memoirs of Mrs. Woolstonecraft,* which strikingly evince that love, even in a modern philosopher, *emollit mores, nec sinet esse feros.* This austere moralist, from whose forbidding frown we should expect that Cupid would shrink away abashed, becomes quite bland, obsequious, and gallant, under his fascinating influence. THOMAS GREEN, 5 June 1798: *Extracts from the Diary of a Lover of Literature* (1810), 81.

I don't talk, I can't flatter, and won't listen, except to a pretty or a foolish woman. LORD BYRON, 16 January 1814: *Journal,* ii, 379.

I have read this book in your garden;—my love, you were absent, or else I could not have read it. It is a favourite book of yours, and the writer was a friend of mine. You will not under-

stand these English words, and *others* will not understand them
—which is the reason I have not scrawled them in Italian. But
you will recognise the handwriting of him who passionately
loved you, and you will divine that, over a book which was yours,
he could only think of love. In that word, beautiful in all
languages, but most so in yours—*Amor mio*—is comprised my
existence here and hereafter. I feel I exist here, and I fear that
I shall exist hereafter,—to *what* purpose you will decide; my
destiny rests with you, and you are a woman, seventeen years of
age, and two out of a convent. I wish that you had stayed there,
with all my heart,—or, at least, that I had never met you in your
married state. But all this is too late. I love you, and you love
me,—at least, you *say so*, and *act* as if you *did* so, which last is a
great consolation in all events. But *I* more than love you, and
cannot cease to love you. Think of me sometimes, when the Alps
and the ocean divide us,—but they never will, unless you *wish* it.
LORD BYRON to the MARCHESA GUICCIOLI, written in a copy
of *Corinne* which he found in her garden at Bologna, 25 August
1819: *Letters and Journals* (1900), iv, 350.

I never wrote anything worth mentioning till I was in love.
Dante dates his passion for Beatrice at twelve. I was almost as
young when I fell over head and ears in love. . . . I was sent to
Harrow at twelve, and spent my vacations at Newstead. It was
there that I first saw Mary C——. She was several years older
than myself; but, at my age, boys like something older than
themselves, as they do younger, later in life. Our estates joined.
. . . She was the *beau idéal* of all that my youthful fancy could
paint of beautiful; and I have taken all my fables about the celestial nature of women from the perfection my imagination created
in her—I say created, for I found her, like the rest of the sex,
anything but angelic. LORD BYRON, *Conversations*, Medwin
(1824), 57–9.

You ask if Lady Byron were ever in love with me? . . . No! I was
the fashion when she first came out: I had the character of being
a great rake, and was a great dandy—both of which young ladies

like. She married me from vanity and the hope of reforming and fixing me. LORD BYRON, *Conversations*, Medwin (1824), 45–6.

I have prejudices about women: I do not like to see them eat. Rousseau makes Julie *un peu gourmande*; but that is not at all according to my taste. I do not like to be interrupted when I am writing. Lady Byron did not attend to these whims of mine. The only harsh thing I ever remember saying to her was one evening shortly before our parting. I was standing before the fire, ruminating upon the embarrassment of my affairs, and other annoyances, when Lady Byron came up to me and said, 'Byron, am I in your way?' to which I replied 'damnably!' I was afterwards sorry and reproached myself for the expression: but it escaped me unconsciously—involuntarily; I hardly knew what I said. LORD BYRON, *Conversations*, Medwin (1824), 41–2.

I understand with a deep sense of sorrow of the indisposition of your son: I fear he hath too much *mind* for his body, and that superabounds with fancy, which brings him to these fits of distemper, proceeding from the black humour of Melancholy: Moreover, I have observed that he is too much given to his study and self-society, 'specially to converse with dead Men, I mean Books: You know anything in excess is naught. Now, Sir, were I worthy to give you advice, I could wish he were well married, and it may wean him from that bookish and thoughtful humour: Women were created for the comfort of Men, and I have known that to some they have proved the best *Helleborum* against Melancholy. JAMES HOWELL to MAJOR SERJEANT D., 13 June 1632: *Familiar Letters*.

I leave you to judge whether Holland can be said to be wanting in gallantry, when it is customary there to inclose a *billet doux* to a lady in a letter to her husband; I have not so much as made mention of this to yours; and if you tell first, let the sin fall upon your head instead of his. For my part I keep the Commandments; I love my neighbour as myself, and to avoid coveting my neighbour's wife I desire to be coveted by her; which you know is another thing. WILLIAM CONGREVE at Rotterdam, to MRS.

This Love

EDWARD PORTER 1700: *Letters of Eminent Literary Men* (1843), 300.

In his *Utopia* his [Sir Thomas More's] law is that the young people are to see each other stark-naked before marriage. Sir William Roper, of . . . Eltham, in Kent, came one morning, pretty early, to my lord, with a proposal to marry one of his daughters. My lord's daughters were then both together abed in a truckle-bed in their father's chamber asleep. He carries Sir William into the chamber and takes the sheet by the corner and suddenly whips it off. They lay on their backs, and their smocks up as high as their armpits. This awakened them, and immediately they turned on their bellies. Quoth Roper, I have seen both sides, and so gave a pat on her buttock, he made choice of, saying, 'Thou art mine.' Here was all the trouble of the wooing. JOHN AUBREY, *The Scandal and Credulities of John Aubrey* (1931), 1–2.

I am sorry to say the generality of women who have exceeded in wit have failed in chastity. ELIZABETH MONTAGUE, *Letters* (1813), iii, 97.

She must be intellectual enough to sympathize with my pursuits; orderly and resolute enough to fill up those two vacant apartments in my character. It may be as well for her to know German, and to read Goethe. Pretty, though this is of less consequence, as I shall certainly fancy her so after six months; a good housekeeper, with a little money to aid in floating our Noah's Ark, with its future Shems and Japhets. J. R. GREEN to W. BOYD DAWKINS, 2 October 1860: *Letters* (1901), 47.

I will tell you what sort of a man I desire, which is above ten times as good as I deserve; for gratitude is a great virtue, and I would have cause to be thankful. He should have a great deal of sense and prudence to direct and instruct me, much wit to divert me, beauty to please me, good humour to indulge me in the right, and reprove me gently when I am in the wrong; money enough to afford me more than I can want, and as much as I can wish;

and constancy to like me as long as other people do, that is, till my face is wrinkled by age, or scarred by the small-pox; and after that I shall expect only civility in the room of love, for as Mrs. Clive sings,

> All I hope of mortal man,
> Is to love me whilst he can.

When I can meet all these things in a man above the trivial consideration of money, you may expect to hear I am going to change the easy tranquillity of mind I enjoy at present for a prospect of happiness; for I am, like Pygmalion, in love with a picture of my own drawing, but I never saw an original like it in my life; I hope when I do, I shall, as some poets say, find the statue warm. ELIZABETH ROBINSON (Mrs. Montague) to the DUCHESS OF PORTLAND, 11 November 1738. *Letters* (1810), i, 38–9.

I am not surprised by what you tell me of Miss ——'s new attachment. Your pale and peevish nymphs are always amorous. The snow about their hearts resembles that of our English mountains, rather than the snows of Taurus or Mount Jura. Sun-beams from a lover's eye, seldom play in vain upon the white bosom of a prude. ANNA SEWARD to JOSEPH SYKES, 13 April 1787: *Letters* (1811), i, 284–5.

Love is the great softener of savage dispositions. Johnson had always a metaphysic passion for one princess or other—first, the rustic Lucy Porter, before he married her nauseous mother;—next, the handsome, but haughty Molly Aston;—next, the sublimated, methodistic Hill Boothby, who read her bible in Hebrew; —and, lastly, the more charming Mrs. Thrale, with the beauty of the first, the learning of the second, and with more wit than a bushel of such sinners and such saints. It is ridiculously diverting to see the old elephant forsaking his nature before these princesses. ANNA SEWARD to MRS. KNOWLES, 20 April 1788: *Letters* (1811), ii, 103.

It is the hardest thing in the world to be in love and yet attend business. As for me, all who speak to me find me out, and I must lock myself up, or other people will do it for me. A gentleman ask'd me this morning what news from Lisbon, and I answer'd, She's exquisitely handsome. Another desir'd to know when I had been last at Hampton-Court, I reply'd Twill be on Tuesday come se'nnight. Prithee allow me at least to kiss your hand before that day, that my mind may be in some composure. Oh love!

> A thousand torments dwell about thee,
> Yet who would live to live without thee?

Methinks I could write a volume to you, but all the language on earth would fail in saying how much, and with what disinterested passion. RICHARD STEELE to MARY SCURLOCK, 1 September 1707: *Life*, Aitken (1889), i, 188.

Up to the time I was 29, actually twenty-nine, I was too shabby for any woman to tolerate me. I stalked about in a decaying green coat, cuffs trimmed with the scissors, terrible boots, and so on. Then I got a job to do and bought a suit of clothes with the proceeds. A lady immediately invited me to tea, threw her arms round me, and said she adored me. I permitted her to adore, being intensely curious on the subject. Never having regarded myself as an attractive man, I was surprised; but I kept up appearances successfully. Since that time, whenever I have been left alone in a room with a female, she has invariably thrown her arms round me and declared she adored me. It is fate. Therefore beware. If you allow yourself to be left alone with me for a single moment, you will certainly throw your arms round me and declare you adore me; and I am not prepared to guarantee that my usual melancholy forbearance will be available in your case. BERNARD SHAW to ELLEN TERRY, 12 October 1896: *Ellen Terry and Bernard Shaw: a Correspondence* (1931), 98–9.

I make it a habit when I get restless over my work to seize the nearest woman and squeeze all the breath out of her stays. She does not feel neglected under these circumstances, nor is she much scandalized after the first few shocks. And when she does anything for me I always have a stock of fantastic complaints to make of it which are much more interesting than if I insulted her with delicate acknowledgments. It is not the small things that women miss in me, but the big things. My pockets are always full of the small change of lovemaking; but it is magic money, not real money. BERNARD SHAW to ELLEN TERRY, 8 September 1897: *Ellen Terry and Bernard Shaw: a Correspondence* (1931), 253.

I took your advice; and some time ago took to love and made some advances to the lady you sent me to in Soho, but met no return; so I have given up all thoughts of it, and have now no pursuit or amusement. JOHN GAY to DEAN SWIFT, 4 July 1730: *Life and Letters of Gay* (1921), 119.

BOSWELL. 'Pray, Sir, do you not suppose that there are fifty women in the world, with any one of whom a man may be as happy, as with any one woman in particular?' JOHNSON. 'Ay, Sir, fifty thousand.' BOSWELL. 'Then, Sir, you are not of opinion with some who imagine that certain men and certain women are made for each other; and that they cannot be happy if they miss their counterparts?' JOHNSON. 'To be sure not, Sir. I believe marriages would in general be as happy, and often more so, if they were all made by the Lord Chancellor, upon a due consideration of characters and circumstances, without the parties having any choice in the matter.' 22 March 1776: *Boswell's Life of Johnson* (1887), ii, 461.

In our way, Johnson strongly expressed his love of driving fast in a post-chaise. 'If (said he) I had no duties, and no reference to futurity, I would spend my life in driving briskly in a post-chaise with a pretty woman; but she should be one who could understand me, and would add something to the conversation.' *Boswell's Life of Johnson* (1887), iii, 162.

Went to Lady Mildmay for the MS. of Lord Byron I had lent her to read; sat some time with her. Mentioned how much she felt afraid of Lord Byron, when she used to meet him in society in London; and that once, when he spoke to her in a doorway, her heart beat so violently that she could hardly answer him. She said it was not only her awe of his great talents, but the peculiarity of a sort of *under* look he used to give, that produced this effect upon her. THOMAS MOORE, 2 July 1821: *Memoirs* (1853), iii, 247.

Do not be over-persuaded to marry a man you can never respect —I do not say *love*; because, I think, if you can respect a person before marriage, moderate love at least will come after; and as to intense *passion*, I am convinced that that is no desirable feeling. In the first place, it seldom or never meets with a requital; and, in the second place, if it did, the feeling would be only temporary: it would last the honeymoon, and then, perhaps, give place to disgust, or indifference worse, perhaps, than disgust. Certainly this would be the case of the man's part; and on the woman's—God help her, if she is left to love passionately and alone. CHARLOTTE BRONTË, 1840: *Life*, Gaskell (1857), i, 216.

Mrs. Buchanan talked about Mrs. Carlyle, whom she had known at Fort Augustus as Jeannie Welsh. She and her very pretty widowed mother were staying there; a clergyman went to call one morning, and finding Greek and Hebrew books scattered about the parlour, he asked, 'What young student have you here?' 'Oh, it is only Jeannie Welsh,' was the answer. Another who called reported that the mother would get two husbands before the daughter had one; however, this was a mistake, for news came before long that Jeannie had married, 'just a bookish man like herself'. CAROLINE FOX, 15 September 1847: *Memories of Old Friends* (1882), 223.

'The Last Speech and *marrying* words of that unfortunate young woman Jane Baillie Welsh,' I received on Friday morning; and truly a most delightful and swan-like melody was in them; a tenderness and warm devoted trust, worthy of such a maiden bidding farewell to the (unmarried) Earth, of which she was the fairest ornament. Dear little child! How is it that I have deserved

This Love

thee; deserved a purer and nobler heart than falls to the lot of millions? I swear I will love thee with *my* whole heart, and think my life well spent if it can make thine happy. Thomas Carlyle to Miss Welsh, 9 October 1826: *Early Letters* (1886), 353.

Yes, that is very sweet about the kissing. I have done it to rocks so often, seldom to flowers, not being sure that they would like it. I recollect giving a very reverent little kiss to a young sapling that was behaving beautifully in an awkward chink, between two great big ones that were ill-treating it. Poor me (I'm old enough, I hope, to write grammar my own way), my own little self, meantime, never by any chance got a kiss when I wanted it, —and the better I behaved, the less chance I had, it seemed. John Ruskin, *Hortus inclusus* (1887), 132.

I have read the Master's [Benjamin Jowett's] essay on immortality with much admiration, especially of its inconclusive conclusion. As to his defence of the marriage-tie . . . I can only say that I have always defended that institution on the same ground that Mr. Fitzjames Stephen takes in support of the kindred institution—merely as a salutary check on the vulgar propensities of our natural inferiors; but when I hear that a personal friend has fallen into matrimonial courses, I feel the same sorrow as if I had heard of his lapsing into theism—a holy sorrow, unmixed with anger, for who am I to judge him? I think at such a sight as the preacher—was it not Baxter?—at sight of a thief or murderer led to the gallows, 'There, but for the grace of ——, goes A. C. S.,' and drop a tear over fallen man. Algernon Charles Swinburne to Edwin Harrison, 13 February 1878: *Letters* (1918), 62.

We hear that Lord Byron is going to be a good boy, and will never be naughty no more, and he is really and truly writing a new version of the *Psalms*. Emily Eden to Lady Buckinghamshire, 25 October 1814: *Miss Eden's Letters* (1919), 3.

I know of nothing that will be so interesting to you at present, as some circumstances of the last act of that eminent comic poet, and our friend, Wycherly. He had often told me, as I doubt not he did all his acquaintance, that he would marry as soon as his life was despaired of: Accordingly a few days before his death he underwent the ceremony; and join'd together those two sacraments which, wise men say, should be the last we receive; for, if you observe, Matrimony is placed after Extreme unction in our Catechism, as a kind of hint of the order of time in which they are to be taken. The old man then lay down, satisfy'd in the conscience of having by this one act paid his just debts, obliged a woman, who (he was told) had merit, and shown an heroic resentment of the ill usage of his next heir. Some hundred pounds which he had with the Lady, discharged those debts; a jointure of four hundred a year made her a recompense; and the nephew he left to comfort himself as well as he could, with the miserable remains of a mortgaged estate. ALEXANDER POPE to EDWARD BLOUNT, 21 January 1715: *Works* (1753), viii, 8.

'Lord, Mr. Dryden, how can you be always poring over those musty books? I wish I were a book, and then I should have more of your company.' 'Pray, my dear,' replied old John, 'if you do become a book let it be an almanack, for then I shall change you every year.' EDWARD MALONE: *Life* (1860), 436–7.

But, Madam, let me say, that, dearly as I love your sex; I am so well satisfied with the laws of my country, that it would be criminal in me, in my own eye, to hint at any doctrine, much more at any license, (whether criminal or not, in other respects), that should tend to enslave the one, as the doctrine of polygamy must do, or weaken the laws of my country. But when, in this country, the sex is so generally running into licentiousness; when home is found to be the place that is most irksome to them; when Ranelaghs, Vauxhalls, Marybones, assemblies, routs, drums, hurricanes, and a rabble of such-like amusements, carry them out of all domestic duty and usefulness into infinite riot and expense; day and night inverted; and that sex, in which virtue, modesty, sobriety, ought to be characteristically found, in order to save a corrupted world, were those qualities and graces to be lost in the generality of the other;—then would I beg leave to remind the wild pigeons of the sex, that they are not the doves they were designed to be; and that such cannot claim the privileges allowed to English wives, with any justice. SAMUEL RICHARDSON to LADY BRADSHAIGH, 17 August 1752: *Correspondence* (1804), vi, 210–11.

Such is the nature of woman, if she be not a vixen indeed, that if if the man sets out right with her; if he lets her early know that he is her lord, and that she is but his vassal; and that he has a stronger sense of his prerogative than of her merit and beauty; she will succumb: and, after a few struggles, a few tears, will make him a more humble, a more passive wife, for his insolent bravery, and high opinion of himself. SAMUEL RICHARDSON to LADY BRADSHAIGH, 26 December 1751: *Correspondence* (1804), vi, 129–30.

He [Robert Browning], as you say, had done everything for me, had loved me for reasons which had helped to weary me of myself, loved me heart to heart persistently—in spite of my own will —drawn me back to life and hope again when I had done with both. My life seemed to belong to him and to none other at least, and I had no power to speak a word. Have faith in me, my dearest friend, till you can know him. The intellect is so little in comparison to all the rest, to the womanly tenderness, the inexhaustible goodness, the high and noble aspiration of every hour. Temper, spirits, manners: there is not a flaw anywhere. I shut my eyes sometimes and fancy it all a dream of my guardian angel. Only, if it had been a dream, the pain of some parts of it would have awakened me before now; it is not a dream. ELIZABETH BARRETT BROWNING to MISS MITFORD, 2 October 1846: *Letters* (1897), i, 298.

The Reverend Mr. John M'Aulay, one of the Ministers of Inverary . . . came to us this morning, and accompanied us to the castle, where I presented Dr. Johnson to the Duke of Argyle. We were shown through the house; and I shall never forget the impression made upon my fancy by some of the ladies' maids tripping about in neat morning dresses. After seeing for a long time little but rusticity, their lively manner, and gay inviting appearance, pleased me so much, that I thought for the moment, I could have been a knight-errant for them. JAMES BOSWELL at Inverary, 25 October 1773: 'A Tour in the Hebrides', *Boswell's Life of Johnson* (1887), v, 355.

VIII

TALK AND TALKERS

I like a man who talks me to death, provided he is amusing; it saves so much trouble. Mrs. Shelley to Abraham Hayward, *Mr. Hayward's Letters* (1886), i, 83.

Too much talking is ever the index of the fool. Ben Jonson, *Discoveries* (1641), xlvi.

HAZLITT HAS A BAD PLATFORM MANNER. Heard Hazlitt's first lecture on the *History of English Philosophy*. He seems to have no conception of the difference between a lecture and a book. What he said was sensible and excellent, but he delivered himself in a low monotonous voice, with his eyes fixed on his MS., not once daring to look at his audience; and he read so rapidly that no one could possibly give the matter the attention it required. HENRY CRABB ROBINSON, 14 January 1812: *Diary* (1872), i, 192.

LANDOR OVERWHELMS THE CARLYLES. Walter Savage Landor . . . called . . . and talked us almost into syncope. THOMAS CARLYLE to his brother DR. CARLYLE, 26 May 1839: *New Letters* (1904), i, 162.

COLERIDGE ORATES. Coleridge cannot *con*verse. He addresses himself *to* his hearers. HENRY CRABB ROBINSON to DOROTHY WORDSWORTH, 23 December 1810: *Diary* (1872), i, 165.

COLERIDGE WALKS AND TALKS TO KEATS. Last Sunday I took a walk towards Highgate and in the lane that winds by the side of Lord Mansfield's park I met Mr. Green our Demonstrator at Guy's in conversation with Coleridge—I joined them, after enquiring by a look whether it would be agreeable—I walked with him at his alderman-after-dinner pace for near two miles I suppose. In those two Miles he broached a thousand things—let me see if I can give you a list—Nightingales, Poetry—on Poetical Sensation—Metaphysics—Different genera and species of Dreams —Nightmare—a dream accompanied with a sense of touch— single and double touch—a dream related—First and second consciousness—the difference explained between will and Voli- tion—so many metaphysicians from a want of smoking the second consciousness—Monsters—the Kraken—Mermaids— Southey believes in them—Southey's belief too much diluted— a Ghost story—Good morning—I heard his voice as he came to- wards me—I heard it as he moved away—I had heard it all the interval—if it may be called so. JOHN KEATS to GEORGE and GEORGIANA KEATS, 15 April 1819: *Letters* (1895), 312–3.

TALK FOR TALK'S SAKE. Coleridge is the only person who can talk to all sorts of people, on all sorts of subjects, without caring a farthing for their understanding one word he says. WILLIAM HAZLITT, *London Magazine*, September 1820.

THE MUSES LISTEN WHEN COLERIDGE TALKS. I dined in Par- nassus, with Wordsworth, Coleridge, Rogers, and Tom Moore, —half the poetry of England constellated and cluster'd in Gloucester Place. It was a delightful Even! Coleridge was in his finest vein of talk, had all the talk, and let 'em talk as evilly as they do of the envy of Poets, I am sure not one there but was content to be nothing but a listener. The Muses were dumb while Apollo lectured. CHARLES LAMB to BERNARD BARTON, 5 April 1823: *Letters* (1905), ii, 605.

WORDSWORTH PURRS. He talks in a manner very peculiar. As for duration, it is from the rising up of the sun to the going down of the same. As for quality, a sort of thinking aloud, a perpetual purring of satisfaction. He murmurs like a tree in the breeze; as softly and as incessantly; it seems as natural to him to talk as to breathe. He is by nature audible, as well as visible, and goes on thus uttering his being just as a fountain continues to flow, or a star to shine. In his discourse I was at first principally struck by the extraordinary purity of his language, and the absolute perfection of his sentences; but by degrees I came to find a great charm in observing the exquisite balance of his mind, and the train of associations in which his thoughts followed each other. He does not put forward thoughts like those of Coleridge which astonished his hearers by their depth or vastness, but you gradually discover that there is a sort of inspiration in the mode in which his thoughts flow out of each other, and connect themselves with outward things. He is the voice and Nature the instrument; and they always keep in perfect tune. AUBREY DE VERE to his sister, 25 June 1841: *Memoir*, (1904), 64.

MRS. CARLYLE AND HER CAT'S TONGUE. She had, when she was angry, a tongue like a cat's, which would take the skin off at a touch. SIR JAMES CRICHTON BROWNE, *New Letters* (1903), lxiii.

MACAULAY OVERWHELMS BUT—— Macaulay is a most extraordinary man, and his astonishing knowledge is every moment exhibited, but (as far as I have yet seen of him, which is not sufficient to judge) he is not *agreeable*. His propositions and his allusions are rather too abrupt; he starts topics not altogether naturally; then he has none of the graces of conversation, none of that exquisite tact and refinement which are the result of a felicitous intuition or a long acquaintance with good society, or more probably a mixture of both. The mighty mass of his knowledge is not animated by that subtle spirit of taste and discretion which alone can give it the qualities of lightness and elasticity and without which, though he may have the power of instructing and astonishing, he never will attain that of delighting and captivating his hearers. CHARLES C. F. GREVILLE, 12 August 1832: *The Greville Memoirs* (1875), ii, 317–18.

DEVELOPS FLASHES OF SILENCE. Yes, he is certainly more agreeable since his return from India. His enemies might perhaps have said before (though I never did so) that he talked rather too much; but now he has occasional flashes of silence, that makes his conversation perfectly delightful. SYDNEY SMITH: *Life and Letters of Macaulay*, Trevelyan (1876), ii, 273.

Talk and Talkers

CARLYLE AND MACAULAY COMPARED. I can imagine no better fun than to have Carlyle and himself [Macaulay] meet accidentally at the same dinner-table with a small company. It would be like two locomotives, each with a long train, coming against each other at express speed. Both, I have no doubt, could be smashed into silence at the first collision. Macaulay, however, is not so dogmatic, or so outrageously absurd as Carlyle often is, neither is he half so grotesque or amusing. His whole manner has the smoothness and polished surface of the man of the world, the politician, and the new poet, spread over the man of letters within. I do not know that I can repeat any of his conversation, for there was nothing to excite very particular attention in its even flow. . . . It is the perfection of the commonplace, without sparkle or flash, but at the same time always interesting and agreeable. JOHN LOTHROP MOTLEY to his Wife, 30 May 1858: *Correspondence* (1889), i, 237.

CHARLES KINGSLEY IS RACY AND CORRECT. Kingsley's conversational powers were very remarkable. In the first place he has, as may be easily understood by the readers of his books, a rare command of racy and correct English, while he was so many sided that he could take keen interest in almost any subject which attracted those about him. He had read, and read much, not only in matters which every one ought to know, but had gone deeply into many out-of-the-way and unexpected studies. Old medicine, magic, the occult properties of plants, folk-lore, mesmerism, nooks and bye-ways of history, old legends; on all these he was at home. On the habits and dispositions of animals he would talk as though he were that king in the *Arabian Nights* who understood the language of beasts, or at least had lived among the gipsies who loved him so well. The stammer, which in those days was so much more marked than in later years, and which was a serious discomfort to himself, was no drawback to the charm of his conversation. Rather the hesitation before some brilliant flash of words served to lend point to and intensify what he was saying; and when, as he sometimes did, he fell into a monologue, or recited a poem in his sonorous voice, the stammer left him wholly, as it did when he read or preached in church. C. KEGAN PAUL, *Charles Kingsley*, by his Wife (1877), i, 225.

THACKERAY A DRY LECTURER. Went to Thackeray's lecture on the *Humorists* at Willis's Rooms. It was a very large assembly, including Mrs. Carlyle, Dickens, Leslie, and innumerable noteworthy people. Thackeray is a much older-looking man than I had expected; a square, powerful face, and most acute and sparkling eyes, greyish hair and eyebrows. He reads in a definite, rather dry manner, but makes you understand thoroughly what he is about. CAROLINE FOX, 12 June 1851: *Memories* (1882), 269.

EMERSON STEPS DELICATELY AMONG WORDS. I went to the Club last Saturday, and . . . sat by the side of Emerson, who always charms me with his delicious voice, his fine sense and wit, and the delicate way he steps about among the words of his vocabulary,—if you have seen a cat picking her footsteps in wet weather, you have seen the picture of Emerson's exquisite intelligence, feeling for its phrase or epithet,—sometimes I think of an ant-eater singling out his insects, as I see him looking about and at last seizing his noun or adjective,—the best, the only one which would serve the need of his thought. OLIVER WENDELL HOLMES to JOHN LOTHROP MOTLEY, 3 April 1870: *Life* (1896), ii, 188–9.

LOWES DICKINSON MORE SOCRATIC THAN SOCRATES. In his talk, as in writing, he had the evenness of temper, and the power to state the other side fairly which are supposed to characterize Socrates. Indeed, to a Goth like myself he seems much more Socratic than Socrates. Socrates—as Plato presents him—would have emptied any modern room at once. Dickinson kept every room full, never nagging, never setting traps, never reducing the company to silence while he demonstrated the supremacy of his intellect, the justness of his opinion, the aptness of his wit, the profundity of his vision. E. M. FORSTER, *Goldsworthy Lowes Dickinson* (1934), 46.

Talk and Talkers

ARNOLD BENNETT REPORTS SHAW AND BELLOC CIRCUS. (Political Debate between G. B. Shaw and Hilaire Belloc as to Connection between Private Property and Servitude. At Queen's Hall.) Went with Vaughan. Crammed, at concert prices. Not a seat unsold. Shaw very pale with white hair, and straight. His wife beside him. Effect too conjugal for a man at work. Sidney and Beatrice Webb next to them. Effect also too conjugal here. Maurice Baring supporting Belloc, both very shabby. Maurice with loose brown boots and creased socks. They spoke thus. Belloc 30 mins. Shaw 30. Belloc 20. Shaw 20. Belloc 10. Shaw 10. Time was kept to three minutes. Belloc's first was pretty good. Shaw's first was a first-class performance, couldn't have been better; the perfection of public speaking (not oratory); not a word wrong. But then afterwards the impression that it was a gladiatorial show or circus performance gained on one, and at the end was a sense of disappointment, as the affair degenerated into a mere rivalry in 'scoring'. Still I have never seen Shaw emotional before, as he was then. ARNOLD BENNETT, 28 January 1913: *Journals* (1932), ii, 57–8.

IX

CONVERSATION PIECES

A conversation among literary men is muddy. R. W. Emerson, *Journals*, Perry, 145.

I have always rather tried to escape the acquaintance and conversation of authors. An author talking of his own works, or censuring those of others, is to me a dose of ipecacuanha. Horace Walpole, *Walpoliana* (1800), 17.

Talking of conversation, he [Johnson] said, 'There must, in the first place, be knowledge, there must be materials;—in the second place, there must be a command of words; in the third place, there must be imagination, to place things in such views as they are not commonly seen in;—and in the fourth place, there must be presence of mind, and a resolution that is not to be overcome by failures: this last is an essential requisite; for want of it many people do not excel in conversation. Now *I* want it: I throw up the game upon losing a trick.' I wondered to hear him talk thus of himself, and said, 'I don't know, Sir, how this may be; but I am sure you beat other people's cards out of their hands.' I doubt whether he heard this remark. 21 March 1783: *Boswell's Johnson* (1887), iv, 166.

6 APRIL 1772. Fielding being mentioned, Johnson exclaimed 'he was a blockhead'; and upon my expressing my astonishment at so strange an assertion,

JOHNSON: 'What I mean by his being a blockhead is that he was a barren rascal.'

BOSWELL: 'Will you not allow, Sir, that he draws very natural pictures of human life?'

Conversation Pieces

JOHNSON: 'Why, Sir, it is of very low life. Richardson used to say, that had he not known who Fielding was, he should have believed he was an ostler. Sir, there is more knowledge of the heart in one letter of Richardson's, than in all *Tom Jones*. I, indeed, never read *Joseph Andrews*.'

ERSKINE: 'Surely, Sir, Richardson is very tedious.'

JOHNSON: 'Why, Sir, if you were to read Richardson for the story, your impatience would be so much fretted that you would hang yourself. But you must read him for the sentiment, and consider the story as only giving occasion to the sentiment.' *Boswell's Johnson* (1887), ii, 173–5.

MAURICE MORGANN [Author of the *Essay on the Character of Sir John Falstaff*, 1777]. 'Pray, Sir, whether do you reckon Derrick or Smart the best poet?'

DR. JOHNSON. 'Sir, there is no settling the point of precedency between a louse and a flea.' 1783: *Boswell's Johnson* (1887), iv, 192.

Dr. Johnson no sooner saw [Adam] Smith than he brought forward a charge against him for something in his famous letter on the death of Hume. Smith said he had vindicated the truth of the statement. 'And what did the Doctor say?' was the universal query: 'why, he said—he said——' said Smith, with the deepest impression of resentment, 'he said, "*You lie!*"' 'And what did you reply?' 'I said, "You are a son of a bitch!"' On these terms the two great moralists meet and part. SIR WALTER SCOTT to JOHN WILSON CROKER, 30 January 1829: *The Croker Papers* (1884), ii, 31.

Boswell, that quintessence of busybodies, called on me last week, and was let in, which he should not have been could I have foreseen it. After tapping many topics, to which I made as dry answers as an unbribed oracle, he vented his errand. 'Had I seen Dr. Johnson's *Lives of the Poets*?' I said slightly, 'No, not yet,' and so overlaid his whole impertinence. HORACE WALPOLE to REV. WILLIAM MASON, 22 May 1781: *Letters* (1891), viii, 44.

Conversation Pieces

I remember going into his [Scott's] library shortly after the publication of *The Lady of the Lake*, and finding Miss Scott (who was then a very young girl) there by herself. I asked her, 'Well, Miss Sophia, how do you like *The Lady of the Lake*?' Her answer was given with perfect simplicity. 'Oh, I have not read it; papa says there's nothing so bad for young people as reading bad poetry.' JAMES BALLANTYNE, *Life of Scott*, Lockhart (1837–8), ii, 306.

Once before I had ever seen Wordsworth . . . I met a person who had enjoyed the signal honour of travelling with him to London. It was in a stage-coach. . . . Immediately he was glorified in my eyes. 'And', said I, to this glorified gentleman (who, *par parenthèse*, was also a donkey), 'Now, as you travelled nearly three hundred miles in the company of Mr. Wordsworth, consequently (for this was in 1805) during two nights and two days, doubtless you must have heard many profound remarks that would inevitably fall from his lips.' 'Nay, Coleridge had also been of the party; and, if Wordsworth *solus* could have been dull, was it within human possibilities that these *gemini* should have been so?' 'Was it possible?' I said; and perhaps my donkey, who looked like one that had been immoderately threatened, at last took courage; his eye brightened; and he intimated that he *did* remember something that Wordsworth had said. . . .

'Ay, indeed; and what was it now? What did the great man say?'

'Why sir, in fact, and to make a long story short, on coming near London, we breakfasted at Baldock. . . . Well, now, sir, would you believe it, though we were quite on regular time, the breakfast was precisely good for nothing?'

'And Wordsworth?'

'He observed——'

'What did he observe?'

'That the buttered toast looked, for all the world, as if it had been soaked in hot water.' THOMAS DE QUINCEY, *Collected Writings* (1889), ii, 314–15.

One morning, when Hookham Frere breakfasted with me, Coleridge talked for three hours without intermission about poetry, and so admirably, that I wish every word he uttered had been written down. But sometimes his harangues were quite unintelligible, not only to myself, but to others. Wordsworth and I called upon him one forenoon, when he was in a lodging off Pall Mall. He talked uninterruptedly for about two hours, during which Wordsworth listened to him with profound attention, every now and then nodding his head as if in assent. On quitting the lodging, I said to Wordsworth, 'Well, for my own part, I could not make head or tail of Coleridge's oration: pray, did you understand it?' 'Not one syllable of it,' was Wordsworth's reply. SAMUEL ROGERS, *Table-Talk* (1856), 205.

Wordsworth called to-day, and we went to church together. There was no seat to be got at the chapel near us, belonging to the rectory of Paddington, and we sat among publicans and sinners. I determined to try him, so advised our staying, as we could hear more easily. He agreed like a Christian; and I was much interested in seeing his venerable white head close to a servant in livery, and on the same level. The servant in livery fell asleep, and so did Wordsworth. I jogged him at the Gospel, and he opened his eyes and read well. A preacher preached when we expected another, so it was a disappointment. We afterwards walked to Rogers's across the park. He had a party to lunch, so I went into the pictures, and sucked Rembrandt, Reynolds, Veronese, Raffaele, Hassan and Tintoretto. Wordsworth said, 'Haydon is down stairs.' 'Ah,' said Rogers, 'he is better employed than chattering nonsense upstairs.' As Wordsworth and I crossed the park, we said, 'Scott, Wilkie, Keats, Hazlitt, Beaumont, Jackson, Charles Lamb, are all gone;—we only are left.' He said, 'How old are you?' 'Fifty-six,' I replied. 'How old are you?' 'Seventy-three,' he said; 'in my seventy-third year. I was born in 1770.' 'And I in 1786.' 'You have many years before you.' 'I trust I have; and you, too, I hope. Let us cut out Titian, who was ninety-nine.' 'Was he ninety-nine?' said Wordsworth. 'Yes,' said I, 'and his death was a moral; for as he lay dying of the plague, he was plundered, and could not help himself.' . . . I quoted his own beautiful address to the stock dove. He said, once in a wood, Mrs. Wordsworth and a lady were walking, when the stock dove was cooing. A farmer's wife coming by said to herself, 'Oh, I do like stock doves!' Mrs. Wordsworth, in all her enthusiasm for Wordsworth's poetry, took the old woman to her heart; 'but' continued the old woman, 'some like them in a pie; for my part there's nothing like 'em stewed in onions.' BENJAMIN ROBERT HAYDON, 22 May 1842: *Autobiography* (1853), iii, 218–19.

Passing along a long dim passage, I came on a tall man leant to the wall, with his head touching the ceiling like a caryatid, to all appearance asleep, or resolutely trying it under the most unfavourable circumstances. 'Alfred Tennyson!' I exclaimed in joyful surprise. 'Well!' said he, taking the hand I held out to him, and forgetting to let it go again. 'I did not know you were in town', said I. 'I should like to know who you are,' said he; 'I know that I know you, but I cannot tell your name.' And I had actually to name myself to him. Then he woke up in good earnest, and said he had been meaning to come to Chelsea. 'But Carlyle is in Scotland,' I told him with humility. 'So I heard from Spedding already, but I asked Spedding, would he go with me to see Mrs. Carlyle? and he said he would.' I told him if he really meant to come, he had better not wait for backing, under the present circumstances. . . . Craik arrived next evening (Sunday) to make his compliments . . . I was lying on the sofa headachey leaving Craik to put himself to the chief expenditure of wind when a cab drove up. Mr. Strachey? No. Alfred Tennyson alone! Actually, by a superhuman effort of volition he had put himself into a cab, nay, brought himself away from a dinner party, and was there to smoke and talk with me!—by myself—me! But no such blessedness was in store for him. Craik prosed, and John babbled for his entertainment, and I, whom he had come to see, got scarcely any speech with him. The exertion, however, of having to provide him with tea, through my own unassisted ingenuity (Helen being gone for the evening) drove away my headache; also perhaps a little feminine vanity at having inspired such a man with the energy to take a cab on his own responsibility, to throw himself on providence for getting away again! He stayed till eleven, Craik sitting him out, as he . . . would sit out the Virgin Mary should he find her here. JANE WELSH CARLYLE to THOMAS CARLYLE, 23 September 1845: *Letters and Memorials* (1883), i, 341.

CARLYLE: 'Do you know De Quincey?'

SOUTHEY: 'Yes, sir, and if you have opportunity, I'll thank you to tell him he is one of the greatest scoundrels living!' CARLYLE, *Reminiscences* (1881), ii, 315.

On returning from a visit to the Lakes, I told Porson that Southey had said to me, 'My *Madoc* has brought me in a mere trifle; but that poem will be a valuable possession to my family.' Porson answered, '*Madoc* will be read,—when Homer and Virgil are forgotten.' SAMUEL ROGERS, *Table-Talk* (1856), 331.

When the demand for the word had assured success to *Jane Eyre*, her sisters urged Charlotte to tell their father of its publication. She accordingly went into his study one afternoon after his early dinner, carrying with her a copy of the book, and two or three reviews, taking care to include a notice adverse to it. She informed me that something like the following conversation took place between her and him. (I wrote down her words the day after I heard them; and I am pretty sure they are quite accurate.)

'Papa, I've been writing a book.'

'Have you, my dear?'

'Yes, and I want you to read it.'

'I am afraid it will try my eyes too much.'

'But it is not in manuscript; it is printed.'

'My dear! you've never thought of the expense it will be! It will almost sure to be a loss, for how can you get a book sold? No one knows you or your name.'

'But, papa, I don't think it will be a loss; no more will you, if you will just let me read you a review or two, and tell you more about it.'

So she sate down and read some of the reviews to her father; and then, giving him the copy of *Jane Eyre* that she intended for him, she left him to read it. When he came in to tea, he said, 'Girls, do you know Charlotte has been writing a book, and it is much better than likely?' MRS. GASKELL, *Life of Charlotte Brontë* (1857), ii, 36–7.

Last night at dinner I saw Lady Oxford again. I had a great time with her at the Aeolian Hall, sitting next her. The quartette was appalling and lasted 50 minutes. I said: 'There's only one word—"bloody".' She roared and passed it along the row to her son and others. Dame Ethel Smyth sat in front of us. She was far worse. She said to me: 'If this goes on much longer I shall be taken short.' In short, a lively evening. I can't write any more now. ARNOLD BENNETT, 4 February 1930: *Letters to his Nephew* (1936), 289.

Went to breakfast with George Lewis to meet Ranke, the author of *The Popes of the Sixteenth and Seventeenth Century*. He had got Macaulay, who had reviewed his book, to meet him, Sir Alexander Duff Gordon and his wife (daughter of Mrs. Austin, his translator), and Sir Edmund Head. I went prepared to listen to some first-rate literary talk between such luminaries as Ranke and Macaulay, but there never was a greater failure. The professor, a vivacious little man, not distinguished in appearance, could talk no English, and his French, though spoken fluently, was quite unintelligible. On the other hand, Macaulay could not speak German, and he spoke French without any facility and with a very vile accent. It was comical to see the abundance of his matter struggling with his embarrassment in giving utterance to it, to hear the torrent of knowledge trying to force its way through the impediment of a limited acquaintance with the French language and the want of habit of conversing in it. But the struggle was of short duration. He began in French, but very soon could bear the restraint no longer, and broke into English, pouring forth his stores to the utterly unconscious and uncomprehending professor. This babel of a breakfast, at which it was impossible for seven people to converse in any common language, soon came to an end, and Ranke was evidently glad to go off to the State Paper Office, where he was working every day. After he had gone, Macaulay held forth, and was as usual very well worth listening to. CHARLES C. F. GREVILLE, *The Greville Memoirs* (1885), ii, 203.

X

DESIGNS FOR LIVING

Man has unrivalled powers of self-adaptation—ay, of adapting himself to wanting everything; just as easily as to wanting nothing; there's the plague. Rev. Charles Kingsley to Rev. R. C. Powles, 1846: *Letters and Memories* (1877), i, 140.

ROGER ASCHAM DESIRES TO BE QUIET WITH HIS BOOKS. I am more desirous to have your help for my stay at Cambridge . . . than for any kind of living elsewhere. I having now some experience of life at home and abroad, and knowing what I can do most fitly, and how I would live most gladly, do well perceive there is no such quietness in England, nor pleasure in strange centres, as even in S. Johns College than to keep company with the *Bible*, *Plato*, *Aristotle*, *Demosthenes* and *Tully*. ROGER ASCHAM to SIR WILLIAM CECIL one of the two Principal Secretaries to the King's Majesty, 24 March 1553: *Original Letters of Literary Men* (1843), 13–14.

GOOD ADVICE FROM GEORGE HERBERT. Let there be a kind of excellency which it is possible for you to attain to, which you seek not; and have a good conceit of your wit, mark what I say, have a good conceit of your wit; that is, be proud, not with a foolish vaunting of yourself when there is no cause, but by setting a just price of your qualities . . . And it is the part of a poor spirit to undervalue himself and blush. GEORGE HERBERT to his brother 1618: *Remains* (1848), 298.

MRS. MONTAGU AND THE GARDEN CURE. I think one should put one's son apprentice to a gardener before he goes into the House of Commons, that when he is an unsuccessful politician he may retire to his garden with some pleasure and skill to boot. ELIZABETH MONTAGU to HON. MRS. BOSCAWEN, 25 October 1757: *Letters* (1813), ix, 72.

HORACE WALPOLE IS SICK OF VISIONS AND SYSTEMS. Roehampton is a delightful spot, at once cheerful and retired. You will amble in your chaise about Richmond-park: and we shall see one another as often as we like; I shall frequently peep at London, and bring you tales of it, and we shall sometimes touch a card with the Clive, and laugh our fill; for I must tell you, I desire to die when I have nobody left to laugh with me. I have never yet seen or heard anything serious, that was not ridiculous. Jesuits, methodists, philosophers, politicians, the hypocrite Rousseau, the scoffer Voltaire, the encyclopedists, the Humes, the Lyttletons, the Grenvilles, the atheist tyrant of Prussia, and the mountebank of history, Mr. Pitt, all are to me but imposters in their various ways. Fame or interest is their object; and after all their parade, I think a ploughman who sows, reads his almanack, and believes the stars but so many farthing candles, created to prevent his falling into a ditch as he goes home at night, a wiser and more rational being, and I am sure an honester than any of them. Oh! I am sick of visions and systems, that shove one another aside, and come over again, like the figures in a moving picture. Rabelais brightens up to me as I see more of the world; he treated it as it deserved, laughed at it all, and as I judge from myself, ceased to hate it; for I find hatred an unjust preference. HORACE WALPOLE to GEORGE MONTAGU, 21 November 1765: *Letters* (1891), iv, 440.

COWPER FINDS PEACE AND HAPPINESS IN HIS ORCHARD. For the sake of a longer visit, my dearest coz, I can be well content to wait. The country, this country at least, is pleasant at all times, and when winter is come, or near at hand, we shall have the better chance for being snug. I know your passion for retirement indeed, or for what we call *deedy* retirement, and the F——s intending to return to Bath with their mother, when her visit at the Hall is over, you will then find here exactly the retirement in question. I have made in the orchard the best winterwalk in all the parish, sheltered from the east, and from the north-east, and open to the sun, except at his rising, all the day. Then we will have Homer and *Don Quixote*: and then we will have saunter and chat, and one laugh more before we die. Our orchard is alive with creatures of all kinds; poultry of every denomination swarms in it, and pigs, the drollest in the world! WILLIAM COWPER at Weston Underwood to his cousin LADY HESKETH, 27 June 1788: *Letters* (1912), ii, 196.

WORDSWORTH HAS FAITH IN NATURE AND BOOKS. Do your duty to yourself immediately; love Nature and Books; seek these, and you will be happy; for virtuous friendship, and love, and knowledge of mankind must inevitably accompany these, all things thus ripening in their due season. WILLIAM WORDSWORTH at Grasmere to THOMAS DE QUINCEY at Worcester College, Oxford, 6 March 1804: *Early Letters of William and Dorothy Wordsworth* (1935), 370.

MACAULAY DREAMS OF ESCAPE FROM PUBLIC LIFE. I begin to wonder what the fascination is which attracts men, who could sit over their tea and their books in their own cool, quiet room, to breathe bad air, hear bad speeches, lounge up and down the long gallery, and doze uneasily on the green benches till three in the morning. Thank God, these luxuries are not necessary to me. My pen is sufficient for my support, and my sister's company is sufficient for my happiness. Only let me see her well and cheerful; and let offices in the Government, and seats in Parliament, go to those who care for them. If I were to leave public life to-morrow, I declare that, except for the vexation it might give you and one or two others, the event would not be in the slightest degree painful to me. T. B. MACAULAY to his sister HANNAH, 17 June 1833: *Life* (1909), i, 270–1.

CARLYLE SEEKS SOLITUDE. Solitude is what I long and pray for. In the babble of men my own soul goes all to babble: like soil you were forever *screening*, tumbling over with shovels and riddles;

in which soil no fruit can grow! My trust in Heaven is, I shall yet get away 'to some cottage by the sea-shore'; far enough from all the mad and mad-making things that dance around me here, which I shall then look on only as a theatrical phantasmagory, with an eye only to the meaning that lies hidden in it. You, friend Emerson, are to be a Farmer, you say, and dig Earth for your living, Well; I envy you that as much as any other of your blessednesses. Meanwhile I sit shrunk together here in a small dressing-closet, alôft in the back part of the house, excluding all cackle and cockneys; and, looking out over the similitude of a May grove (with little brick in it, and only the minarets of West-minster and gilt cross of St. Paul's visible in the distance, and the enormous roar of London softened into an enormous hum), en-deavour to await what will betide. I am busy with Luther in one Marheinecke's very long-winded Book. I think of innumerable things; steal out westward at sunset among the Kensington lanes; would this *May* weather last, I might be as well here as in any attainable place. But June comes; the rabid dogs get muzzles; all is brown-parched, dusty, suffocating, desperate, and I shall have to run! THOMAS CARLYLE to RALPH WALDO EMERSON, 21 May 1841: *Correspondence of Carlyle and Emerson, 1834–1872* (1883), i, 330.

THOREAU'S AMORALIST IDEAL. Pursue, keep up with, circle round and round your life, as a dog does his master's chaise. Do what you love. Know your own bone; gnaw at it, bury it, un-earth it, and gnaw it still. Do not be too moral. You may cheat yourself out of much life so. Aim above morality. Be not simply good; be good for something. All fables, indeed, have their morals; but the innocent enjoy the story. Let nothing come be-tween you and the light. Respect men and brothers only. When you travel to the Celestial City, carry no letter of introduction. When you knock, ask to see God,—none of the servants. In what concerns you much, do not think that you have companions: know that you are alone in the world. H. D. THOREAU, 27 March 1848: *Essays and Other Writings* [n.d.], 197.

Designs for Living

RUSKIN UPHOLDS REAL WEALTH. Free-heartedness, and graciousness, and undisturbed trust, and requited love, and the sight of the peace of others, and the ministry to their pain; these,—and the blue sky above you, and the sweet waters and flowers of the earth beneath; and mysteries and presences, innumerable, of living things,—may yet be here your riches; untormenting and divine: serviceable for the life that now is; nor, it may be, without promise of that which is to come. JOHN RUSKIN, *The Crown of Wild Olive* (1866), Intro. 22–3.

JOHN ADDINGTON SYMONDS AIMS AT SELF-DEPENDENCE. To study, to acquire facts, gain style, lose the faults of youth, form a standard of taste, throw off dependence on authority, learn to be sincere, try to see clearly, refuse to speak before I feel, grow logical, must be my aim. JOHN ADDINGTON SYMONDS, 1865: *Biography* (1908), 186.

CHARLES ELIOT NORTON PLANS A PERFECT FARM FOR HIMSELF AND LOWELL. I propose that when you retire from Cambridge you should come up here to live. We will buy together five or six hundred acres, and have a great sheep and stock farm. We can get a good head man for overseer, and then we will raise prize merinoes, and have a herd of Dutch cattle, and of shorthorns, and such stables as have not been imagined north of Pennsylvania. I have already selected the place, and only want you to approve the choice. . . . There is a lovely trout stream running through the farm; bordered with deep woods of beech and maple in which are great ledges of rock and enormous boulders covered with moss and ferns; the woods stretch up the hillside and from the top of the hill one can look anywhere,—even in Canaan. There is a sunny slope for the orchard, and the meadows stretch away smooth and green below. Here one can live in luxury on the salary of a German professor;—and here we would have our books as well as our farm, and would build on the solid earth of actual performance those castles which in Cambridge are only of the air. Here we would welcome the tax-gatherer as a messenger from our dear country,—we would not dread our annual bills;

Designs for Living

but we would live in content and in peace and grow old, loving each other. . . . CHARLES ELIOT NORTON to J. R. LOWELL, 26 May 1866: *Letters* (1913), i, 290.

JOHN RICHARD GREEN ON HARMONIOUS LIVING. Remember my theory of life is no mere indolence theory. I have worked hard and mean to work hard on things which have a worthy end and use. What I protest against is mere asceticism, a blindness to what is really beautiful and pleasurable in life, a preference for the disagreeable as if it were in *itself* better than the agreeable, above all a parting of life into this element and that, and a contempt of half the life we have to live as if it were something which hindered us from living the other half. Mind and soul and body—I would have all harmoniously develop together—neither intellectualism nor spiritualism, nor sensualism, but a broad humanity. J. R. GREEN to MISS STOPFORD, 24 March 1877: *Letters* (1901), 450.

LOWELL WOULD LIVE ON INCOME FROM FLOWERS AND DIVIDENDS OF THE SEASONS. Good heavens, of what uncostly material is our earthly happiness composed—if we only knew it! What incomes have we not had from a flower, and how unfailing are the dividends of the seasons! JAMES RUSSELL LOWELL to THOMAS HUGHES, 10 April 1890: *Letters* (1894), ii, 446.

BERNARD SHAW'S RECEIPT FOR TRUE JOY. This is the true joy in life, the being used for a purpose recognized by yourself as a mighty one; the being thoroughly worn out before you are thrown on the scrap heap; the being a force of Nature instead of a feverish selfish little clod of ailment and grieving complaining that the world will not devote itself to making you happy. And also the only real tragedy in life is the being used by personally minded men for purposes which you recognize to be base. All the rest is mere misfortune or mortality: this alone is misery, slavery, hell on earth; and the revolt against it is the only force that offers a man's work to the poor artist, whom our personally minded rich people would so willingly employ as pander, buffoon, beauty monger, sentimentalizer and the like. BERNARD SHAW, Pref. *Man and Superman* (1903), xxxii.

A COUNTRY LIFE AND A LIBRARY FOR GEORGE WYNDHAM. I have a wife, a son, a home, six good hunters and a library of Romance literature. I mean to enjoy them. If I am wanted, I can be found. GEORGE WYNDHAM at Saighton Grange, Cheshire, to CHARLES BOYD, 23 February 1908: *Life and Letters* [N.D.], ii, 602.

XI

SMALL TALK FROM HELICON

The variations of life consist of little things. Dr. Johnson to Mrs. Thrale, *Piozzi Letters* (1861), i, 354.

Though fate has denied to me the honour of suckling fools, the inferior female office of chronicling small beer, remains to me in full force. Elizabeth Montague, 1756: *Letters* (1813), iv, 42.

And do write chatty letters. There is none I like so much. Tell me about everybody. J. R. Green at San Remo to Miss von Glehn, 28 November 1870: *Letters* (1901), 271.

THE INDOLENCE OF GIBBON. Mr. Gibbon, the historian, is so exceedingly indolent that he never even pares his nails. His servant, while Gibbon is reading, takes up one of his hands, and when he has performed the operation lays it down, and then manages the other—the patient in the meanwhile scarcely knowing what is going on, and quietly pursuing his studies. EDMOND MALONE, *Life* (1860), 382.

COVENTRY PATMORE AND THE ORGAN BOY. You will be glad to hear that I am very comfortable in my new place. . . . I have had to call the policeman many times to the organ boys who prevent me from reading and writing and thinking. One was very rude, and would not go away, and I could not find a policeman; so I had to go out to him and pour some water over him, and that made him go away. COVENTRY PATMORE in Percy Street, Tottenham Court Road, 1863: *Portrait of My Family*, Derek Patmore (1935), 117.

DR. JOHNSON'S GOOD-HUMOURED GROWL. Johnson's laugh was as remarkable as any circumstance in his manner. It was a kind of good-humoured growl. Tom Davies described it drolly enough: 'He laughs like a rhinoceros.' JAMES BOSWELL, *Life of Johnson* (1887), ii, 378.

MRS. BURNS PRESENTS ROBERT WITH A MASTERPIECE. On Saturday morning last Mrs. Burns made me a present of a fine boy; rather stouter, but not so handsome as your godson was at his time of life. Indeed, I look on your little namesake to be my *chef d'œuvre* in that species of manufacture, as I look upon *Tam o' Shanter* to be my standard performance in the poetical line. ROBERT BURNS at Ellisland to MRS. DUNLOP, 11 April 1791: Letters (1931), ii, 68.

THE BEST-LOOKING BARD. Yesterday, at Holland House, I was introduced to Southey—the best-looking bard I have seen for some time. To have that poet's head and shoulders, I would almost have written his Sapphics. LORD BYRON to THOMAS MOORE, 27 September 1813: *Letters and Journals* (1898), ii, 266.

THE WORDSWORTHS GO TO CHURCH. I must tell you that I saw Mr. & Mrs. Wordsworth at Chapel on Sunday, pretty well. Dr. Christopher Wordsworth preached!!!!!!!! Alas too. HARTLEY COLERIDGE at Grasmere to MRS. HENRY NELSON COLERIDGE, 16 November 1847: *Letters* (1936), 297.

SIR WALTER ENTERTAINS MRS. HEMANS. We called at Chiefswood and asked Captain Hamilton, and Mrs. H. and Mrs. Hemans, to dinner on Monday. She is a clever person, and has been pretty. I had a long walk with her *tête-à-tête*. She told me of the peculiar melancholy attached to the words *no more*. I could not help telling, as a different application of the words, how an old dame riding home along Cockenzie Sands, pretty bowsy, fell off the pillion, and her husband, being in good order also, did not miss her till he came to Prestonpans. He instantly returned with some neighbours, and found the good woman seated amidst the advancing tide, which began to rise, with her lips ejaculating to her cummers, who she supposed were still pressing her to

another cup, 'Nae ae drap mair, I thank you kindly.' SIR WALTER
Scott, 17 July 1829: *Journal* (1890), ii, 319.

ALL THE STRICTURES. In yesterday's paper, immediately under
an advertisement on 'Strictures in the Urethra', I see—most
appropriately consequent—a poem with '*strictures* on Ld. B.,
Mr. Southey and others', though I am afraid neither 'Mr. S's'
poetical distemper, nor 'mine', nor 'others', is of the suppres-
sive or strangulary kind. LORD BYRON to JOHN MURRAY, 12
June 1813: *Letters* (1898), ii, 216.

THE LAMBS SETTLE IN COVENT GARDEN. Here we are, trans-
planted from our native soil. I thought we never could have been
torn up from the Temple. Indeed it is an ugly wrench, but like a
tooth, now 'tis out, and I am easy. We never can strike root so
deep in any other ground. This, where we are, is a light bit of
gardener's mould, and if they take us up from it, it will cost no
blood and groans, like man-drakes pulled up. We are in the individual spot I like best, in all this great city. The theatres, with
all their noises. Covent Garden, dearer to me than any gardens
of Alcinoüs, where we are morally sure of the earliest peas and
'sparagus. Bow Street, where the thieves are examined, within a
few yards of us. Mary had not been here four-and-twenty hours
before she saw a thief. She sits at the window working; and
casually throwing out her eyes, she sees a concourse of people
coming this way, with a constable to conduct the solemnity.
These little incidents agreeably diversify a female life. CHARLES
LAMB to DOROTHY WORDSWORTH, 21 November 1817: *Letters*
(1905), i, 505.

WORDSWORTH OPPOSES THE RAILWAY. Wordsworth is in a
fever about the railroad which people are going to drive through
the middle of the Lake School. So excited was he, that his wife
persuaded him to go from home for a time, and *compose* his mind.
He went, like an obedient husband—but he has come back again
with ten fevers instead of one—and the time of his absence he
spent in canvassing for Members of Parliament who would not
say 'aye' to it. Fifty have promised, he says, to protect him—

although Monckton Milnes, having caught corruption from the Utilitarians, dares to oppose the master-poet front to front, and sonnet to sonnet. ELIZABETH BARRETT BROWNING to RICHARD HENGIST HORNE, 3 October 1844: *Letters, to Richard Hengist Horne* (1877), ii, 172–3.

HAWTHORNE BUYS THOREAU'S CANOE. After dinner (at which we cut the first water-melon and musk-melon that our garden has grown), Mr. Thoreau and I walked up the bank of the river, and at a certain point he shouted for his boat. Forthwith a young man paddled it across, and Mr. Thoreau and I voyaged farther up the stream, which soon became more beautiful than any picture, with its dark and quiet sheet of water, half shaded, half sunny, between high and wooded banks. The late rains have swollen the stream so much that many trees are standing up to their knees, as it were, in the water; and boughs, which lately swung high in air, now dip and drink deep of the passing wave. As to the poor cardinals which glowed upon the bank a few days since, I could see only a few of their scarlet hats peeping above the tide. Mr. Thoreau managed the boat so perfectly, either with two paddles or with one, that it seemed instinct with his own will, and to require no physical effort to guide it. He said that, when some Indians visited Concord a few years ago, he found that he had acquired, without a teacher, their precise method of propelling and steering a canoe. Nevertheless he was desirous of selling the boat of which he was so fit a pilot, and which was built by his own hands; so I agreed to take it, and accordingly became possessor of the *Musketaquid*. I wish I could acquire the aquatic skill of the original owner. NATHANIEL HAWTHORNE at Concord, 1 September 1842: *Note-Books* (1869), 190–1.

RUSKIN'S PENWIPER. But, Susie, do you know, I'm greatly horrified at the penwipers of peacocks' feathers! *I* always use my left-hand coat tail, indeed, and if only I were a peacock and a pet of yours, how you'd scold me. JOHN RUSKIN to MISS SUSAN BEEVER, *Hortus Inclusus* (1887), 26.

Small Talk from Helicon

LOWELL CONDEMNS TYPEWRITERS AND POST CARDS. Typewriters quotha! They are as bad as postal cards. Both of them are unclean things I have never touched . . . I could never say what I would if I had to pick out my letters like a learned pig. JAMES RUSSELL LOWELL to MRS. W. K. CLIFFORD, 11 June 1889: *Letters* (1894), ii, 419.

TENNYSON AMONG FLEAS AND FOREIGNERS. Alfred Tennyson is at his very dirty hotel in Leicester Square: filled with fleas and foreigners. He looks thin and ill: and no wonder, from his habits. EDWARD FITZGERALD in London to BERNARD BARTON, 8 May 1847: *New Letters* (1923), 137.

MACAULAY PROMOTES HIMSELF TO A CARRIAGE. At half-past seven the brougham came, and I went to dine at Lord John Russell's, pleased and proud, and thinking how unjustly poor Pepys was abused for noting in his diary the satisfaction it gave him to ride in his own coach. This is the first time I ever had a carriage of my own, except when in office. T. B. MACAULAY, 16 January 1851: *Life* (1876), ii, 291–2.

BYRON SWIMS THE HELLESPONT. This morning I *swam* from *Sestos* to *Abydos*. The immediate distance is not above a mile, but the current renders it hazardous;—so much so that I doubt whether Leander's conjugal affection must not have been a little chilled in his passage to Paradise. I attempted it a week ago, and failed—owing to the north wind, and the wonderful rapidity of the tide,—though I have been from my childhood a strong swimmer. But, this morning being calmer, I succeeded, and crossed the 'broad Hellespont' in an hour and ten minutes. LORD BYRON to HENRY DRURY, 3 May 1810: *Letters* (1898), i, 263–4.

SWINBURNE DEIFIES CAPTAIN WEBB. What a glorious thing is this triumph of Captain Webb, and what a lyric Pindar would have written on him! If only I could beg, borrow, or steal the Theban lyre for half an hour I would try at an ode myself. There never was such a subject of the kind even in Greece itself: it is above all Olympian, Pythian, Isthmian, of Nemean fame. I consider it as the greatest glory that has befallen England since the publication of Shelley's greatest poem, whichever that may be. Its hero is the only man among strangers to me personally in England that I would go much out of my way to shake hands with, if permitted that honour: or, if not, even to see. Jowett himself hurrahed mildly (*ne pas lire* 'wildly') when the news came (I had the pleasure of announcing it), and observed what a supremely great man he would have been in Greece. Man, indeed! he would (and should) have been deified on the spot. ALGERNON CHARLES SWINBURNE to THEODORE WATTS-DUNTON, 27 August 1875: *Letters*, (1918), 58–9.

ODD NEWS ABOUT RUSKIN. I hear odd news from Oxford about Ruskin and his lectures. The last was attended by more than 1,000 people, and he electrified the Dons by telling them that a chalk-stream did more for the education of the people than their prim 'national school with its well-taught doctrine of Baptism and gabbled Catechism'. Also 'that God was in the poorest man's cottage, and that it was advisable He should be well housed'. I think we were ten years too soon for the fun! J. R. GREEN to W. BOYD DAWKINS, 5 March 1870: *Letters* (1901), 246.

TENNYSON CHANGES HATS WITH HIS GRANDSON. Tennyson had kindly called for us. He was in the carriage with his little grandson Alfred, on his nurse's lap, and Mr. Fields, an American guest. Little Alfred, aged 2, had on the great Alfred's black sombrero, and the child's straw hat with a blue ribbon was stuck on the top of the poet's huge head, and so they drove gravely along. WILLIAM ALLINGHAM at Haslemere, 5 August 1880: *Tennyson: A Memoir*, by his Son (1897), ii, 259.

TOM JONES TEACHES LADY LOUISA STUART HOW TO SWEAR. Mrs. S. and I have been quite alone these ten days, and are not at all tired of one another, nor of a wicked book we have been reading (*Tom Jones*, if you won't tell). Neither of us had read it for a great while, and, oh, what good writing it is. No modern *stuff* can possibly do after it. But I am in great fear it will have taught me to swear. LADY LOUISA STUART to MISS LOUISA CLINTON, 3 August 1831: *Letters* (Second Series, 1903), 289.

COLERIDGE ATTACKED BY COW. Coleridge came in with a sack full of books, etc. and a branch of Mountain ash. He had been attacked by a cow. DOROTHY WORDSWORTH at Dove Cottage, Grasmere, 10 June 1802: *Journals* (1924).

MAYTIME AT DOVE COTTAGE. We sate in the orchard. The sky cloudy, the air sweet and cool. The young bullfinches, in their party-coloured raiment, bustle about among the blossoms, and poise themselves like wire-dancers or tumblers, shaking the twigs and dashing off the blossoms. There is yet one primrose in the orchard. The stitchwort is fading. The vetches are in abundance, blossoming and seeding. That pretty little wavy-looking dial-like yellow flower, the speedwell, and some others, whose names I do not yet know. In the garden we have lilies and many other flowers. The scarlet beans are up in crowds. It is now between eight and nine o'clock. It has rained sweetly for two hours and a half; the air is very mild. The heckberry blossoms are dropping off fast, almost gone; barberries are in beauty; snowballs coming forward; May roses blossoming. DOROTHY WORDSWORTH at Grasmere, 28 May 1802: *Journals* (1924), 124–5.

TENNYSON IMPRESSES ANNE GILCHRIST. I was sitting under the yew tree yesterday, when Fanny [the maidservant] came to me and put a card into my hand. And whose name do you think was on that card? If I were talking instead of writing, I should make you guess and keep you in suspense a long while, but that is no use in a letter, because you can peep forward. It was, 'Mr. Alfred Tennyson'. He looks older than I expected, because of course the portraits one was early familiar with have stood still in one's mind as the image to be associated with that great name. But he is to my thinking far nobler looking now; every inch a king; features are massive, eyes very grave and penetrating, hair long, still very dark and, though getting thin, falls in such a way as to give a peculiar beauty to the mystic head. ANNE GILCHRIST

Small Talk from Helicon

to WILLIAM HAINES, 16 September 1866: *Life and Writings* (1887), 161–2.

MACAULAY VERSUS HIPPOPOTAMUS. I have seen the hippopotamus, both asleep and awake; and I can assure you that, awake or asleep, he is the ugliest of the works of God. But you must hear of my triumphs. Thackeray swears that he was eye-witness and ear-witness of the proudest event of my life. Two damsels were just about to pass that door-way which we, on Monday, in vain attempted to enter, when I was pointed out to them. 'Mr. Macaulay!' cried the lovely pair. 'Is that Mr. Macaulay? Never mind the hippopotamus.' And, having paid a shilling to see Behemoth, they left him in the very moment at which he was about to display himself to them, in order to see—but spare my modesty. T. B. MACAULAY, 9 March 1850: *Life* (1876), ii, 254–5.

MR. KINGSLEY FASCINATES MISS MITFORD. Mr. Kingsley took me quite by surprise in his extraordinary fascination. I have never seen a man of letters in the least like him, for, in general, the beau ideal of a young poet remains a beau ideal. They are mostly middle-aged, (sometimes elderly), conceited, affected, foppish, vulgar. Mr. Kingsley is not only a high-bred gentleman, but has the most charming admixture of softness and gentleness, with spirit, manliness and frankness—a frankness quite transparent—and a cordiality and courtesy that would win any heart. MISS MITFORD to MRS. JENNINGS, 31 December 1850: *Life* (1870), iii, 223.

AFTER THE BALL—JANE AUSTEN IS CATTY. There were very few beauties, and such as there were were not very handsome. Miss Iremonger did not look well, and Mrs. Blount was the only one much admired. She appeared exactly as she did in September, with the same broad face, diamond bandeau, white shoes, pink husband and fat neck. The two Miss Coxes were there: I traced in one the remains of the vulgar, broad-featured girl who danced at Enham eight years ago; the other is refined into a nice, composed-looking girl, like Catherine Bigg. I looked at Sir Thomas Champneys and thought of poor Rosalie; I looked at his daughter, and thought her a queer animal with a white neck. Mrs. Warren, I was constrained to think a very fine young woman, which I much regret. She danced away with great activity. Her husband is ugly enough, uglier even than his cousin John; but he does not look so *very* old. The Miss Maitlands are both prettyish, very like Anne, with brown skins, large dark eyes, and a good deal of nose. The General has got the gout, and Mrs. Maitland the jaundice. Miss Debary, Susan, and Sally, all in black, but without any statues, made their appearance, and I was as civil to them as circumstances would allow me. JANE AUSTEN to her sister CASSANDRA, 20 November 1800: *Letters* (1884), i, 242-3.

CHARLOTTE BRONTË SEES THE QUEEN AT BRUSSELS. You ask about Queen Victoria's visit to Brussels. I saw her for an instant flashing through the Rue Royale in a carriage and six, surrounded by soldiers. She was laughing and talking very gaily. She looked a little stout, vivacious lady, very plainly dressed, not much dignity or pretension about her. The Belgians liked her very well on the whole. They said she enlivened the sombre court of King Leopold, which is usually as gloomy as a conventicle. CHARLOTTE BRONTË to her sister EMILY, 1 December 1843: *Life* (1857), i, 303.

MR. AND MRS. GLADSTONE FRISK AMONG THE HEATHER. After luncheon A. [Tennyson], Hallam [Tennyson], and the Gladstones walked to the end of Blackdown. Mr. & Mrs. Gladstone frisked about like boy and girl in the heather. EMILY, LADY TENNYSON, 1871: *Tennyson: A Memoir*, by his Son (1897), 108.

GEORGE ELIOT TOO PLAIN FOR IMPROPRIETY. I went to see Fechter the other night and found myself between Lewes and Miss Evans! [George Eliot]—by Destiny and *not* by my own Deserving. . . . Poor soul! there never was a more absurd miscalculation than her constituting herself an improper *woman*. She looks Propriety personified! Oh so *slow*! JANE WELSH CARLYLE to ALEXANDER GILCHRIST, 31 July 1861: *Anne Gilchrist: Life and Writings* (1887), 86.

JANE AUSTEN READS BYRON AND MENDS HER PETTICOAT. I have read the *Corsair*, mended my petticoat, and have nothing else to do. Getting out is impossible. It is a nasty day for everybody. JANE AUSTEN to her sister CASSANDRA, 5 March 1814: *Letters* (1884), ii, 222.

WORDSWORTH READS WORDSWORTH TO HIS HAIRDRESSER. It is now 5 o'clock—We have our Haircutter below stairs, William [Wordsworth] is reading the *Leech-gatherer* to him. DOROTHY WORDSWORTH at Grasmere, 14 June 1802: *Early Letters of William and Dorothy Wordsworth* (1935), 303–4.

THERE BUT FOR THE GRACE OF GOD GOES HANNAH MORE. Heard of John Wilkes' death—awful event! talents how abused! Lord, who hath made *me* to differ; but for thy grace, I might have blasphemed thee like him. In early youth I read *Hume, Voltaire, Rousseau*. . . . HANNAH MORE, 2 February 1798: *Memoirs* (1835), iii, 56.

BROWNING AT THE POP. Friends are truly kind. Miss Mundella sent two season tickets for the Monday 'Pop' . . . I managed to go and stay for most of it . . . sat quite near to Browning, who is a nice-looking old man, delightfully *clean*. He seemed to delight in Naruda and Patti, and followed the music with a score of his own. JOANNA HORATIA EWING to her Husband, 7 November 1879: *J. H. Ewing: Her Books and Letters* (1896), 215.

NEWS OF SPEDDING'S FOREHEAD. You have of course read the account of Spedding's forehead landing in America. English sailors hail it in the Channel, mistaking it for Beachy Head. There is a Shakespeare cliff, and a Spedding cliff. Good old Fellow! I hope he'll come back safe and sound, forehead and all. EDWARD FITZGERALD to SAMUEL LAWRENCE, 22 May 1842: *Letters* (1889), 96.

Small Talk from Helicon

HANNAH MORE GOES RUSTIC. I spent almost my whole time in my little garden . . . employed in raising dejected pinks, and reforming disorderly honeysuckles. HANNAH MORE at Cowslip Green to HORACE WALPOLE at Strawberry Hill, June 1787: *Memoirs* (1835), iv, 73.

MRS. HEMANS AND HER SMALL SINS. I have been very ill-used in several ways since I saw you. Here is a great book on Phrenology, which a gentleman has just sent me and expects that I shall *read*! People really do take me for a sort of literary ogress, I think, or something like the sailor's definition of an epicure, 'a person that can eat *anything*'. To be sure I *did* very much aggravate the Phrenologist lately, by laughing at the whole *Scullery* science and its votaries, so I suppose this is his revenge. And imagine some of my American friends having actually sent me several copies of a Tract, audaciously calling itself *A Sermon on Small Sins*. Did you ever know any thing so scurrilous and personal? 'Small sins' *to me*, who am little better than a grown-up Rosamond, (Miss Edgeworth's naughty girl, you know,) who constantly lie in bed till it is too late to get up early, break my needles, (when I use any,) leave my keys among my necklaces, answer all my amusing letters first and leave the others to their fate; in short, to roll up into one great, immense, *frightful* one at the end of it! MRS. HEMANS, *Memorials* (1836), i, 260–1.

LUTTRELL COMPARES MOORE AND ROGERS. Luttrell was talking of Moore and Rogers—the poetry of the former so licentious, that of the latter so pure; much of its popularity owing to its being so carefully weeded of everything approaching indelicacy; and the contrast between the lives and the works of the two men—the former a pattern of conjugal and domestic regularity, the latter of all men he had ever known the greatest sensualist. CHARLES C. F. GREVILLE, *The Greville Memoirs* (1875), iii, 324.

THE SWAN OF LICHFIELD CONDEMNS THE FRENCH AND THEIR ADMIRERS. My inmost soul detests the bloody French, and abjures all confidence in the humanity or worth of those who vindicate or admire them. Anna Seward, 23 January 1797: *Letters* (1811), iv, 301.

Poets and Philosophers sponge on Shelley. Mr. J. . . . lives at Marlow, and is exceedingly intimate with Peacock and Shelley. . . . He says the system of plunder exercised upon poor Mr. Shelley exceeds all belief. Leigh Hunt went to Marlow once for money, and finding Mr. S. without any family, took off a load of the good man's furniture—chairs and tables and bedsteads! Is it not incredible? And Mr. Godwin, his papa-in-law, was much worse; he used to threaten to stab himself if his dutiful son-in-law would not accept his bills. Only fancy him down on his knees, flourishing a drawn dagger and talking tragedy! It's really better than *Tom Thumb*. But it was no joke to poor Mr. Shelley. He used to send for Mr. Peacock to protect him, and is fairly gone abroad to get rid of this fine grand sort of sentimental persecution. Well, great authors are great people—but I believe they are best seen at a distance. Miss Mitford to Mrs. Hofland, 18 March 1819: *Letters* (1925), 157–8.

XII

TRAVEL PICTURES

Why is there more merit in having travelled one's eyes over so many reams of papers, than having carried one's legs over so many acres of ground? Horace Walpole to Richard Bentley, 6 May 1755: *Letters* (1891), ii, 438.

BATH GAY IN GRAVE TIMES. Grave as the times are, Bath never was so gay: princes and kings that will be, and princes and kings that have been, pop upon you at every corner. HANNAH MORE to MRS. BOSCAWEN, 1797: *Memoirs* (1835), iii, 12.

NIGHT FALLS ON THE JUNGFRAU. Mürren faces the Jungfrau. This glorious creature is your one object of interest from morning to night. It seems so near that you could fancy a stone might be thrown across to it. Between you and it is a broad valley: but so deep, and with sides so precipitous, that it is entirely out of sight. So the Jungfrau *vis-à-vis*-es you frankly through the bright sweet intervening air. And then she has such moods; such unutterable smiles, such inscrutable sulks, such growls of rage suppressed, such thunder of avalanches, such crown of stars. One evening our sunset was the real rose-pink you have heard of so much. It fades, you know, into a deathlike chalk-white. That is the most *awful* thing. A sort of spasm seems to come over her face, and in an instant she is a corpse, rigid, and oh so cold! Well, so she died, and you felt as if a great soul had ebbed away into the Heaven of Heavens: and thankful, but very sad, I went up to my room. I was reading by candle-light, for it gets dark immediately after sunset, when A. shrieked to me to come to the window. What a Resurrection—so gentle, so tender—like that sonnet of Milton's about his dead wife returning in vision! The moon had risen; and there was the Jungfrau—oh chaste, oh blessed saint in glory everlasting! Then all the elemental spirits that haunt crevasses, and hover around peaks, all the patient powers that bear up the rock buttresses, and labour to sustain great slopes, all streams, and drifts, and flowers, and vapours, made a symphony, a time most solemn and rapturous. It was there, unheard, perhaps, unheard, I will not deny it; but there, nevertheless. A young Swiss felt it, and with exquisite delicacy feeling his way, as it were, to some expression however inadequate, he played a sonata of Schumann, and one or two of the songs, such as the *Frühlingsnacht*. . . . The abyss below was a pot of boiling blackness, and on to this, and down into this, and all over this, the moonlight fell as meal falls on to porridge from nimbly sifting fingers. Moon-meal! that was it. THOMAS EDWARD BROWN, 18 October 1874: *Letters* (1900), i, 75–6.

MACAULAY FINDS ST. MARK'S ENTERTAINING BUT NOT BEAUTIFUL. I do not think it [St. Mark's, Venice], nobody can think it, beautiful, and yet I never was more entertained by any building. I never saw a building except St. Peter's where I could be content to pass so many hours in looking about me. There is something attractive to me in the very badness of the rhyming monkish hexameters, and in the queer designs and false drawing of the pictures. Everything carries back the mind to a remote age; to a time when Cicero and Virgil were hardly known in Italy; to a time compared with which the time of Politan and even the time of Petrarch is modern. I returned in the course of the day, and spent an hour in making out the histories of Moses and Joseph, and the mottoes. They amused me as the pictures in very old Bibles used to amuse me when I was a child. T. B. MACAULAY, 1856: *Life* (1876), ii, 407.

NATURE AND ART. I love hills, but I have discovered by deep reflection that we are such artificial animals, that the recollections of art are much more pleasing and stronger in my mind than those of nature. In thinking over past travels, Rubens' 'Descent from the Cross' at Antwerp, and Canova's 'Magdalene', and one or two Vandycks at Amsterdam, and parts of Westminster Abbey and of York Minster, come constantly into my thoughts; and I can see all the pictures at Penshanger, particularly the Correggio, and many of those at Woburn and Bowood, as clearly as if they were hanging in this room. There is a bit of grey sky in that 'Descent from the Cross' I shall never forget, whereas Killarney, and the Rhine, and the Pyrenees are all confused recollections, pleasant but not clear. And I am sure that in this country, though I do not admire Indian architecture, I shall recollect every stone of the Kootûb and every arch about it, when these mountains will be all indistinct. In short, notwithstanding that 'God made the country and man made the town', I, after the fashion of human nature, enjoy most what God has given, and remember best what man has done. EMILY EDEN, at Simla, to her Sister, 17 June 1838: *Up the Country* (1866), 146–7. (Oxford ed., 1937.)

TOM MOORE IN A MIDLANDS COACH. Left Leamington to return home by way of Birmingham. In the coach as far as Hatton, a gentleman, who had gone for two successive Sundays, and breakfasted and dined at a little public-house in the village, for the purpose of seeing Parr, and hearing him read prayers, but was disappointed each time, both morning and evening, was going now to make a third trial. Alone from thence to Birmingham, reading *Horace* all the way. From Birmingham had a Quaker lady in the coach, who had been poisoned by applying nightshade to her arm for the *tic douloureux*. A cloddish beau, who could not speak a word of decent English, joined us, with a little footman in gaudy livery, of whom he seemed to be more careful than if it had been his wife; had him inside the coach, and brought him into the same room with us at supper,—a footman evidently a new circumstance to him. This dandy found me out by the name on my trunk, and my having said I lived sometime in Leicestershire—proved to be the son of the extraordinary man alluded to by Southey in his Espriella letters, who had a museum of the ropes in which various malefactors had been hanged, all ticketed and hung in order round his room. If I recollect right, Southey says *his own* ought to have completed the collection. He was, notwithstanding this ferocious taste, a poor, weak, squeaking, unmanly mannered old creature; for I knew him a little. The hopeful son left us at Tewkesbury, where we took in a young man, who became very lively and intelligent in the morning. When we arrived at the Bush Inn at Bristol, the Quaker lady, who was a very amiable kind of person, and had been very attentive to my conversation with the rope-virtuoso's son, told the gentleman who I was; upon which he pressed me very cordially either to stay in Bristol, or come over to his father's house within the following month, that he might show me the country. THOMAS MOORE, 23 August 1818: *Memoirs* (1853), ii, 149–51.

OLIVER GOLDSMITH BRAVES SEA-SICKNESS AND CALAIS PORTERS. We had a very quick passage from Dover to Calais which we performed in three hours and twenty minutes, all of us extremely sea-sick, which must necessarily have happened as my machine to prevent sea-sickness was not completed. We were glad to leave Dover, because we hated to be imposed upon, so were in high spirits at coming to Calais where we were told that a little money would go a great way. Upon landing two little trunks, which was all we carried with us we were surprised to see fourteen or fifteen fellows all running down to the ship to lay their hands upon them, four got under each trunk, the rest surrounded and held the hasps, and in this manner our little baggage was conducted with a kind of funeral solemnity till it was safely lodged at the custom house. We were well enough pleased with the people's civility till they came to be paid; every creature that had the happiness of but touching our trunks with their finger expected six-pence, and they had so pretty civil a manner of demanding it that there was no refusing them. OLIVER GOLDSMITH to SIR JOSHUA REYNOLDS, 27 July 1770: *Collected Letters* (1928), 91–2.

GRAY ON THE KENTISH COAST. I went to Margate for a day;

one would think it was Bartholomew fair that had *flown* down from Smithfield to Kent in the London machine, like my Lady Stuffdamask: (to be sure you have read the *New Bath Guide*, the most fashionable of books) so then I did *not* go to Kingsgate, because it belonged to my Lord Holland; but to Ramsgate I did, and so to Sandwich, and Deal, and Dover, and Folkestone, and Hythe, all along the coast, very delightful. I do not tell you of the great and small beasts, and creeping things innumerable that I met with, because you do not suspect that this world is inhabited by any thing but men and women and clergy, and such two-legged cattle. THOMAS GRAY to the REV. NORTON NICHOLLS, 26 August 1766: *Letters* (1900), iii, 110.

G. B. S. IS NOT AMUSED BY ATHENS AND THE GREEK ISLES. Good God, Ellen, the Grecian Archipelago! Can't you see it in your mind's eye, a group of exquisite islands in a turquoise setting? Ugh! Cold, storm, sleety grey, pitching and rolling, misery, headaches, horrors of universal belchings! A moment's respite in the Dardanelles enables me to write to you: soon we shall be in the sea of Marmora, reputed, as I learn for the first time, the coldest and windiest in the world. However, I am at least quit of Athens, with its stupid classic Acropolis and smashed pillars. BERNARD SHAW to ELLEN TERRY, 12 October 1899: *Ellen Terry and Bernard Shaw: A Correspondence* (1931), 365.

FIRST IMPRESSIONS OF PARIS FROM GEORGE GISSING. I am vastly at home and the sights of this unspeakably beautiful town are rejoicing me. I imagine what it would be if one found oneself suddenly in the middle of the Athens of Pericles. No whit less interesting is this—incredible, unimaginable. I have been on the 'Place de la Bastille'. No trace of the Bastille remains. I have mused strangely over the things that quiet place has seen. This morning I went to the 'Morgue', which was at once very horrible and very simple. This Latin civilization is astonishingly different from our own. I could tell you curious things. Wonderful scene in the great markets. Astonishing good humour of all and sundry. Women of the lower classes seldom wear anything on their heads, but have the most elaborate method of hair dressing. It is the beginning of a new life. Ah, if you saw the bookstalls, illimitable, not to be counted. But the Opera crowns everything in modern architecture. I never knew what a public building could be. GEORGE GISSING to his brother ALGERNON, 22 March 1886: *Letters* (1926), 177.

VENICE BETTER IN REALITY THAN IN MEMORY. I was surprised to find what pleasure it gave me to be in Venice again. It was like coming home, when sounds and smells which one had forgotten stole upon one's senses; and certainly there is no place like it in the world: everything there is better in reality than in memory. I first saw it on a romantic evening after sunset in 1900, and I left it on a sunshiny morning, and I shall not go there again. A. E. HOUSMAN to his sister MRS. E. W. SYMONS, 23 June 1926: *A.E.H.* (1937), 151.

MRS. MONTAGU COMPARES TUNBRIDGE WELLS WITH BATH. In many respects this place is inferior to the Bath, in some it is better. We are not confined here in streets; the houses are scattered irregularly, and Tunbridge Wells looks, from the window I now sit by, a little like the village you see from our terrace at Sandleford, only that the inhabitants, instead of Jack and Joan, are my Lord and Lady. ELIZABETH MONTAGU to the REV. MR. FREIND, 1749: *Letters* (1913), iii, 128.

LOWELL IN PASTORAL LONDON. I have just come in from Hyde Park, whither I go to smoke my cigar after breakfast. The day is as fine as they can make 'em in London: the sun shines and the air is meadowy. I sat and watched the sheep crawl through the filmy distance, unreal as in a pastoral of the last century, as if they might have walked out of a London eclogue of Gay. Fancy saw them watched by beribboned shepherdesses and swains. Now and then a scarlet coat would cross my eye like a stain of blood on the innocent green. The trees lifted their cumulous outlines like clouds, and all around was the ceaseless hum of wheels that never sleep. . . . This scene in the Park is one of which I never tire. I like it better than anything in London. If I look westward I am in the country. If I turn about, there is the never-ebbing stream of coaches and walkers, the latter with more violent contrasts of costume and condition than are to be seen anywhere else, and with oddities of face and figure that make Dickens seem no caricaturist. The landscape has the quiet far-offness of *Chaucer*. The town is still the town of Johnson's London. . . . JAMES RUSSELL LOWELL to MISS GRACE NORTON, 29 July 1877: *Letters* (1894), 222–3.

THE SAGE OF CHELSEA IN CHEAPSIDE. I was hurrying along Cheapside into Newgate Street among a thousand bustling pigmies and the innumerable jinglings and rollings and crashings of many-coloured Labour, when all at once in passing from the abode of John Gilpin, stunned by the tumult of his restless compeers, I looked up from the boiling through a little opening at the corner of the street—and there stood St. Paul's—with its columns and friezes, and massy wings of bleached yet unworn stone; with its statues and its graves around it; with its solemn dome four hundred feet above me, and its gilded ball and cross gleaming in the evening sun, piercing up into the heaven through the vapours of our earthly home! It was silent as Tadmor of the Wilderness; gigantic, beautiful, enduring; it seemed to frown with a rebuking pity on the vain scramble which it overlooked: at its feet were tombstones, above it was the everlasting sky, within priests perhaps were chanting hymns; it seemed to transmit with a stern voice the sounds of Death, Judgment, and Eternity through all the frivolous and fluctuating city. THOMAS CARLYLE to ALEXANDER CARLYLE, 25 June 1824: *Early Letters* (1886), 312.

CARLYLE GRUMBLES ABOUT EDINBURGH. This accursed, stinking, reeky mass of stones and lime and dung. THOMAS CARLYLE to his brother JOHN, 10 February 1821: *Early Letters* (1886), 153.

ARNOLD BENNETT ENJOYS VENICE. Venice is the finest holiday place I was ever in—bar none. You have town life, with terrific cafés in a superb square (Piazza San Marco), many restaurants, etc. You have architecture, antiquities and pictures of the finest sort. You have gondoliering on the canals, unique. The port is full of big yachts. And you take a steamer or a launch and in ten minutes are on the Lido beach, which is splendidly organized for bathing and is infested by the most putrid plutocrats. You don't need much food, and not much sleep: but you can drink all day. We were at the Hotel Commercio; but it is on two narrow canals complete with odours, and so yesterday we moved to this hotel, which is dearer, on the Grand Canal, with superb views. A gondola would only cost 16s. a day. They are lovely objects. I must go home on Sunday. We know quantities of people here, and meet far more in the chief café (Florian) than we should meet in any London restaurant. The snag is mosquitoes. But I don't suffer from them. Moreover all beds are of course netted. Mosquitoes prefer blondes. Italians prefer blondes. 9 September 1926: *Arnold Bennett's Letters to his Nephew* (1936), 168–9.

CHARLOTTE BRONTË STIRRED BY CRYSTAL PALACE—BUT . . .
On Friday, I went to the Crystal Palace; it is a marvellous, stirring, bewildering sight—a mixture of a genii palace, and a mighty bazaar, but it is not much in my way; I liked the lecture [Thackeray's] much better. CHARLOTTE BRONTË, 2 June 1851: *Life*, Gaskell (1857), ii, 211.

MACAULAY'S FIRST SIGHT OF ST. PETER'S. Nov. 14. Up and off by half-past four. The sun triumphed over the mist just as I reached Narni. The scenery was really glorious; far finer than that of Matlock or the Wye, in something of the same style. The pale line of the river which brawled below, though in itself not agreeable, was interesting from classical recollections. I thought how happily Virgil had touched the most striking and characteristic features of Italian landscape. As the day wore on, I saw the Tiber for the first time. I saw Mount Soracte, and, unlike Lord Byron, I loved the sight for Horace's sake. And so I came to Civita Castellana, where I determined to stop, though it was not much after two. I did not wish to enter Rome by night. I wanted to see the dome of St. Peter's from a distance, and to observe the city disclosing itself by degrees.

Nov. 15. On arriving this morning, I walked straight from the hotel door to St. Peter's. I was so much excited by the expectation of what I was to see, that I could notice nothing else. I was quite nervous. The colonnade in front is noble—very, very noble—yet it disappointed me, and I was for a minute fairly stunned by the magnificence and harmony of the interior. I never in my life saw, and never, I suppose, shall again see, any thing so astonishingly beautiful. I really could have cried with pleasure. I rambled about for half an hour or more, paying little or no attention to details, but enjoying the effect of the sublime whole. T. B. MACAULAY, *Life* (1876), ii, 28.

TROLLOPE CREATES A SENSATION IN VERONA. It was on a previous visit to Milan, when the telegraph-wires were only just opened to the public by the Austrian authorities, that we had decided one day at dinner that we would go to Verona that night. There was a train at six, reaching Verona at midnight, and we asked some servant of the hotel to telegraph for us, ordering supper and beds. The demand seemed to create some surprise; but we persisted, and were only mildly grieved when we found ourselves charged twenty zwanzigers for the message. Telegraphy was new at Milan, and the prices were intended to be almost prohibitory. We paid our twenty zwanzigers and went on, consoling ourselves with the thought of our ready supper and our assured beds. When we reached Verona, there arose a great cry along the platform for Signor Trollope. I put out my head and declared my identity, when I was waited upon by a glorious personage dressed like a beau for a ball, with half-a-dozen others almost as glorious behind him, who informed me, with his hat in his hand, that he was the landlord of the 'Due Torre'. It was a heating moment, but it became more hot when he asked me after my people,—'mes gens'. I could only turn round, and point to my wife and brother-in-law. I had no other 'people'. There were three carriages provided for us, each with a pair of grey horses.

Travel Pictures

When we reached the house it was all lit up. We were not allowed to move without anattendant with a lighted candle. It was only gradually that the mistake came to be understood. On us there was still the horror of the bill, the extent of which could not be known till the hour of departure had come. The landlord, however, had acknowledged to himself that his inductions had been ill-founded, and he treated us with clemency. He had never before received a telegram. ANTHONY TROLLOPE, *Autobiography* (1923), 104–5.

BYRONIC CARAVAN. His [Byron's] travelling equipage was rather a singular one, and afforded a strange catalogue for the *Dogana*: seven servants, five carriages, nine horses, a monkey, a bull-dog and a mastiff, two cats, three pea-fowls and some hens . . . formed part of his live-stock; these and all his books, consisting of a very large library of modern works (for he bought all the best that came out,) together with a vast quantity of furniture. THOMAS MEDWIN, *Conversations of Lord Byron* (1824), 9–10.

MARK RUTHERFORD AT THE BIRTHPLACE OF THE 'LYRICAL BALLADS'. Molly and I left home to escape house-cleaning and came here, partly to see the Quantocks, and partly to see the birth-place of so many of the *Lyrical Ballads*. It was a pilgrimage I have long purposed. We are about 600 feet up the hills, in complete solitude. A mere track, not a road, leads to the cottage, and behind us are the moors, rising near the sea they seem much higher. Deep combs run through them, each with its little beck. The lanes in the lowlands are the true west-country lanes smothered in foliage and flowers. Within a short distance is the shrine, the house in which Dorothy and her brother lived, which Coleridge so often visited, and three miles away is Nether Stowey. Every path in Dorothy's *Journal* can be traced, and the Ancient Mariner hove in sight hard by when the immortal Three set out on that memorable November walk to Linton. It is very affecting, but my emotions or thoughts—properly a kind of thought-feeling—are of the inarticulate kind. The silence of the place strikes me. I have never before known, that is to say for and length of time, what pure silence is. The birds certainly, any especially the cuckoo, sing incessantly, but they do not interrupt the quietude. They rather add to it. MARK RUTHERFORD to MISS PARTRIDGE, 14 May 1899: *Letters to Three Friends* (1924), 183–4.

'IONICA' CORY MAKES PILGRIMAGE TO HAWORTH. We saw the little parsonage, altered by the substitution of plate-glass for the very small panes: a miserable homestead, choked with big gravestones, with no garden but the merest strip, no bigger than a bedroom passage; hardly a courtyard of any kind; behind it, ugly stone fences shutting off Emily's moor. Out of that prison the little Charlotte put forth a hand to feel for the world of human emotion. I wish she would come back to us, and count up the myriads to whom she has given new souls. WILLIAM CORY, 23 April 1867: *Letters and Journals* (1897), 187.

KEATS AT BURNS'S COTTAGE. We went to the Cottage and took some Whisky. I wrote a sonnet for the mere sake of writing some lines under the roof—they are so bad I cannot transcribe them. The Man at the Cottage was a great Bore with his Anecdotes—I hate the rascal—his life consists in fuz, fuzzy, fuzziest. He drinks glasses five for the Quarter and twelve for the hour— he is a mahogany-faced old Jackass who knew Burns. He ought to have been kicked for having spoken to him. He calls himself 'a curious old Bitch'—but he is a flat old dog—I should like to employ Caliph Vathek to kick him. O the flummery of a birth-place! Cant! Cant! Cant! It is enough to give a spirit the guts-ache. Many a true word, they say, is spoken in jest—this may be because his gab hindered my sublimity: the flat dog made me write a flat sonnet. JOHN KEATS to JOHN HAMILTON REYNOLDS, 13 July 1818: *Letters* (1895), 159–60.

PHILADELPHIA FLATTERS TOM MOORE. My reception at Phila-delphia was extremely flattering: it is the only place in America which can boast any literary society, and my name had prepos-sessed them more strongly than I deserve. But their affectionate attentions went far beyond this deference to reputation; I was quite caressed while there; and their anxiety to make me known, by introductory letters, to all their friends on my way, and two or three little poems of a very flattering kind, which some of their choicest men addressed to me, all went so warmly to my heart, that I felt quite a regret in leaving them; and the only place I have seen, which I had one wish to pause in, was Philadelphia. THOMAS MOORE at Passaick Falls to his Mother, 26 June 1804: *Memoirs* (1853), i, 164.

LONDON FROM A HANSOM. I am as fond of London as Charles Lamb. The rattle of a hansom shakes new life into my old bones, and I ruin myself in them. I love such evanescent and unimportant glimpses of the world as I catch from my flying perch. I envy the birds no longer, and learn better to converse with them. Our views of life are the same. JAMES RUSSELL LOWELL to CHARLES ELIOT NORTON, 25 July 1886: *Letters* (1894), ii, 353.

RICHARD LE GALLIENNE DISCOVERS KELMSCOTT. Kelmscott! When at last I stood beneath a finger-post which said 'To Kelmscott', I stood and looked a long while. It was as though in some green lane I had come upon a finger-post: 'To the Moon' —in fact, was not Kelmscott 'East of the Sun and West of the Moon'? It is strange how a great man first of all makes a place so real, and then turns it to utter fairyland. Once Kelmscott was an unknown cluster of farms and pigstyes; then it became real with the daylight of contemporary fame; now it is a dream-village, bathed in the moonlight of immortality. 'To Kelmscott!' O my bicycle—wheel very softly thither. And shall we not wreath us in green boughs, and thus enter the village—very strangely? The villagers would not fear us so, for they have seen many strange and moon-like things at Kelmscott. As in some Italian village once obscure, but suddenly wild with fame because the Madonna has appeared to a goatherd in a great radiance, the peasants are learned in holy things; so at Kelmscott, one might fancy, the very pigs must know somewhat of the ways of poets. RICHARD LE GALLIENNE, *Travels in England* (1900), 210–11.

Travel Pictures

MOTLEY AT CHARLOTTE BRONTË'S COFFEE HOUSE. Friday morning I went down to the City with the Amorys. I acted as cicerone to show them the Chapter Coffee-House in Paternoster Row, which . . . is the place of all others in the world in London which Charlotte Brontë selected when she came suddenly from Yorkshire to London to make a two days' visit. The place is as gloomy and forbidding as it is described to be by Mrs. Gaskell, and certainly no house in all the town could be imagined more forlorn for any woman to select as even a temporary residence. The alley is so narrow that one can almost touch the houses on both sides, and the whole expression of the locality is disconsolate in the last degree. The inscription is 'Chapter Coffee House—Faithful'; and I asked a man who is there to superintend the premises, which are to be let, whether he had ever heard of Miss Brontë. 'Can't say I ever heard the name, sir. Was she here in Mr. Faithful's time?' was the only reply. The slender furrow made by little Jane Eyre in the ocean of London had long been effaced. JOHN LOTHROP MOTLEY to his Wife, 6 June 1858: *Correspondence* (1889), i, 253.

CHARLES KINGSLEY AT SALISBURY. The first thing which strikes you in it, (spiritually, I mean) is its severe and unstudied calm, even to 'primness'—nothing luscious, very little or no variation. Then you begin to feel how *one* it is; how the high slated roof and the double lancet windows, and the ranges of graduating lancet arches filling every gable, and the continued repetition of the same simple forms even in the buttresses and string courses, and corbal tables, and the extreme harsh angular simplicity of the mouldings—all are developments of one idea, and the idea so well expressing the tone of its date, the end of the thirteenth and beginning of the fourteenth centuries, I suppose, when the 'revival' of the age of St. Francis, St. Dominic, and dear St Elizabeth had formed itself, from the many private fancies of its great minds, into one clear dark system of stern, elegant, soul-crushing asceticism. And then from the centre of all this, that glorious spire rises—the work of a slightly later hand

—too huge, I believe, for the rest of the cathedral, its weight having split and crushed its supporters. Fit emblem of the result of curbing systems. The moment the tower escapes above the level of the roof, it bursts into the wildest luxuriances, retaining the general character of the building below, but disguising it in a thousand fantastic excrescences—like the mind of man, crushed by human systems, and then suddenly asserting its own will in some burst of extravagance, yet unconsciously retaining the harsh and severe lineaments of the school in which it had been bred. And then its self-willed fancies exhaust themselves, and it makes one final struggle upward, in a vast simple pyramid like that spire; emblem of the return, the revulsion rather, to 'pure' and naked spirituality. CHARLES KINGSLEY to his Wife, 28 March 1844: *Letters and Memories,* (1877), i, 117–18.

BYRON SUMS UP FALMOUTH. The town contains many Quakers and salt fish—the oysters have a taste of copper, owing to the soil of a mining country—the women (blessed by the Corporation therefor!) are flogged at the cart's tail when they pick and steal, as happened to one of the fair sex yesterday noon. She was pertinacious in her behaviour, and damned the Mayor. This is all I know of Falmouth. LORD BYRON to FRANCIS HODGSON, 25 June 1890: *Letters and Journals* (1898), i, 228.

MOTLEY TELLS THE AUTOCRAT ABOUT BRUSSELS. Nothing can be more exquisite in its way than the Grande Place in the very heart of the city, surrounded with those toppling, zig-zag, ten storied buildings, bedizened all over with ornaments and emblems so peculiar to the Netherlands, with the brocaded Hôtel de Ville on one side, with its impossible spire, rising some three hundred and seventy feet into the air, and embroidered on the top with the delicacy of needlework, sugar-work, spiderwork, or what you will. I haunt this place because it is my scene, my theatre. Here were enacted so many deep tragedies, so many stately dramas, and even so many farces, which have been so familiar to me so long, that I have got to imagine myself invested with a kind of property in the place, and look at it as if it were merely the theatre with the *coulisses*, machinery, drapery, etc., for representing scenes which have long since vanished, and which no more enter the minds of men and women who are actually moving across its pavement than if they had occurred in the moon. When I say that I know no soul in Brussels I am perhaps wrong. With the present generation I am not familiar. *En revanche* the dead men of the place are my intimate friends. I am at home in any cemetery. With the fellows of the sixteenth century I am on the most familiar terms. Any ghost that ever flits by night across the moonlight square is at once hailed by me as a man and a brother. I call him by his Christian name at once. JOHN LOTHROP MOTLEY to OLIVER WENDELL HOLMES, 20 November 1853: *Correspondence* (1889), i, 162.

HAWTHORNE BATHES IN WALDEN POND. Walden Pond . . . lies embosomed among wooded hills,—it is not very extensive, but large enough for waves to dance upon its surface, and to look like a piece of blue firmament, earth-encircled. The shore has a narrow, pebbly strand, which it was worth a day's journey to look at, for the sake of the contrast between it and the weedy, oozy margin of the river. Farther within its depths, you perceive a bottom of pure white sand, sparkling through the transparent water, which, methought, was the very purest liquid in the world. After Mr. Emerson left us, Hillard and I bathed in the pond; and it does really seem as if my spirit, as well as corporeal person, were refreshed by that bath. A good deal of mud and river-slime had accumulated on my soul; but these bright waters washed it all away. NATHANIEL HAWTHORNE, 15 August 1842: *Note-Books* (1869), 175.

GEORGE GISSING AT WELLS. Wells itself is ideally situated, amid the hills which break away from the windy Mendips to the great Somerset level. A peaceful village, little more; and at a turn of the street you come upon that glorious Cathedral, set amid surely the most beautiful Close that exists; the entrance at each corner through archways of grey crumbling stone. Anything like the Bishop's Palace I never saw. It is surrounded by a wall and

a moat: the wall embattled and loop-holed, overgrown with ivy,
and in places with peach and apricot; the entrance a drawbridge
and portcullis; and the moat very wide, supplied with water that
rushes into it foaming and roaring from St. Andrew's well, a
great spring coming somehow from the hidden depths of the
Mendips. Swans and ducks swim about on the olive-green water.
Close by is a walk shadowed by huge, dense elms, and all around
are lawns, meadows, hills, rising to woodland and heath. A marvellous spot, civilized with the culture of centuries, yet quite unlike the trimness of other cathedral towns. GEORGE GISSING to
his Brother, 4 August 1894: *Letters* (1926), 338-9.

WASHINGTON IRVING IN SHAKESPEARE'S HOMETOWN. To a
homeless man who has no spot on this wide world which he can
truly call his own, there is a momentary feeling of something like
independence and territorial consequence, when, after a weary
day's travel, he kicks off his boots, thrusts his feet into slippers,
and stretches himself before an inn fire. Let the world without
go as it may; let kingdoms rise or fall, so long as he has the
wherewithal to pay his bill, he is, for the time being, the very
monarch of all he surveys. The arm-chair is his throne; the poker
his sceptre, and the little parlour of some twelve feet square his
undisputed empire. It is a morsel of certainty, snatched from the
midst of the uncertainties of life; it is a sunny moment gleaming
out kindly on a cloudy day; and he who has advanced some way
on the pilgrimage of existence knows the importance of husband-
ing even morsels and moments of enjoyment. 'Shall I not take
mine ease in mine inn?' thought I, as I gave the fire a stir,
lolled back in my elbow chair, and cast a complaisant look about
the little parlour of the Red Horse, at Stratford-on-Avon. The
Words of sweet Shakespeare were just passing through my mind,
as the clock struck midnight from the tower of the church in
which he lies buried. There was a gentle tap at the door, and a
pretty chambermaid, putting in her smiling face, enquired with
a hesitating air whether I had rung. I understood it as a modest
hint that it was time to retire. My dream of absolute dominion

131

was at an end: so abdicating my throne, like a prudent potentate, to avoid being deposed, and putting the *Stratford Guide Book* under my arm as a pillow companion, I went to bed, and dreamt all night of Shakespeare, the Jubilee, and David Garrick. WASHINGTON IRVING, *The Sketch Book* (1859), 192.

CLOUGH MEETS EMERSON AT CONCORD. Loads of talk with Emerson all morning. Breakfast at 8 displays two girls and a boy, the family. Dinner at 2.30. Walk with Emerson to a wood with a prettyish pool. Concord is very bare (so is the country in general); it is a small sort of village, almost entirely of wood houses, painted white, with Venetian blinds, green outside, with two white wooden churches—one with a stone façade of Doric columns, however. Emerson's ancestors brought his congregation here from Gloucestershire (I think) in the year 1635. There are some American elms, of a weeping kind, and sycamores, i.e. planes; but the wood is mostly pine—white and yellow pine—somewhat scrubby, occupying the tops of the low banks and marshy hay land between. . . . A little brook runs through to the Concord river. ARTHUR HUGH CLOUGH, 1852: *Letters* (1865), 234.

XIII

INTERIORS

*The candles are burnt down and I am using the last wax taper—
which has a long snuff on it—the fire is at its last click—I am sitting
with my back to it with one foot rather askew upon the rug and the
other with the heel a little elevated from the carpet—I am writing
this on the* Maid's Tragedy, *which I have read since tea with great
pleasure. Besides this volume of Beaumont and Fletcher—there are on
the table two volumes of* Chaucer, *and a new work of Tom Moore's
called* Tom Cribb's Memorial to Congress—*nothing in it. These
are trifles but I require nothing so much of you but that you will give
me a like description of yourselves, however it may be when you are
writing to me. Could I see the same thing done of any great Man
long since dead it would be a great delight: As to know in what position Shakespeare sat when he began ' To be or not to be'—such things
become interesting from distance of time or place.* John Keats at
Wentworth Place to George and Georgiana Keats, 12 March
1819: *Letters* (1901), v, 31.

Sir Walter Raleigh's Study. Durham House was a noble
palace; after he came to his greatness he lived there, or in some
apartment of it. I well remember his study, which was a little
turret that looked into and over the Thames, and had the prospect
which is pleasant perhaps as any in the world, and which not only
refreshes the eyesight but cheers the spirits, and . . . I believe en-
larges an ingenious man's thoughts. John Aubrey, 1680: *Brief
Lives* (1898), ii, 183.

John Bunyan's Library. I heard Mr. Bagford . . . say, that he
walked once into the country on purpose to see the study of John
Bunyan. When he came, John received him very civilly and cour-

teously, but his study consisted only of a Bible and a parcel of books, written by himself, all lying on a shelf. THOMAS HEARNE, 7 April 1723: *Reliquiae Hearnianae* (1869), ii, 157.

DR. JOHNSON'S GARRET IN GOUGH SQUARE. Mr. Levet this day showed me Dr. Johnson's library, which was contained in two garrets over his chambers, where Lintot, son of the celebrated bookseller of that name, had formerly his warehouse. I found a number of good books, but very dusty and in great confusion. The floor was strewn with manuscript leaves, in Johnson's own handwriting, which I beheld with a degree of veneration, supposing they perhaps might contain portions of the *Rambler* or of *Rasselas*. I observed an apparatus for chemical experiments, of which Johnson was all his life very fond. The place seemed to be very favourable for retirement and meditation. Johnson told me that he went up thither without mentioning it to his servant when he wanted to study, secure from interruption; for he would not allow his servant to say he was not at home when he really was. 18 July 1763. JAMES BOSWELL: *Life of Johnson* (1887), i, 435–6.

COWPER'S WINTER SNUGGERY AT OLNEY—I see the winter approaching without much concern, though a passionate lover of fine weather and the pleasant scenes of summer; but the long evenings have their comforts too, and there is hardly to be found upon the earth, I suppose, so snug a creature as an Englishman by his fireside in the winter. I mean however an Englishman that lives in the country, for in London it is not very easy to avoid intrusion. I have two ladies to read to, sometimes more, but never less. At present we are circumnavigating the globe, and I find the old story with which I amused myself some years since, through the great felicity of a memory not very retentive, almost new. I am however sadly at a loss for Cook's voyage, can you send it? I shall be glad of Foster's too. These together will make the winter pass merrily, and you will much oblige me. WILLIAM COWPER to JOSEPH HILL, 20 October 1783: *Letters* (1912), i, 250–1.

Interiors

AND HIS SUMMER BOUDOIR. I write in a nook that I call my *Boudoir*. It is a summerhouse not much bigger than a sedan chair, the door of which opens into the garden, that is now crowded with pinks, roses, and honeysuckles, and the window into my neighbour's orchard. It formerly served an apothecary, now dead, as a smoking room; and under my feet is a trap-door, which once covered a hole in the ground, where he kept his bottles. At present, however, it is dedicated to sublimer uses. Having lined it with garden mats, and furnished it with a table and two chairs, here I write all that I write in summer-time, whether to my friends, or to the public. It is secure from all noise, and a refuge from all intrusion; for intruders sometimes trouble me in the winter evenings at Olney. But (thanks to my *Boudoir*!) I can now hide myself from them. A poet's retreat is sacred. They acknowledge the truth of that proposition, and never presume to violate it. WILLIAM COWPER to JOSEPH HILL, 25 June 1785: *Letters* (1912), i, 355–6.

WHERE ROBERT BURNS LIVED. Went to the churchyard where Burns is buried. A bookseller accompanied us. He showed us the outside of Burns' house, where he had lived the last three years of his life, and where he died. It has a mean appearance, and is in a bye situation, whitewashed; dirty about the doors, as almost all Scotch houses are; flowering plants in the windows. . . . Mrs. Burns was gone to spend some time by the sea-shore with her children. We spoke to the servant-maid at the door, who invited us forward, and we sate down in the parlour. The walls were coloured with a blue wash; on one side of the fire was a mahogany desk, opposite to the window a clock, and over the desk a print from the *Cotter's Saturday Night*, which Burns mentions in one of his letters having received as a present. The house was cleanly and neat in the inside, the stairs of stone, scoured white, the kitchen on the right side of the passage, the parlour on the left. In the room above the parlour the Poet died, and his son after him in the same room. DOROTHY WORDSWORTH, 18 August 1803: *Journals* (1924), 167–8.

Interiors

WORDSWORTH AT DOVE COTTAGE. A mild morning. William worked at *The Cuckoo* poem. I sewed beside him . . . I read German, and, at the closing-in of day, went to sit in the orchard. William came to me, and walked backwards and forwards. We talked about C. Wm. repeated the poem to me. I left him there, and in 20 minutes he came in, rather tired with attempting to write. He is now reading *Ben Jonson*. I am going to read German. It is about 10 o'clock, a quiet night. The fire flutters, and the watch ticks. I hear nothing save the breathing of my Beloved, as he now and then pushes his book forward, and turns over a leaf. DOROTHY WORDSWORTH at Dove Cottage, Grasmere, 23 March 1802: *Journals* (1924), 103–4.

WORDSWORTH'S STUDY. This evening Wordsworth related a pretty anecdote of his cookmaid. A stranger, who was shown about the grounds (of Rydal Mount), asked to see his study. The servant took him to the library, and said, 'This is the master's *library*, but he *studies* in the *fields.*' HENRY CRABB ROBINSON, at Rydal, 7 January 1864: *Diary* (1872), ii, 270.

SHELLEY INTERIOR AT OXFORD. Books, boots, papers, shoes, philosophical instruments, clothes, pistols, linen, crockery, ammunition and phials innumerable, with money, stockings, prints, crucibles, bags and boxes were scattered on the floor and in every place; as if the young chemist in order to analyse the mystery of creation, had endeavoured first to re-construct the primeval chaos. The tables, and especially the carpet, were already stained with large spots of various hues, which frequently proclaimed the agency of fire. An electrical machine, an air-pump, the galvanic trough, a solar microscope, and large glass jars and receivers, were conspicuous amidst the mass of matter. Upon the table by his side were some books lying open, several letters, a bundle of new pens and a bottle of japan ink that served as an inkstand; a piece of deal, lately part of the lid of a box, with many chips, and a handsome razor that had been used as a knife. There were bottles of soda water, sugar, pieces of lemon, and the traces of an effervescent beverage. Two piles of books supported the tongs, and these upheld a small glass retort about an argand lamp. I had not been seated many minutes before the liquor in the vessel boiled over, adding fresh stains to the table, and rising in fumes with a most disagreeable odour. Shelley snatched the glass quickly, and dashing it in pieces among the ashes under the grate, increased the unpleasant and penetrating effluvium. THOMAS JEFFERSON HOGG, *Shelley* (1853), 169–70.

THE LADIES OF LLANGOLLEN AT HOME. At Llangollen we waited on 'the Ladies', as they are called, and found them and everything about their habitation odd, extravagant, crazy beyond even report, not to speak of imagination. Imagine two women, one apparently 70, the other 65, dressed in heavy blue riding-habits, enormous shoes, large men's hats, more for show than use, a world of brooches, rings, etc. and Lady Eleanor Butler positively *orders*, stars, crosses, and red ribbon exactly like a K.C.B.: and to crown all, crop-heads, shaggy, rough, bushy, as white as snow, one with age alone, the other (Lady E.) partly with age and partly with a 'tait o'powther'. The elder lady is almost quite blind, and twaddles fearfully; the other is very pleasing. But, O Lord! the prints, the dogs, the cram of *bijouterie*, and cabinets, and glass cases, and books, and whirligigs of every shape and hue, and the whole house, outside and in, *covered* with carved oak, very rich and fine, much of it, and the illustrated copies of Sir W.'s Poems, and the joking compliments about Waverley, and the anxiety to know who MacIvor really was, and the absolute devouring of the poor Unknown who had his dose of butter to carry away, including one small bit of butter dug up in a cask lately from the bottom of an Irish bog! Great *romance, alias* absurd innocence, of character visible in these old girls; high— very highly bred—but queer, and indeed the elder mad beyond all dreaming. Such curiosity and such an enormous knowledge of the scandal of all towns and villages, even among the Antipodes, I believe. Their luncheon was more beautiful than satisfactory; however, having swallowed it, and taken the tenderest of adieus, we proceeded by the magnificent aqueduct bridge of the Ellesmere Canal, along which Sir W. and I walked,—I think the greatest human edifice I have seen,—and so to Chester. J. G. LOCKHART to his Wife, 21 August 1825: *Familiar Letters of Sir Walter Scott* (1894), ii, 334–5.

SAMUEL ROGERS'S HOUSE. What a delightful house it is! It looks out on the Green Park just at the most pleasant point. The furniture has been selected with a delicacy of taste quite unique. Its value does not depend on fashion, but must be the same while the fine arts are held in any esteem. In the drawing-room, for example, the chimney-pieces are carved by Flaxman into the most beautiful Grecian forms. The book-case is painted by Stothard, in his very best manner, with groups from *Chaucer, Shakspeare,* and *Boccaccio.* The pictures are not numerous; but every one is excellent. In the dining-room there are also some beautiful paintings. But the three most remarkable objects in that room are, I think, a cast of Pope, taken after death by Roubiliac; a noble model in terra-cotta by Michael Angelo, from which he afterward made one of his finest statues, that of Lorenzo de' Medici; and, lastly, a mahogany table on which stands an antique vase. T. B. MACAULAY to HANNAH MACAULAY, 25 June 1831: *Life* (1876), i, 225.

MACAULAY'S COMFORTABLE ALBANY SUITE. I have taken a very comfortable suite of chambers in The Albany; and I hope to lead, during some years, a sort of life peculiarly suited to my taste,—college life at the West End of London. I have an entrance-hall, two sitting-rooms, a bedroom, cellars, and two rooms for servants—all for ninety guineas a year: and this in a situation which no younger son of a duke need be ashamed to put on his card. We shall have, I hope, some very pleasant breakfasts there, to say nothing of dinners. My own housekeeper will do very well for a few plain dishes, and The Clarendon is within a hundred yards. T. B. MACAULAY to T. F. ELLIS, 12 July 1841: *Life* (1876), ii, 93.

CHARLES KINGSLEY AT EVERSLEY. The picturesque bow-windowed Rectory rises to memory as it stood with all its doors and windows open on certain hot summer days, the sloping bank with its great fir-tree, the garden—a gravel sweep before the drawing-room and dining rooms, a grass-plat before the study hedged off from the walk—and the tall active figure of the Rector tramping up and down one or the other. His energy made him seem everywhere, and to pervade every part of house and garden. The MS. of the book he was writing lay open on a rough standing desk, which was merely a shelf projecting from the wall; his pupils—two in number, and treated like his own sons —were working in the dining-room; his guests perhaps lounging on the lawn, or reading in the study. And he had time for all, going from writing to lecturing on optics, or to a passage in *Virgil*, from this to a vehement conversation with a guest, or tender care for his wife—who was far from strong—or a romp with his children. He would work himself into a sort of white heat over his book, till, too excited to write more, he would calm himself down by a pipe, pacing his grass-plat in thought and with long strides. C. KEGAN PAUL, *Charles Kingsley*, by his Wife (1877), i, 226.

CHARLOTTE BRONTË'S PARLOUR. The parlour has been evidently refurnished within the last few years, since Miss Brontë's success has enabled her to have a little more money to spend. Everything fits into, and is in harmony with, the idea of a country parsonage, possessed by people of very moderate means. The prevailing colour of the room is crimson, to make a warm setting for the cold grey landscape without. There is her likeness by Richmond, and an engraving from Lawrence's picture of Thackeray; and two recesses, on each side of the high, narrow, old-fashioned mantel-piece, filled with books,—books given to her, books she has bought, and which tell of her individual pursuits and tastes; *not* standard books. MRS. GASKELL, *Life of Charlotte Brontë* (1857), ii, 298.

JOHN FORSTER'S LIBRARY. His library is the pleasantest room in a private house which I have seen in London. He built it for himself, and it is large enough to hold 18,000 volumes. It is high, and a gallery runs around it, reached by a stairway in one corner, so that all the books are easily at hand. The collection is really a splendid one. Such books as there are in it! The first folio, I mean the folio of 1623, which is to you and me in the true sense the first. The copy of the *Dunciad* which Pope gave to Swift, with Pope's inscription in it; from Swift it went to Warburton, from him to Mason, at length it came to Rogers and from him through Daniels to Forster. Addison's *Letters from Italy* with his inscription to Swift, as 'the greatest genius' of the time. Johnson's *Lives of the Poets*,—the proof-sheets,—crammed with Johnson's corrections and emendations. A whole heap of Swift's account books and memorandum books, filled with most characteristic entries; and such a collection of manuscripts and letters of the Civil War time as I have never seen before. CHARLES ELIOT NORTON to J. R. LOWELL, 22 February 1869: *Letters* (1913), i, 321.

J. R. GREEN'S ROOMS GO PRE-RAPHAELITE. I had a sort of instinct I should be a prisoner soon. So a few weeks back I turned out of my rooms and turned in a very Preraphaelite friend with carte-blanche as to money and design. The result is wonderful. The end of my room reminds me of a conflagration,—beneath, heaven; above, a brilliant red! The doors are the sea-sickness style, green picked out with a sickly blue! My poor old writing desk, dear from many an association, had been clothed in light blue with lines of red. When I re-entered my rooms for the first time, my artistic friend had just begun covering it with black dragons. I 'yowled' and dashed the paint-boxes downstairs, but the dragons had already been completed, and yawn on me whenever I want to write a gay little note. 'Is it nice?' I asked my landlady 'sarcastic'. That venerable woman stood gazing on the scene. 'Not nice,' replied the critic of the kitchen, 'not nice, sir, no! but certainly spruce!' J. R. GREEN to MRS. A COURT, 1872: *Letters* (1901), 320–1.

GEORGE WYNDHAM'S TOWER. I have invaded the upper room in the tower—the 'girls' schoolroom'—*eheu fugaces*! There I feel like the Greek tyrant who slept in the top storey and pulled the ladder up after him through a hole in the floor. The room is cleared and whitewashed. I retain my own, old, lower room also. I started to sort my books on the broad principle of poetry, literature, books of reference, upstairs; history, politics, philosophy, science, downstairs. I found that nine-tenths of the books in each class were *not* in the storey of their ultimate destination, but in the other. So I spent 2½ days on the turret stairs, perspiring freely, with 10 volumes on each journey clasped between my hands and chin. Now order reigns, and it is mighty pleasant. GEORGE WYNDHAM at Saighton Grange, Chester, to CHARLES T. GATTY, 18 August 1905: *Life and Letters*, [n.d.] ii, 511.

MEREDITH'S CHALET ON BOX HILL. I want you to see my cottage—annexe—chalet on the terrace. I think you will agree with me, that it is the prettiest to be found, the view is without a match in Surrey. The interior full of light, which can be moderated; and while surrounded by firs, I look over the slope of our green hill to the ridges of Reith, round to Ranmore, and half of Norbury. GEORGE MEREDITH to JOHN MORLEY: *Letters* (1912), i, 272.

W. H. HUDSON'S APARTMENT IN PADDINGTON. The big sitting-room . . . was a gloomy place. It was furnished with derelicts from boarding-houses: there was nothing beautiful in it, no gleam of brightness or spot of colour save in one glass-covered case which held his best books. In the centre of the room stood a gigantic circular settee covered with horsehair. It might have been salved from Dickens's *Mugby Junction*. It filled and blocked the centre of the room, a comfortless and dreadful thing of which he seemed unconscious, though its preposterous construction made my blood run cold when I saw it or had to sit upon it. The outdoor colours of Nature he bathed in: he cared, it seemed, as little for colour in his house . . . it was not poverty which kept him from some attempt at decoration. Indoors did not matter. Some of the brightest birds live in the closest nests. Tomorrow and tomorrow he would go where there was light. Truly he had no real sense of colour or decoration. MORLEY ROBERTS, *W. H. Hudson* (1924), 83–4.

CHARLES AND MARY LAMB IN COLERIDGE'S LAKELAND STUDY. I set out with Mary to Keswick, without giving Coleridge any notice. . . . He received us with all the hospitality in the world, and gave up his time to show us all the wonders of the country. He dwells upon a small hill by the side of Keswick, in a comfortable house, quite enveloped on all sides by a net of mountains: great floundering bears and monsters they seemed, all couchant and asleep. We got in in the evening, travelling in a post-chaise from Penrith, in the midst of a gorgeous sunshine, which transmuted all the mountains into colours, purple, &c. &c. We thought we had got into fairy-land. But that went off . . . and we entered Coleridge's comfortable study just in the dusk, when the mountains were all dark with clouds upon their heads. Such an impression I never received from objects of sight before, nor do I suppose I can ever again. Glorious creatures, fine old fellows, Skiddaw, &c. I never shall forget ye, how ye lay about that night, but promising that ye were to be seen in the morning. Coleridge had got a blazing fire in his study; which is a large, antique, ill-shaped room, with an old-fashioned organ, never played upon, big enough for a church, shelves of scattered folios, an Aeolian harp, and an old sofa, half bed, &c. And all looking out upon the last fading view of Skiddaw, and his broad-breasted brethren: what a night! CHARLES LAMB to THOMAS MANNING, 24 September 1802: *Letters* (1905), i, 243–4.

SHELLEY'S NEST NEAR PISA. 'L'Inglese *malincolico* haunts the wood *maladetta*. I will show you his nest.' As we advanced, the ground swelled into mounds and hollows. By-and-by the old fellow pointed with his stick to a hat, books, and loose papers lying about, and then to a deep pool of dark glimmering water. . . . The strong light streamed through the opening of the trees. One of the pines, undermined by the water, had fallen into it. Under its lea, and nearly hidden, sat the Poet, gazing on the dark mirror beneath, so lost in his bardish reverie that he did not hear my approach. There the trees were stunted and bent, and their crowns were shorn like friars by the sea breezes, excepting a cluster of three, under which Shelley's traps were lying; these over-topped the rest. To avoid startling the Poet out of his dream, I squatted under the lofty trees, and opened his books. One was a volume of his favourite Greek dramatist, *Aeschylus*— the same that I found in his pocket after death—and the other was a volume of *Shakespeare*. I then hailed him, and, turning his head, he answered faintly, 'Hollo! come in.' 'Is this your study?' I asked. 'Yes,' he answered; 'and these trees are my books— they tell no lies. In composing one's faculties must not be divided; in a house there is no solitude: a door shutting, a footstep heard, a bell ringing, a voice, causes an echo in your brain and dissolves your visions.' I said, 'Here you have the river rushing by you, the birds chattering, and the beasts bellowing.' He answered 'The river flows by like Time, and all the sounds of Nature harmonize; they soothe: it is only the human animal that is discordant with Nature and disturbs me.' EDWARD JOHN TRE-LAWNEY, *Records of Shelley, Byron and the Author* (1878), 58–9.

DICKENS'S CHÂLET. Divers birds sing here all day, and the nightingales all night. The place is lovely, and in perfect order. I have put five mirrors in the Swiss châlet (where I write) and they reflect and refract in all kinds of ways the leaves that are quivering at the windows, and the great fields of waving corn, and the sail-dotted river. My room is up among the branches of the trees; and the birds and the butterflies fly in and out, and the green branches shoot in, at the open windows, and the lights and shadows of the clouds come and go with the rest of the company. The scent of the flowers, and indeed of every thing that is growing for miles and miles, is most delicious. CHARLES DICKENS at Gad's Hill to MRS. JAMES T. FIELDS, 25 May 1868: *Letters* (1882), iii, 256.

XIV

GOOD COMPANY

Good company is like good wine, and improves by keeping. Anne Thackeray (Lady Ritchie), *Records* (1892), 64.

Put in at my Lord's lodgings, where we stayed late, eating a part of his turkey-pie, and reading Quarles' *Emblems*. SAMUEL PEPYS, 7 January 1659: *Diary* (1893), i, 12.

To-day I dined with Lewis and Prior at an eating-house, but with Lewis's wine. Lewis went away, and Prior and I sat on, where we complimented one another for an hour or two upon our mutual wit and poetry. JONATHAN SWIFT, 17 November 1710: *Journal to Stella* 1710–1713 (Bohn Lib. 1924), 55.

Coleridge came in to dinner. . . . We were very merry . . . Wm. read *Ruth* etc. after supper. Coleridge *Christabel*. DOROTHY WORDSWORTH at Grasmere, 22 October 1800: *Journals* (1924), 55.

Late at C. Lamb's. Found a large party there. Southey had been with Blake, and admired both his designs and his poetic talents. At the same time he held him to be a decided madman. . . . He showed Southey a perfectly mad poem, called 'Jerusalem'. Oxford Street is in Jerusalem. HENRY CRABB ROBINSON, 24 July 1811: *Diary* (1872), i, 176.

THE IMMORTAL DINNER PARTY

Scene: Benjamin Robert Haydon's Studio. Guests: Charles Lamb, John Keats, Wordsworth, Ritchie, Monkhouse—and a stranger.

On December 28th the immortal dinner came off in my painting-room, with Jerusalem towering up behind us as a background. Wordsworth was in fine cue, and we had a glorious set-to,—on Homer, Shakespeare, Milton and Virgil. Lamb got exceedingly merry and exquisitely witty; and his fun in the midst of Wordsworth's solemn intonations of oratory was like the sarcasm and wit of the fool in the intervals of Lear's passion. He made a speech and voted me absent, and made them drink my health. 'Now', said Lamb, 'you old lake poet, you rascally poet, why do you call Voltaire dull?' We all defended Wordsworth, and affirmed there was a state of mind when Voltaire would be dull. 'Well', said Lamb, 'here's to Voltaire—the Messiah of the French nation, and a very proper one too.'

He then, in a strain of humour beyond description, abused me for putting Newton's head into my picture,—'a fellow', said he, 'who believed nothing unless it was as clear as the three sides of a triangle.' And then he and Keats agreed he had destroyed all the poetry of the rainbow by reducing it to the prismatic colours. It was impossible to resist him, and we all drank 'Newton's health, and confusion to mathematics'. It was delightful to see the good-humour of Wordsworth in giving in to all our frolics without affectation and laughing as heartily as the best of us.

By this time other friends joined, amongst them poor Ritchie who was going to penetrate by Fezzan to Timbuctoo. I introduced him to all as 'a gentleman going to Africa'. Lamb seemed to take no notice; but all of a sudden he roared out, 'Which is the gentleman we are going to lose?' We then drank the victim's health, in which Ritchie joined.

In the morning of this delightful day, a gentleman, a perfect stranger, had called on me. He said he knew my friends, had an enthusiasm for Wordsworth and begged I would procure him the happiness of an introduction. He told me he was a Comptroller of stamps, and often had correspondence with the poet. I thought it a liberty; but still, as he seemed a gentleman, I told him he might come.

When we retired to tea we found the comptroller. In introducing him to Wordsworth I forgot to say who he was. After a little time the comptroller looked down, looked up and said to

Wordsworth, 'Don't you think, sir, Milton was a great genius?'
Keats looked at me, Wordsworth looked at the comptroller.
Lamb who was dozing by the fire turned round and said, 'Pray,
sir, did you say Milton was a great genius?' 'No, Sir; I asked
Mr. Wordsworth if he were not.' 'Oh,' said Lamb, 'then you are
a silly fellow.' 'Charles! my dear Charles!' said Wordsworth;
but Lamb, perfectly innocent of the confusion he had created, was
off again by the fire.

After an awful pause the comptroller said, 'Don't you think
Newton a great genius?' I could not stand it any longer. Keats
put his head into my books. Ritchie squeezed in a laugh. Wordsworth seemed asking himself, 'Who is this?' Lamb got up, and
taking a candle, said, 'Sir, will you allow me to look at your
phrenological development?' He then turned his back on the
poor man, and at every question of the comptroller he chaunted—

> 'Diddle diddle dumpling, my son John
> Went to bed with his breeches on.'

The man in office, finding Wordsworth did not know who he
was, said in a spasmodic and half-chuckling anticipation of assured victory, 'I have had the honour of some correspondence
with you, Mr. Wordsworth.' 'With me, sir?' said Wordsworth,
'not that I remember.' 'Don't you, sir? I am a Comptroller of
Stamps.' There was a dead silence;—the comptroller evidently
thinking that was enough. While we were waiting for Wordsworth's reply, Lamb sung out

> 'Hey diddle diddle,
> The cat and the fiddle.'

'My dear Charles!' said Worthworth,—

> 'Diddle diddle dumpling, my son John,'

chaunted Lamb, and then rising, exclaimed, 'Do let me have another look at that gentleman's organs'. Keats and I hurried Lamb
into the painting-room, shut the door and gave way to inex-
tinguishable laughter. Monkhouse followed and tried to get

Lamb away. We went back but the comptroller was irreconcilable. We soothed and smiled and asked him to supper. He stayed though his dignity was sorely affected. However, being a good-natured man, we parted all in good-humour, and no illeffects followed.

All the while, until Monkhouse succeeded, we could hear Lamb struggling in the painting-room and calling at intervals, 'Who is that fellow? Allow me to see his organs once more.'

It was indeed an immortal evening. Wordsworth's fine intonation as he quoted Milton and Virgil, Keats' eager inspired look, Lamb's quaint spark of lambent humour, so speeded the stream of conversation, that in my life I have never passed a more delightful time. All our fun was within bounds. Not a word passed that an apostle might not have listened to. It was a night worthy of the Elizabethan age, and my solemn Jerusalem flashing up by the flame of the fire, with Christ hanging over us like a vision, all made up a picture which will long glow upon—

> 'that inward eye
> Which is the bliss of solitude.'

Keats made Ritchie promise he would carry his *Endymion* to the great desert of Sahara and fling it in the midst. BENJAMIN ROBERT HAYDON, *Autobiography* (1853), i, 384–8.

At present I can only talk of Sir Walter Scott, with whom I have been just taking a long, delightful walk through the 'Rhymour's Glen'. I came home, to be sure, in rather a disastrous state after my adventure, and was greeted by my maid, with that most disconsolate visage of hers, which invariably moves my hard heart to laughter; for I had got wet above my ankles in the haunted burn, torn my gown in making my way through thickets of wild roses, stained my gloves with wood strawberries, and even— direst misfortune of all! scratched my face with a rowan branch. But what of all this? Had I not been walking with Sir Walter Scott, and listening to tales of elves and bogles and brownies, and hearing him recite some of the Spanish ballads till they 'stirred the heart like the sound of a trumpet'? I must reserve many of these things to tell you when we meet, but one very important trait, (since it proves a sympathy between the Great Unknown and myself), I cannot possibly defer to that period, but must record it now . . . Well, we had reached a rustic seat in the wood, and were to rest there, but I, out of pure perverseness, chose to establish myself comfortably on a grass bank. 'Would it not be more prudent for you, Mrs. Hemans,' said Sir Walter, 'to take the seat?' 'I have no doubt that it would, Sir Walter, but, somehow or other, I always prefer the grass.' 'And so do I', replied the dear old gentleman, coming to sit there beside me, 'and I really believe that I do it chiefly out of a wicked wilfulness, because all my good advisers say that it will give me the rheumatism.' Now was it not delightful? I mean for the future to take exactly my own way in all matters of this kind, and to say that Sir Walter Scott particularly recommended me to do so. I was rather agreeably surprised by his appearance, after all I had heard of its homeliness; the predominant expression of countenance, is, I think, a sort of arch good-nature, conveying a mingled expression of penetration and benevolence. MRS. HEMANS to ——, 13 July 1829: *Memorials* (1836), ii, 31–3.

Had the pleasure of a long walk with a lady, well known in the world of poetry, Mrs. Hemans. She is young and pretty, though the mother of five children, as she tells me. There is taste and spirit in her conversation. My daughters are critical, and call her blue, but I think they are hypercritical. I will know better when we meet again. SIR WALTER SCOTT, 13 July 1829: *Journal* (1890), ii, 317.

I spent one evening with Carlyle, but was very dull somehow and delighted to get out into the street. An organ was playing a polka even so late in the street: and Carlyle was rather amazed to see me polka down the pavement—He shut his street door—to which he always accompanies you—with a kind of groan—He was looking well—but he says he gets no sleep of nights. This comes of having a great idea, which germinating once in the mind, grows like a tape worm, and consumes the vitals. What a nasty idea.—EDWARD FITZGERALD to BERNARD BARTON, 11 January 1845: *New Letters* (1923), 94.

Yesterday morning I breakfasted with Taylor to meet Southey: the party was Southey; Strutt, member for Derby, a Radical; young Mill, a political economist; Charles Villiers, young Elliot, and myself. Southey is remarkably pleasing in his manner and appearance, unaffected, unassuming, and agreeable; at least such was my impression for the hour or two I saw him. Young Mill is the son of Mill who wrote the *History of British India*, and said to be cleverer than his father. He has written many excellent articles in reviews, pamphlets, &c. but though powerful with a pen in his hand, in conversation he has not the art of managing his ideas, and is consequently hesitating and slow, and has the appearance of being always working in his mind propositions or a syllogism. CHARLES C. F. GREVILLE, 15 November 1830: *The Greville Memoirs* (1875), ii, 58–9.

Breakfasted the day before yesterday with Rogers, Sydney Smith, Luttrell, John Russell, and Moore; excessively agreeable. I never heard anything more entertaining than Sydney Smith; such bursts of merriment and so dramatic. Breakfasts are the meals for poets. I met Wordsworth and Southey at breakfast. Rogers' are always agreeable. CHARLES C. F. GREVILLE, 10 June 1831: *The Greville Memoirs* (1875), ii, 150.

I found a very different party here from what I left at Woburn. There nothing but idle, ignorant, ordinary people, among whom there was not an attempt at anything like society or talk; here though not many, almost all distinguished more or less—Moore, Rogers, Macaulay, Westmacott, Butler and Mrs. Butler [Fanny Kemble], Dr. Fowler and his wife, Lady H. Baring, Miss Fox. Mrs. Butler read the last three acts of *Much Ado About Nothing*. Her reading is admirable, voice beautiful, great variety, and equally happy in the humorous and pathetic parts . . . Charles Austin came yesterday, Dundas and John Russell today. Last night, Mrs. Butler read the first three acts of *The Hunchback*, which she was to have finished to-night, but she ran restive and pretended that some of the party did not like it, and no persuasion could induce her to go on. Another night Moore sang some of his Melodies, and Macaulay has been always talking. . . . The drollest thing is to see the effect upon Rogers, who is nearly extinguished, and can neither make himself heard, nor find an interval to get in a word. He is exceedingly provoked, though he can't help admiring, and he will revive tomorrow when Macaulay goes. . . . I never passed a week with so much good talk, literary and miscellaneous, no scandal or gossip. CHARLES C. F. GREVILLE at Bowood, Lord Lansdowne's seat in Wiltshire, Christmas 1841: *The Greville Memoirs* (1885), ii, 69–71.

At half-past seven on Friday evening last, an omnibus set me down in Great Cheyne Row. Shown up into the large, comfortable drawing-room, I found Mrs. Carlyle alone (Carlyle downstairs fetching a short allowance of sleep over night), and was more favourably impressed by her than I had expected. After exchanging a few words, as she was making the tea, Carlyle appeared in his long brown indoors coat, and shook me cordially by the hand; was from that moment to the last *very* kind. 'I have brought you here on false pretences.' Ruskin was coming the *following* night; Mrs. Carlyle was engaged out to a party. 'You must not suppose', she had said before, 'the wife of a philosopher sits at home over the fire in white satin shoes.' . . . After tea, Mrs. Carlyle left. And for the rest of the evening, (till twelve) I sat with him alone, he pouring himself out as is his wont; sitting the latter part of the time on a footstool by the fire, smoking, and looking in his old long brown kind of greatcoat, as he was bewailing the pass men and things had come to, and as he thought of it hardly caring to live,—looking like a veritable Prophet, mourning in sackcloth and ashes the sins of the world. ALEXANDER GILCHRIST to WILLIAM HAINES, 29 November 1855: *Anne Gilchrist's Life and Writings* (1887), 41–2.

Leslie Stephen and Morris dined with us,—they had never met before. Morris complained of feeling old. Monday was his thirty-ninth birthday; his hair, he said, was turning gray. He was as usual a surprising piece of nature; certainly one of the most unconventional and original of men. His talk was much of old Northern stories, and sagas, very vivid, picturesque and entertaining from its contents and from its character. Stephen was pleasant, but he is at his best and shows his worth most in tête-à-tête. CHARLES ELIOT NORTON, 26 March 1873: *Letters* (1913), i, 470.

Went with George Wyndham to a dinner given by Henley to the *New Review* contributors, a deadly dull affair, as all men's dinners are—the most interesting person I met there was the Dane Brandes, who has the honour of having invented Ibsen. WILFRID SCAWEN BLUNT, 10 July 1896: *Diaries* (1910), i, 232.

At the dinner given to Anatole France I sate with Wells to the back of me, Mrs. Humphry Ward to the front of me, and Marie Corelli (in pale blue baby-dress, a pink rose over the ear, an immense barrel-bulk, a mighty atom indeed) to the side of me. And straight into the ocean of soup swam the two hundred. EDITH SICHEL to LADY ROBERT CECIL, 1914: *Letters, Verses and Other Writings* (1918), 180.

Dined at Osbert Sitwell's. Good dinner. Fish before soup. Present, W. H. Davies, Lytton Strachey, Woolf, Nichols, S. Sassoon, Aldous Huxley, Atkin (a very young caricaturist), W. J. Turner, and Herbert Read (a very young poet). The faces of Woolf, Atkin, and Read, were particularly charming in their ingenuousness. Davies I liked. He had walked all the way from Tottenham Court Road to Swan Walk. A house with much better pictures and bric-à-brac than furniture. But lots of very modern pictures, of which I liked a number. Bright walls and bright cloths and bright glass everywhere. A fine Rowlandson drawing. Osbert is young. He is already a very good host. I enjoyed this evening, though I knew I should have indigestion after the creamy sweet, and I have got it. ARNOLD BENNETT, 5 June 1919: *Journals* (1932), ii, 251.

XV

TABLE TALK

If you are ever at a loss to support a flagging conversation, introduce the subject of eating. Leigh Hunt, *Table Talk* (1851), 104.

Tell me what you eat, and I will tell you what you are. Brillat-Savarin, *Physiologie du Goût* (1827).

Home to dinner, and there I took occasion, from the blackness of the meat as it came out of the pot, to fall out with my wife and my maid for their sluttery, and so left the table, and went up to read in Mr. Selden till church time, and then my wife and I to church. SAMUEL PEPYS, 22 December 1661: *Diary* (1893), ii, 157.

I was at a loss to-day for a dinner, unless I would have gone a great way, so I dined with some friends that board hereabout, as a spunger; and this evening Sir Andrew Fountaine would needs have me go to the tavern, where, for two bottles of wine, Portugal and Florence, among three of us, we had sixteen shilling to pay; and if ever he catches me so again, I'll spend as many pounds; and therefore I have put it among my extraordinaries; but we had a neck of mutton dressed à la Maintenon, that the dog could not eat. JONATHAN SWIFT, 8 October 1710: *Journal to Stella* 1710–1713 (Bohn Lib. 1924), 25.

Pope hastened his death by feeding much on high-seasoned dishes, and drinking spirits. Joseph Spence, *Anecdotes* (1858), 105.

We breakfasted at Cullen. They set down fried haddocks broiled, along with our tea. I ate one; but Dr. Johnson was disgusted by the sight of them, so they were removed. JAMES

Table Talk

BOSWELL, 26 August 1773: 'Tour to the Hebrides', *Boswell's Life of Johnson* (1887), v, 110.

Some people have a foolish way of not minding, or pretending not to mind, what they eat: For my part, I mind my belly very studiously, and very carefully; for I look upon it, that he who does not mind his belly will hardly mind anything else. DR. JOHNSON, *Boswell's Life of Johnson* (1887), i, 467.

Gluttony is less common among women than among men. Women commonly eat more sparingly, and are less curious in the choice of meat; but if once you find a woman gluttonous, expect from her very little virtue. DR. JOHNSON, *Autobiography of Mrs. Piozzi* (1861), i, 320.

The Wordsworths never dine . . . they hate such doings; when they are hungry, they go to the cupboard and eat . . . Mr. Wordsworth . . . will live for a month on cold beef, and the next on cold bacon. MRS. HOFLAND to MISS MITFORD, 13 September 1817. *Letters of Mary Russell Mitford* (1925).

Towards freshness or presumption he was unmerciful. . . . There was a lady once who ventured an impertinence. Sitting next Trollope at dinner she noticed that he partook largely of every dish offered to him. 'You seem to have a very good appetite, Mr. Trollope,' she observed. 'None at all, madam,' he replied, 'but, thank God, I am very greedy.' MICHAEL SADLEIR, *Trollope: A Commentary* (1927), 331.

I am very fond of experimental housekeeping, such as having an ox-cheek now and then; I shall have one next week, and I mean to have some little dumplings put into it, that I may fancy myself at Godmersham. JANE AUSTEN to her sister CASSANDRA, 17 November 1798: *Letters* (1884), i, 166

Talking of Pleasure, this moment I was writing with one hand, and with the other holding to my Mouth a Nectarine—good God how fine. It went down soft, pulpy, slushy, oozy—all its delicious embonpoint melted down my throat like a large Beatified strawberry. I shall certainly breed. John Keats to Charles Wentworth Dilke, 22 September 1819: *Letters* (1895), 77.

If you can come next Sunday we shall be equally glad to see you. ... Leg of Lamb, as before, hot at 4. And the heart of Lamb ever. Charles Lamb to Thomas Allsop, 30 March 1821: *Letters* (1905), ii, 551.

My digestion is weak; I am too bilious to eat more than once a day, and generally live on vegetables. To be sure I drink two bottles of wine at dinner, but they form only a vegetable diet. Just now I live on claret and soda-water. Lord Byron, *Conversations*, Medwin (1824), 14–15.

My little Jeannie [Mrs. Carlyle] was in hands with the marmalade that day: none ever made such marmalade for me, pure as liquid amber, in taste and in look almost poetically delicate, and it was the only one of her pretty and industrious confitures that I individually cared for; which made her doubly diligent and punctual about it. Thomas Carlyle, *Reminiscences* (1881), ii, 324.

We have our dinner from the Trattoria at two o'clock, and can dine our favourite way on thrushes and Chianti with a miraculous cheapness, and no trouble, no cook, no kitchen; the prophet Elijah or the lilies of the field took as little thought for their dining, which exactly suits us. It is a continental fashion which we never cease commending. Then at six we have coffee, and rolls of milk, made of milk, I mean, and at nine our supper (call it supper, if you please) of roast chestnuts and grapes. So you see how primitive we are, and how I forget to praise the eggs at breakfast. Elizabeth Barrett Browning to Mrs. Martin, 5 November 1846: *Letters* (1897), i, 303.

Tennyson does not like his eggs too lightly cooked. To-day at breakfast there was a pretty waitress, and he sent his eggs to be more boiled, and then, in the damsel's native tongue, expostulated with her as to the softness of her eggs and the apparent

Table Talk

hardness of her heart. It was very pleasant to hear his grave but gallant remonstrance and her merry laugh. He is delightful. FREDERICK LOCKER-LAMPSON, at the Hotel d'Angleterre, Strasbourg, 3 July 1869: *Memoir of Tennyson* (1897), 77.

We dine at 2.0 and have tea with potted meat at 6.30, and no soda, no brandy, no wine save Marsala, not even thick cream, as milk is scarce; but we have health and no stuffiness, stodginess, or formulae. We don't talk about the weather much. WILLIAM CORY at Halsdon, 31 December 1877: *Letters and Journals* (1897), 436.

What *can* it be, that subtle treachery that lurks in tea-cakes, and is wholly absent in the rude honesty of toast? JOHN RUSKIN to MISS SUSAN REEVER, *Hortus Inclusus* (1887), 119.

Don't talk to me about taverns! There is just one genuine, clean, decent, palatable thing occasionally to be had in them—namely, a boiled egg. The soups taste pretty good sometimes, but their sources are involved in a darker mystery than that of the Nile. Omelettes taste as if they had been carried in the waiter's hat, or fried in an old boot. I ordered scrambled eggs one day. It must be that they had been scrambled for by *somebody*, but who—who in the possession of a sound reason *could* have scrambled for what I had set before me under that name? Butter! I am thinking just now of those exquisite little pellets I have so often seen at your table, and wondering why the taverns *always* keep it until it is old. Fool that I am! As if the taverns did not know that if it was good it would be eaten, which is not what they want. Then the waiters with the napkins—what don't they do with those napkins! Mention any one thing of which you think you can say with truth 'That they do not do'. OLIVER WENDELL HOLMES at Montreal to JAMES T. FIELDS, 23 October 1867: *Life and Letters* (1896), ii, 292-3.

Mr. Lyford was here yesterday; he came while we were at dinner, and partook of our elegant entertainment. I was not ashamed at asking him to sit down to table, for we had some pease-soup,

a sparerib, and a pudding. JANE AUSTEN to her sister CASSAN-
DRA, 1 December 1897: *Letters* (1884), i, 172–3.

It is more useful, perhaps, to know my host at the Blue Boar in
Piccadilly died of eating too many oysters, than how Marshal
Turenne was killed in the trenches. ELIZABETH MONTAGU to
LORD LYTTELTON, 23 October 1757: *Letters* (1813), iv, 66.

Yesterday I dined with Alfred Tennyson at the Cock Tavern,
Temple Bar. We had two chops, one pickle, two cheeses, one
pint of stout, one pint of port, and three cigars. JAMES SPEDDING
to RICHARD MONCKTON MILNES, 4 April 1837: *Life of Richard
Monckton Milnes* (1891), i, 192.

The Ritz Hotel sent me some *pâté de foie gras* yesterday. This
means *pâté de foie gras* at every meal as the stuff won't keep.
Auntie Tertia came on Friday with whole suitcases full of presents and Xmas pudding and mince-tarts and cheese-cakes. These
mince-tarts are unsurpassed in my experience—indeed unequalled. This means mince-tarts at every meal. I can only get
along by eating no meat, especially as I have had a lot of oat-
cakes given me: which monopolises my breakfasts. I *adore* oat-
cakes: yet was I glad to have eaten the last one this morning!
ARNOLD BENNETT, 23 December 1929: *Letters to his Nephew*,
(1936), 282.

I have never been anything so refined as a *gourmet*; so I am happy
to say that I am still quite capable of being a glutton. My ignorance of cookery is such that I can even eat the food in the most
fashionable and expensive hotels in London. G. K. CHESTERTON,
Autobiography (1937), 116.

XVI

FILL UP THE GLASS!

The human intellect owes its superiority over that of the lower animals in great measure to the stimulus which alcohol has given to imagination—imagination being little else than another name for illusion. Samuel Butler, *Alps and Sanctuaries* (1881), 46.

Gloriously drunk, obey the important call. William Cowper, *The Task*, iv, 510.

From *Bachrag* the first stock of Vines, which grow now in the grand *Canary* Island, were brought, which with the heat of the Sun and the Soil, is grown now to that height of perfection, that the Wines which they afford are accounted the richest, the most firm, the best bodied and lastingest Wine, and the most defecated from all earthly grossness, of any other whatsoever; it hath little or no sulphur at all in't, and leaves less dregs behind, tho' one drink it to excess. *French* Wines may be said to pickle meat in the stomach; but this is the Wine that digests, and doth not only breed good blood, but it nutrifieth also, being a glutinous substantial liquor. Of this Wine, if of any other, may be verified that merry induction, That good Wine makes good Blood, good Blood causeth good Humours, good Humours cause good Thoughts, good Thoughts bring forth good Works, good Works carry a Man to Heaven; ergo good Wine carrieth a Man to Heaven. If this be true, surely more *English* go to Heaven this way than any other, for I think there's more *Canary* brought into *England* than to all the World besides. JAMES HOWELL, *Familiar Letters* (1737), 366.

Here is admirable Champagne for twelve pence a quart, as good Burgundy for fifteen pence; and I have virtue enough to resolve

Fill up the Glass!

to leave this place to-morrow for St. Omers, where the same wine is half as dear again, and may be not quite so good . . . Charles and Jacob and I have never fail'd drinking your healths since we saw you, nor ever will till we see you again. WILLIAM CONGREVE at Calais to EDWARD PORTER, 11 August 1700: *Letters of Eminent Literary Men* (1843), 299.

Dined with Stratford at a merchant's in the city, where I drank the first Tokay wine I ever saw; and it is admirable, yet not to the degree I expected. JONATHAN SWIFT, 14 September 1710: *Journal to Stella:* 1710–1713 (Bohn Lib. 1924), 9.

I have left off wine and writing; for I really think that a man must be a bold writer who trusts to wit without it. JOHN GAY to DEAN SWIFT, 4 July 1730: *Life and Letters* (1921), 119.

Since I have got over the impediment to a writer, of water drinking, if I can persuade myself that I have any wit, and find I have inclination, I intend to write; though, as yet, I have another impediment: for I have not provided myself with a scheme. Ten to one but I shall have a propensity to write against vice, and who can tell how far that may offend? But an author should consult his genius, rather than his interest, if he cannot reconcile them. JOHN GAY to DEAN SWIFT, 21 April 1731: *Life and Letters* (1921), 126.

We talked of drinking wine. JOHNSON. 'I require wine, only when I am alone. I have then often wished for it, and often taken it.' SPOTTISWOODE. 'What, by way of a companion, Sir?' JOHNSON. 'To get rid of myself, to send myself away. Wine gives great pleasure; and every pleasure is of itself a good. It is a good unless counterbalanced by evil. A man may have a strong reason, not to drink wine; and that may be greater than the pleasure. Wine makes a man better pleased with himself. I do not say that it makes him more pleasing to others. Sometimes it does. But the danger is, that while a man grows better pleased with himself, he may be growing less pleasing to others. Wine gives a man nothing. It neither gives him knowledge nor wit; it only animates a man, and enables him to bring out what a dread of the company has repressed. It only puts in motion what has been locked up in frost. But this may be good, or it may be bad.' SPOTTISWOODE. 'So, Sir, wine is a key which opens a box; but this box may be either full or empty.' JOHNSON. 'Nay, Sir, conversation is the key: wine is a pick-lock, which forces open the box and injures it. A man should cultivate his mind so as to have that confidence and readiness without wine, which wine gives.' JAMES BOSWELL, 28 April 1778: *Life of Johnson* (1887), iii, 327.

I was heartily disgusted with Mr. Boswell, who came upstairs after dinner, much disordered with wine, and addressed me in a manner which drew from me a sharp rebuke, for which I fancy he will not easily forgive me. HANNAH MORE, 1781: *Memoir* (1835), i, 210–11.

The only water drinkers of any use, importance, or merit in human life are your drinkers of Helicon. ELIZABETH MONTAGUE to HANNAH MORE, 1782: *Memoir of Hannah More, Ib.*, i, 268.

I here inclose you my Scotch Drink, and 'may the deil follow with a blessing for your edification.' I hope, sometime before we hear the gowk, to have the pleasure of seeing you at Kilmarnock, when I intend we shall have a gill between us, in a mutchkin-stoup. ROBERT BURNS to ROBERT MUIR, Wine Merchant, Kilmarnock, 20 March 1786: *Letters* (1931).

I believe I drank too much wine last night at Hurstbourne; I know not how else to account for the shaking of my hand to-day. You will kindly make allowance therefore for any indistinctness of writing, by attributing it to this venial error. JANE AUSTEN to her sister CASSANDRA, 20 November 1800: *Letters* (1884), i, 241.

By the Bye, I must not (speaking of your kindness) forget to thank you and Sir George in my own person and for my own particular sake for the benefit and pleasure I have received from drinking of the Brown Stout, of which I take a certain quantity every day, and it seems to make me stronger and do me good.

Fill up the Glass!

DOROTHY WORDSWORTH to LADY BEAUMONT, 25 July 1804: *Early Letters of William and Dorothy Wordsworth* (1935), 405.

I am but just returned to town, from which you may infer that I have been out of it; and I have been boxing, for exercise, with Jackson for this last month daily. I have also been drinking, and, on one occasion, with three other friends at the Cocoa Tree, from six till four, yea, until five in the matin. We clareted and champagned till two—then supped, and finished with a kind of regency punch composed of madeira, brandy, and *green* tea, no *real* water being admitted therein. There was a night for you! without once quitting the table, except to ambulate home, which I did alone, and in utter contempt of a hackney-coach and my own *vis*, both of which were deemed necessary for our conveyance. And so,—I am very well, and they say it will hurt my constitution. LORD BYRON to THOMAS MOORE, 9 April 1814: *Letters and Journals* (1899), ii, 63.

I never drink now above three glasses of wine—and never any spirits and water. Though by the bye, the other day Woodhouse took me to his coffee house and ordered a Bottle of Claret—now I like Claret, whenever I can have Claret I must drink it,—'tis the only palate affair that I am at all sensual in. Would it not be a good spec. to send you some vine roots—could it be done? I'll inquire. If you could make some wine like Claret, to drink on summer evenings in an arbour! For really 'tis so fine—it fills one's mouth with a gushing freshness—then goes down cool and feverless—then you do not feel it quarrelling with your liver—no, it is rather a Peacemaker, and lies as quiet as it did in the grape; then it is as fragrant as the Queen Bee, and the more ethereal Part of it mounts into the brain, not assaulting the cerebral apartments like a bully in a bad-house looking for his trull and hurrying from door to door bouncing against the wainscot, but rather walks like Aladdin about his enchanted palace so gently that you do not feel his step. Other wines of a heavy and spirituous nature transform a man into a Silenus: this makes him a Hermes—and gives a Woman the soul and immortality of an

Fill up the Glass!

Ariadne, for whom Bacchus always kept a good cellar of Claret—and even of that he could never persuade her to take above two cups. I said this same Claret is the only palate-passion I have—I forgot game—I must plead guilty to the breast of a Partridge, the back of a hare, the backbone of a grouse, and wing and side of a Pheasant, and a Woodcock *passim*. JOHN KEATS to GEORGE and GEORGIANA KEATS in America, 24 February 1819: *Letters* (1895), 287–8.

Wrote some more of the tragedy [*Sardanapalus*]. Took a glass of grog. After having ridden hard in rainy weather, and scribbled, and scribbled again, the spirits (at least mine) need a little exhilaration, and I don't like laudanum now as I used to do. So I have mixed a glass of strong waters and single waters which I shall now proceed to empty. . . . The effect of all wines and spirits upon me is, however, strange. It *settles*, but it makes me gloomy —gloomy at the very moment of their effect, and not gay hardly ever. But it composes for a time, though sullenly. LORD BYRON, 14 January 1821: *Letters and Journals* (1901), v, 174.

Gin-and-water is the source of all my inspiration. LORD BYRON, *Conversations*, Medwin (1824), 272.

When Porson dined with me, I used to keep him within bounds; but I frequently met him at various houses where he got completely drunk. He would not scruple to return to the dining-room, after the company had left it, pour into a tumbler, the drops remaining in the wine-glasses, and drink off the omnium gatherum. SAMUEL ROGERS, *Table Talk* (1856), 219.

On the 16 of July (1853) for the first time in his life that distinguished critic and poet (A. H. Clough) tasted Soda Water, and it is the first American institution on which I have heard him bestow unqualified praise. He is not quite sure, however, that it will do in the long run, and seems to have some vague notion that chemicals, however refreshing for the moment, must corrode the vitals. CHARLES ELIOT NORTON at Cambridge, Mass., to F. J. CHILD: *Letters* (1913), i, 90.

Fill up the Glass!

To-day Ford and I set apart to go into the city to buy books; but we only had a scurvy dinner at an alehouse, and he made me go to the tavern, and drink Florence, four and sixpence a flask; damned wine! so I spent my money, which I seldom do, and past an insipid day, and saw nobody. JONATHAN SWIFT, 9 January 1711: *Journal to Stella*: 1710–1713 (1924), 98.

I promised you a glass of wine one day, and you must let me redeem my promise by sending you these half a dozen bottles. They are marked in Judge Jackson's catalogue 'Essex Madeira, bought and imported through Mr. Isaac P. Davis in 1818,' and have been commonly called 'Essex Junior'. Mr. Parker (of P. & Codman) says the wine is well thought of, and I remember Mr. Isaac P. wanted to purchase all the Judge had in his cellar at one time. But good or bad, there is a bouquet of old friendship under every cork, and to borrow the words of a poet of the nineteenth century, an admirer of your genius, and a near relation in the ascending line of the youth who brings you the friendly tribute (or would have brought it if not too heavy)— .

> 'It is not the sunset that glows in the wine,
>   But the smile that beams over it makes it divine.'

Don't answer this note, but nod your acknowledgments over the next glass of wine we drink together. O. W. HOLMES to JOHN LOTHROP MOTLEY, 9 January 1857: *Correspondence of Motley* (1889), i, 197-8.

In my time I have drunk bottled beer with Algernon Charles Swinburne, brandy and dry ginger with Stephen Phillips, whisky and soda with Lionel Johnson, the like with John Davidson, and the like with sundry other poets and multitudes of fictionists now living. I have even taking sparkling wine with Mr. Clement Shorter, sleeping there after in a bed which had been reserved for no less an exaltitude than Sir William Robertson Nicoll, at that time (let me be humble) plain 'Rev. Dr.' And my judgment on the whole matter is this: One does one's easiest and happiest talking on the amber or the rosy, also one's bread-and-butter and

Fill up the Glass!

forced-pressure writing: but to write for oneself 'turn down the empty glass'. T. W. H. CROSLAND, *The Beautiful Teetotaller* (1906).

Thank you, my very dear friend! I write to you drunk with Cyprus. Nothing can be worthier of either gods or demigods; and if, as you say, Achilles did not drink of it, I am sorry for him. I suppose Jupiter had it instead, just then—Hebe pouring it, and Juno's ox-eyes bellowing their splendour at it, if you will forgive me that broken metaphor, for the sake of Aeschylus's genius, and my own particular intoxication.

Indeed, there *never was*, in modern days, such wine. Flush [her spaniel], to whom I offered the last drop in my glass, felt it was supernatural, and ran away. I have an idea that if he had drunk that drop, he would have talked afterwards—either Greek or English.

Never was such wine! The very taste of ideal nectar, only stiller, from keeping. If the bubbles of eternity were on it, *we* should run away, perhaps, like Flush. ELIZABETH BARRETT BROWNING to H. S. BOYD, 16 June 1844: *Letters* (1897), i, 175

Shannon returned from Lincolnshire. I made him drunk, having placed the Puvis on a table during the grub for him to see when he went into the next room. He blundered in, burbled over his coffee, not turning round towards that side of the room where stood the drawing between two candles. When he turned round, he suddenly became quite sober and serious in an instant, and almost white with astonishment and pleasure. CHARLES RICKETTS, 10 August 1901: *Self Portrait of Charles Ricketts, R.A.* (1939), 66.

XVII

AT THE SHRINE OF SAINT NICOTINE

Sublime tobacco! which from east to west
Cheers the tar's labour or the Turkman's rest . . .
Divine in hookas, glorious in a pipe;
When tipp'd with amber, mellow, rich and ripe;
Like other charmers, wooing the caress
More dazzlingly when daring in full dress;
Yet thy true lovers more admire by far
Thy naked beauties—give me a cigar!

Lord Byron, *The Island*, ii, 19.

For thy sake, tobacco, I
Would do anything but die.

Charles Lamb, *A Farewell to Tobacco.*

He [Sir Walter Raleigh] took a pipe of tobacco a little before he went to the scaffold, which some formal persons were scandalised at, but I think 'twas well and properly done, to settle his spirits. JOHN AUBREY, 1680, *Brief Lives* (1898), ii, 189.

Dr. Young, who would not be outdone in good offices, invited the divine to our inn, where we went to dinner; but he excused himself, and came after the meal was over, in hopes of smoking a pipe; but our Doctor hinted to him that it would not be proper to offer any incense, but sweet praise, to such goddesses as Mrs. Rolt and your humble servant. To say the truth, I saw a large horn tobacco box, with Queen Anne's head upon it, peeping out of his pocket, but I did not care to take the hint, and desire him to put in use that magnificent piece of furniture. ELIZABETH

At the Shrine of Saint Nicotine

Montagu at Tunbridge Wells to the Duchess of Portland,
1745: *Letters* (1809), iii, 22.

Porson was very fond of smoking, and said that when smoking
began to go out of fashion, learning began to go out of fashion
also. Samuel Rogers, *Table Talk* (1856), 303.

I don't know that I have acquired anything by my travels but a
smattering of two languages and a habit of chewing Tobacco.
Lord Byron to the Hon. Augusta Leigh, 9 September 1811:
Letters and Journals (1898).

Tennyson does . . . little, and they say will hardly wake out of
tobacco smoke into any sufficient activity. John Sterling to
R. W. Emerson: *Correspondence between Sterling and Emerson*
(1897), 85.

You abuse snuff! Perhaps it is the final cause of the human nose.
S. T. Coleridge, 4 January 1823: *Table Talk* (1874), 11.

Bless you, old Sophist, who next to Human Nature taught me all
the corruption I was capable of knowing. . . . When shall we two
smoke again? Last night I had been in a sad quandary of spirits,
in what they call the evening; but a pipe and some generous
Port, and *King Lear* (being alone), had its effects as a remonstrance. I went to bed pot-valiant. Charles Lamb to S. T.
Coleridge, 13 April 1803: *Letters* (1905), i, 269.

After lunch went to Carlyle's and found him sitting alone in his
study, smoking his long clay pipe. He gave me a pipe and we sat
for an hour by the fireside and then went for a walk to the Park.
Charles Eliot Norton, 17 January 1873: *Letters* (1913), i,
458.

When you come to London, come down to me and let us smoke
a pipe together. With few words, with many, or with none, it
need not be an eloquent pipe! Thomas Carlyle to Alfred
Tennyson, 7 December 1842: *Memoir of Tennyson*, (1897), ii,
18.

At the Shrine of Saint Nicotine

Alfred Tennyson has been with us for the last week. He is looking well and in good spirits, but complains of nervousness. How should he do otherwise, seeing that he smokes the strongest and most stinking tobacco out of a small blackened clay pipe on an average nine hours every day? J. W. BLAKESLEY to RICHARD MONCKTON MILNES, 19 March 1838: *Life, Letters, and Friendships of Richard Monckton Milnes, First Lord Houghton* (1891), vi, 221.

As you are good enough to say that you will manage anything rather than lose my visit, will you manage that I may have my pipe in my room whenever I like? ALFRED TENNYSON to W. E. GLADSTONE, 25 October 1876: *Memoir*, (1897), ii, 214.

He [Charles Kingsley] was a great smoker, and tobacco was to him a needful sedative. He always used a long and clean clay pipe, which lurked in all sorts of unexpected places. But none was ever smoked which was in any degree foul, and when there was a vast accumulation of old pipes, they were sent back again to the kiln to be rebaked, and returned fresh and new. This gave him a striking simile which, in *Alton Locke*, he puts into the mouth of James Crossthwaite. 'Katie here believes in Purgatory, where souls are burnt clean again, like 'bacca pipes.' C. KEGAN PAUL: Qt. *Charles Kingsley*, by his Wife (1877), i, 226.

Don't fire at me about smoking. I do it, because it does me good and I could not (for I have tried again and again) do without it. I smoke very cheap tobacco. In the meantime I am keeping no horse—a most real sacrifice to me. CHARLES KINGSLEY to JOHN LUDLOW, 1850: *Ib.* i, 235.

I was glad to have got out of the towns . . . to have left behind me for a season the bar-rooms of Massachusetts, where the full-grown are not weaned from savage and filthy habits,—still sucking a cigar. . . . The towns need to be ventilated. The gods would be pleased to see some pure flames from their altars. They are not to be appeased with cigar-smoke. H. D. THOREAU, 1864: *Cape Cod* (1893), 47.

XVIII

HOW D'YE DO?

We are so fond of one another, because our ailments are the same.
Jonathan Swift, 1 February 1711: *Journal to Stella.*

Mr. Pepys sports with Amaryllis in a draught and catches cold. At night to supper, though with little comfort, I find myself both head and breast in great pain, and what troubles me most my right ear is almost deaf. It is a cold, which God Almighty in justice did give me while I sat lewdly sporting with Mrs. Lane the other day with the broken window in my neck. I went to bed with a posset, being very melancholy in consideration of the loss of my hearing. Samuel Pepys, 27 September 1663: *Diary* (1893), iii, 289–90.

Mr. Pepys is brought low but recovers. My very worthy and excellent friend Mr. Pepys has been very ill of late, and was brought so low, that we were afraid we should have lost him: but now, God be praised, the danger is over: and he by advice of Physicians and friends is gone into the Country, but not far from London, for full and perfect recovery of his health: which I dare say, you and indeed all others who know what a brave and publick-spirited a gentlemen he is, wish, as well as I. Dr. Thomas Smith to Humphrey Wanley, 15 May 1697: *Letters of Eminent Literary Men* (1843), 241.

Swift sympathizes with Congreve's troubles. I was to-day to see Mr. Congreve, who is almost blind with cataracts growing on his eyes; and his case is, that he must wait two or three years, until the cataracts are riper, and till he is quite blind, and then he must have them couched; and besides he is never rid of the gout, yet he looks young and fresh, and is as cheerful as ever. He is younger by three years or more than I, and I am twenty years younger than he. He gave me a pain in the great toe, by mentioning the gout. I find such suspicions frequently, but they go off again. JONATHAN SWIFT, 26 October 1710: *Journal to Stella: 1710–1713* (Bohn, 1924), 38.

SWIFT COMPLAINS OF MANY ILLS. I have nobody now left but you. Pray be so kind as to outlive me, and then die as soon as you please, but without pain; and let us meet in a better place, if my religion will permit, but rather my virtue, although much unequal to yours. . . . My state of health is not to boast of; my giddiness is more or less too constant; I sleep ill, and have a poor appetite. I can as easily write a poem in the Chinese language as my own. I am as fit for matrimony as invention; and yet I have daily schemes for innumerable essays in prose, and proceed sometimes to no less than half a dozen lines, which the next morning become waste paper. What vexes me most is, that my female friends, who could bear me very well a dozen years ago, have now forsaken me, although I am not so old in proportion to them as I formerly was: which I can prove by arithmetic, for then I was double their age, which now I am not. JONATHAN SWIFT to ALEXANDER POPE, 7 February 1736: *Correspondence* (1913), v, 303.

SAMUEL RICHARDSON RESPONDS TO TAR-WATER. I heartily rejoice that at length you find benefit from your tar-water. Tar by winter, and steel by summer, are the two champions sent forth by Providence to encounter, and subdue the spleen. EDWARD YOUNG to SAMUEL RICHARDSON, 11 November 1746: *Correspondence of Samuel Richardson* (1804), ii, 19.

AARON HILL RECOMMENDS COFFEE FOR A BAD HEAD. Pray, do you ever drink coffee?—I dare almost promise your head some relief, and the sooner, if you drink it as hot as you can; covering the dish (on its outward edge), with your hand, so as to receive the full stream of the vapour at your mouth, nose and eyes, in the drinking. AARON HILL to SAMUEL RICHARDSON, 29 August 1738: *Ib.* (1804), i, 20.

SAMUEL RICHARDSON BELIEVES IN MUSTARD FOR DIZZINESS. As to myself, I am not worse than I have been for three months past, in which I have had a great increase of my nervous tremblings, catchings, and dizziness. As to riding, I must not, at my time of life, think of overcoming a dislike that I never, either as boy or man, could conquer. But I have a great opinion of mustard. Be pleased to give me your process as to that. SAMUEL RICHARDSON to the REV. PHILIP SKELTON, 25 March 1751: *Ib.* (1804), v, 205.

HORACE WALPOLE DEFIES THE GOUT AT PARIS. Mr. Walpole writes me now and then a long and lively letter from Paris; to which place he went last summer with the gout upon him, sometimes in his limbs, often in his stomach and head. He has got somehow well, (not by means of the climate, one would think) goes to all public places, sees all the best company, and is very much in fashion. He says he sunk like Queen Eleanor at Charing Cross, and has arisen again at Paris. THOMAS GRAY to DR. WHARTON, 5 March 1766: *Letters* (1900), iii, 104.

HOW HORACE WALPOLE KEEPS FIT. I am a kind of delicate Hercules; and though made of paper, have, by temperance, by using as much cold water inwardly and outwardly as I can, and by taking no precautions against catching cold, and braving all weathers, become capable of suffering by none. My biennial visitant, the gout, has yielded to the bootikins, and stayed with me this last time but five weeks in lieu of five months. Stronger men perhaps would kill themselves by my practice, but it has done so long with me, I shall trust to it. HORACE WALPOLE to the REV. WILLIAM COLE, 11 April 1775: *Letters* (1891), vi, 198.

JOHN WESLEY CONSIDERS THE SMALL BEER CURE FOR DROPSY. In this journey I read a volume of the *Medical Essays*, lately published at London. I have read a thousand strange things, but none stranger than the account which is here given of three persons who were entirely cured of a confirmed dropsy; one by drinking six quarts a day of cold water, the second by drinking two or three gallons of new cyder, the third by drinking a gallon or two of small beer, and the same quantity of butter-milk. Why then, what are we doing, in keeping dropsical persons from small drink? The same as in keeping persons in the small pox from air. JOHN WESLEY, 23 July 1772: *Journal* [n.d.] v, 480.

HANNAH MORE WOULD SOONER BE ILL IN ENGLAND THAN WELL ABROAD. Lady Herries is here with the full use of her limbs, which I am glad of; though if they had been my limbs, I question if I should have thought the use of them worth purchasing at the expense of living abroad—better be dying in England, than well anywhere else, is my maxim. HANNAH MORE at Bath, 1797: *Memoirs* (1835), iii, 12.

COLERIDGE HAS A VARIETY OF COMPLAINTS. We have had a long letter from poor Coleridge written in the languor of the first moments of ease after suffering the various tortures of toothache, *teeth* drawing, rheumatism, sickness, pains in the bowels, diarrhœa and worst of all shortness of breath which has recently attacked him on the return of the damp weather. His spirits and strength are yet wonderful. . . . DOROTHY WORDSWORTH at Grasmere to CATHERINE CLARKSON, 12 November 1803: *Early Letters of William and Dorothy Wordsworth* (1935), 347.

BYRON ESCAPES FROM DOCTORS AND FEVERS. As I have just escaped from a physician and a fever, which confined me five days to bed, you won't expect much *allegrezza* in the ensuing letter. In this place there is an indigenous distemper, which when the wind blows from the Gulf of Corinth (as it does five months out of six), attacks great and small, and makes woful work with visitors. Here be also two physicians, one of whom trusts to his genius (never having studied)—the other to a campaign of eighteen months against the sick of Otranto, which he made in his youth with great effect. When I was seized with my disorder,

How d'ye do?

I protested against both these assassins;—but what can a helpless, feverish, toast-and-watered poor wretch do? In spite of my teeth and tongue, the English consul, my Tartar, Albanians, dragoman, forced a physician upon me, and in three days vomited and blystered me to the last gasp. In this state I made my epitaph—take it:

> Youth, Nature, and relenting Jove,
> To keep my lamp *in* strongly strove:
> But Romanelli was so stout,
> He beat all three—and blew it *out*.

But Nature and Jove, being piqued at my doubts, did, in fact, at last, beat Romanelli, and here I am, well but weakly, at your service. LORD BYRON at Patras, Morea, to FRANCIS HODGSON, 3 October 1810: *Letters and Journals* (1898), i, 297–8.

BYRON NURSES HIS BOREDOM. What is the reason that I have been, all my lifetime, more or less *ennuyé*? and that, if any thing, I am rather less so now than I was at twenty, as far as my recollection serves? I do not know how to answer this, but presume that it is constitutional,—as well as the waking in low spirits, which I have invariably done for many years. Temperance and exercise, which I have practised at times, and for a long time together vigorously and violently, make little or no difference. Violent passions did;—when under their immediate influence—it is odd, but—I was in agitated, but *not* in depressed, spirits. A dose of salts has the effect of a temporary inebriation, like light champagne, upon me. But wine and spirits make me sullen and savage to ferocity—silent, however, and retiring, and not quarrelsome, if not spoken to. Swimming also raises my spirits,—but in general they are low, and get daily lower. That is *hopeless*; for I do not think I am so much *ennuyé* as I was at nineteen. The proof is, that then I must game, or drink, or be in the motion of some kind, or I was miserable. At present, I can mope in quietness; and like being alone better than any company—except the lady's whom I serve. But I feel a something, which makes me think that, if I ever reach near to old age, like Swift, 'I shall die at top'

171

first. Only I do not dread idiotism or madness so much as he did. On the contrary, I think some quieter stages of both must be preferable to much of what men think the possession of their senses. LORD BYRON, 6 January 1821: *Letters and Journals* (1901), v, 155–6.

CARLYLE'S ADVICE ON HEALTH. I conjure thee, Jack, to watch over thy health as the most precious of earthly things. I believe at this moment I would consent to become as ignorant as a Choctaw—so I were as sound in body. THOMAS CARLYLE to his brother JOHN, 10 February 1821: *Early Letters* (1886), 153.

THOMAS DE QUINCEY SUFFERS FROM THE HEAT. I have been suffering greatly myself for ten days, the cause being, in part, some outrageous heat that the fussy atmosphere put itself into about the beginning of this month—but what *for*, nobody can understand. Heat always untunes the harp of my nervous system. THOMAS DE QUINCEY to his daughter MARGARET, 10 June 1847.

NO COMPLAINTS FROM LANDOR. I have no ailments—but why should I? I have eaten well-prepared food; I have drunk light subacid wines and three glasses instead of ten; I have liked modest better than immodest women, and I have never tried to make a shilling in the world. WALTER SAVAGE LANDOR, 'Landor,' *Monographs*, Houghton (1873), 128.

CARLYLE PRESCRIBES FOR HENRY TAYLOR. Having heard that Henry Taylor was ill, Carlyle rushed off from London to Sheen with a bottle of medicine, which had done Mrs. Carlyle good, without in the least knowing what was ailing Henry Taylor, or for what the medicine was useful. ALFRED TENNYSON, *Memoir* (1897), i, 334.

SAMUEL ROGERS MAKES THE BEST OF IT. The acquaintance I have seen most of is Samuel Rogers. It is marvellous how well he bears his affliction. He knows that he will never be able to stand on his legs again; yet his cheerfulness, and even vivacity, have undergone no diminution. His wealth enables him to partake of many enjoyments which could not otherwise be possessed. Yesterday I took a drive with him through Lord Chichester's park. He has had a carriage made for himself, which deserves to be taken as a model for all in his condition. The back falls down and forms an inclined plane; the sofa-chair in which he sits is pushed in; the back is then closed; and a side-door is opened to the seat in which his servant sits when no friend is with him. In spite of the noise of the carriage, the feebleness of his voice, and his imperfect hearing (as mine is in a less degree), we were enabled to converse. His sister and he now occupy one of the largest houses in Brighton, and they visit each other twice a day. I was present the other day when he was wheeled in *his* sofa-chair to her in *her* sofa-chair, and the servant assisted them to put their hands together. HENRY CRABB ROBINSON, 28 September 1850: *Diary* (1853), ii, 317.

R. L. S. TRIUMPHS OVER BED AND PHYSIC BOTTLE. For fourteen years I have not had a day's real health; I have wakened sick and gone to bed weary; and I have done my work unflinchingly. I have written in bed, and written out of it, written in hemorrhages, written in sickness, written torn by coughing, written when my head swam for weakness; and for so long, it seems to me I have won my wager and recovered my glove. I am better now, have been rightly speaking since first I came to the Pacific; and still, few are the days when I am not in some physical distress. And the battle goes on—ill or well, is a trifle; so as it goes. I was made for a contest, and the Powers have so willed that my battlefield should be this dingy, inglorious one of the bed and the physic bottle. At least I have not failed, but I would have preferred a place of trumpetings and the open air over my head. ROBERT LOUIS STEVENSON at Samoa to GEORGE MEREDITH, 5 September 1893: *Letters* (1899), ii, 303–4.

RUSKIN HAS COLDS IN THE HEAD. Here, not I, but a thing with a dozen of colds in its head, am I. I caught one cold on Wednesday last, another on Thursday, two on Friday, four on Saturday, and one at every station between this and Ingleborough on Monday. I never was in such ignoble misery of cold! I've no cough to speak of, nor anything worse than usual in the way of sneezing, but my hands are cold, my pulse nowhere, my nose tickles and worries me, my ears sing—like kettles, my mouth has no taste, my heart no hope of ever being good for anything, any more. I never passed such a wretched morning by my own fireside in all my days, and I've quite a fiendish pleasure in telling you all this, and thinking how miserable you'll be too. Oh me, if ever I get to feel like myself again, won't I take care of myself. . . . Seven of the eleven colds are better, but the other four are worse, and they were the worst before, and I'm such a wreck and rag and lump of dust being made mud of, that I'm ashamed to let the maids bring me my dinner. JOHN RUSKIN, *Hortus Inclusus* (1887), 135–6.

THOMAS HARDY IS PESSIMISTIC. Hurt my tooth at breakfast-time. I look in the glass. Am conscious of the humiliating sorriness of my earthly tabernacle, and of the sad fact that the best of parents could do no better for me. . . . Why should a man's mind have been thrown into such close, sad, sensational, inexplicable relations with such a precarious object as his body? THOMAS HARDY, *Later Years of Hardy* (1930), 13–14.

EDWARD FITZGERALD BLAMES THE EAST WIND. Yes, this has been a Year indeed for Death and Sickness: Doctors and Chemists hereabout say they never had such demand. I saw in yesterday's *Telegraph* that *Helps* S. A. was seriously ill—with Pleurisy —one form of Cold, I believe. I got on pretty well till last week: when Cold came which began to *wheeze*: but went about till yesterday, when the Doctor, meeting me at my niece's Door, ordered me in, & sent Pill, Draught, and Embrocation after me. I think the East Wind, *plus* sun, is worse than *minus*: I suppose one fries and freezes on different sides at the same time. EDWARD FITZGERALD to WILLIAM BODHAM DONNE, 6 March 1875: *A FitzGerald Friendship* (1930), 121.

MRS. PIOZZI NURSES MISS BURNEY. Fanny Burney has kept her room here in my house seven days, with a fever or something that she called a fever; I gave her every medicine and every slop with my own hand; took away her dirty cups, spoons, &c.; moved her tables: in short, was doctor and nurse and maid—for I did not like the servants should have additional trouble lest they should hate her for it. And now,—with the true gratitude of a wit, she tells me, that the world thinks the better of me for my civilities to her. It does? does it? Mrs. Piozzi (Thrale), 1779: *Autobiography* (1861), ii, 340.

XIX

A LA MODE

Dress is at all times a frivolous distinction, and excessive solicitude about it often destroys its own aim. . . . Woman is fine for her own satisfaction alone. No man will admire her the more, no woman will like her the better for it. Neatness and fashion are enough for the former, and a something of shabbiness or impropriety will be most endearing to the latter. Jane Austen, *Northanger Abbey* (1818), x.

I went home and put on my gray cloth suit and faced white coat, made of one of my wife's petty-coats, the first time I have had it on. SAMUEL PEPYS, 13 June 1661: *Diary* (1893), ii, 54.

This noon I received a letter from the country from my wife, wherein she seems much pleased with the country; God continue that she may have pleasure while she is there. She, by my Lady's advice, desires a new petticoat of the new silk striped stuff, very pretty. So I went to Paternoster Row presently, and bought her one, with Mr. Creed's help, a very fine rich one, the best I did see there, and much better than she desires or expects, and sent it by Creed to Unthanke to be made against tomorrow to send by the carrier, thinking it had been but Wednesday to-day, but I found myself mistaken, and also the taylor being out of the way, it could not be done, but the stuff was sent me back at night by Creed to dispose of some other way to make, but now I shall keep it to next week. SAMUEL PEPYS, 25 June 1663: *Ib.* (1893), iii, 181.

Here's ado and a clutter! I must now answer MD's fifth; but first you must know that I dined at the Portugal envoy's to-day, with Addison, Vanbrugh, Admiral Wager, Sir Richard Temple,

A la Mode

Methuen, &c. I was weary of their company, and stole away at five, and came home like a good boy, and studied till ten, and had a fire; O ho! and now am in bed. I have no fire-place in my bed-chamber; but 'tis very warm weather when one's in bed. Your fine cap, Madam Dingley, is too little, and too hot: I'll have that fur taken off; I wish it were far enough; and my old velvet cap is good for nothing. Is it velvet under the fur? I was feeling, but cannot find: if it be, 'twill do without it, else I will face it; but then I must buy new velvet: but may be I may beg a piece. JONATHAN SWIFT, 8 November 1710: *Journal to Stella:* 1710–1713 (Bohn, 1924), 47.

The whole of my whole purchase here is one silk coat which I have put on and which makes me look like a fool. OLIVER GOLDSMITH in Paris to SIR JOSHUA REYNOLDS, 29 July 1770: *Letters* (1928), 97.

New fashions in dress, furniture, and baubles, I have seen none. Feathers are waning, and almost confined to *filles* and foreigners. I found out an English woman at the Opera last night by her being covered with plumes and no rouge; so well our countrymen contrive to display their virtue. HORACE WALPOLE at Paris to GEORGE SELWYN, 16 September 1775: *Letters* (1891), vi, 258.

We received a visit from Mr. Tom Lefroy and his cousin George. The latter is really very well-behaved now; and as for the other, he has but *one* fault, which time will, I trust, entirely remove— it is that his morning coat is a great deal too light. He is a very great admirer of *Tom Jones*, and therefore wears the same coloured clothes, I imagine, which *he* did when he was wounded. JANE AUSTEN to her sister CASSANDRA, 9 January 1796: *Letters* (1884), i, 128–9.

I am not to wear my white satin cap to-night, after all; I am to wear a mamalone cap instead, which Charles Fowle sent to Mary, and which she lends me. It is all the fashion now; worn at the opera, and by Lady Mildmays at Hackwood balls. I hate describing such things, and I dare say you will be able to guess what it is like. I have got over the dreadful epoch of mantua-making much better than I expected. My gown is made very much like my blue one, which you always told me sat very well, with only these variations: the sleeves are short, the wrap fuller, the apron comes over it, and a band of the same completes the whole. Jane Austen to Cassandra Austen, 8 January 1799: *Letters* (1884), i, 192–3.

My cloak is come home. I like it very much, and can now exclaim with delight, like J. Bond at harvest-time, 'This is what I have been looking for these three years.' I saw some gauzes in a shop in Bath Street yesterday at only 4d. a yard, but they were not so good or so pretty as mine. Flowers are very much worn, and fruit is still more the thing. Elizabeth has a bunch of straw-berries, and I have seen grapes, cherries, plums, and apricots. There are likewise almonds and raisins, French plums, and tamarinds at the grocers', but I have never seen any of them in hats. A plum or greengage would cost three shillings; cherries and grapes about five, I believe, but this is at some of the dearest shops. My aunt has told me of a very cheap one, near Walcot Church, to which I shall go in quest of something for you. Jane Austen at Bath to her sister Cassandra, 2 June 1799: *Ib.*, i, 212–13.

You will find here a bonnet of Imperial chip or Simple chip, or Real chip, or whatever it is, which I hope will arrive safely and be found to suit you. I think it looks like your head. I wish it were fifty times better for your sake: it would still be the most feeble testimony of what I owe to your kind affection, which has followed me unweariedly through good and evil fortune, sooth-ing and sweetening all the days of my existence, and which I trust Providence will yet long, long continue for a blessing to us both. Thomas Carlyle to his Mother, May 1822: *Early Letters* (1886), 210.

I got the bonnet which you sent me. It fits very well; I am cer-tainly highly pleased with this fresh token of your kindness and attention towards me. Amid all this turmoil it soothes me to think that there is one who can sympathise with me; who knows all the little inconveniences I have to struggle with; who is so fond of anticipating all my wants. MRS. CARLYLE to her Son, THOMAS, 26 May 1822: *Ib.* 214.

Before leaving this miserable city, in which I have been destined to experience so many vexations first and last, I determined in packing up my greatcoat to enclose a piece of tartan in it to make you a cloak of. It was the best I could find; but surely the knaves have made me take nearly twice as much as was required. You can make yourself a substantial covering from the winter wind out of it in the first (place), and turn the rest into a scarf or whatever you think fittest. THOMAS CARLYLE at Edinburgh to his Mother, 19 August 1823: *Ib.* 282.

I believe you had better choose me a pair of winter trousers . . . wide enough, long enough; not too heavy, and of a dim colour! I shall then have nothing to do with the Cockney snips for another blessed Winter,—perhaps never more in Time? THOMAS CARLYLE at Chelsea to his Wife in Scotland, 24 July 1836: *New Letters* (1904), i, 20.

The black Collar fits well, and looks respectable—but I am indebted to Mrs. Richardson for fastening it, which my clumsy fingers cannot effect. The shirts are perfection. I thank you for the *Almanack* and other useful things. I am sorry you thought Garnet's bill so unreasonable. The swansdown was for a waistcoat, a useful and needful one it is. The trowzers are stout and indispensable. The hat was very dear, as things go now, but I never got a good one for less. I have however, now got a handsome one, much lower, which may reconcile you to the fact that the hatter is a Papist. Fell says he pays but 10s. for silk hats, but that they last no time. He is, to be sure, out in all weathers, and cannot carry an Umbrella on horseback. HARTLEY COLERIDGE to his Mother, January 1844: *Letters* (1936), 271.

Dined with my dear friend Serjeant Talfourd. He said Wordsworth went to court in Rogers's clothes, buckles and stockings,

and wore Davy's sword. Moxon had hard work to make the
dress fit. It was a squeeze, but by pulling and hauling they got
him in. Fancy the high priest of mountain and of flood on his
knees in a court, the quiz of courtiers, in a dress that did not belong to him, with a sword that was not his own and a coat which
he borrowed. BENJAMIN ROBERT HAYDON, 16 May 1845:
Autobiography (1853), iii, 305.

Do you know that I was in Leeds on the very same day with you
—last Wednesday? I had thought of telling you where I was
going, and having your help and company in buying a bonnet,
etc. but then I reflected that this would merely be making a selfish use of you, so I determined to manage or mismanage the
matter alone. I went to Hurst and Hall's for the bonnet, and got
one which seemed grave and quiet there amongst all the splen-
dours; but now it looks infinitely too gay with its pink lining.
I saw some beautiful silks of pale sweet colours, but had not the
spirit nor the means to launch out at the rate of five shillings per
yard, and went and bought a black silk at three shillings after all.
I rather regret this, because papa says he would have lent me a
sovereign if he had known. I believe, if you had been there, you
would have forced me to get into debt. CHARLOTTE BRONTË,
1851: *Life* (1857), ii, 209–10.

Gibbon took very little exercise. He had been staying some time
with Lord Sheffield in the country; and when he was about to go
away, the servants could not find his hat. 'Bless me,' said Gibbon, 'I certainly left it in the hall on my arrival here.' He had not
stirred out of doors during the whole of the visit. SAMUEL
ROGERS, *Table Talk* (1856), 116.

She (Lady Dufferin) made herself very agreeable all dinner-
time. I told her I had just heard Disraeli speak. She said she had
always known him and liked him in spite of his tergiversations
and absurdities. When he was very young and had made his first
appearance in London society as the author of *Vivian Grey*, there
was something almost incredible in his aspect. She assured me

A la Mode

that she did not exaggerate in the slightest degree in describing to me his dress when she first met him at a dinner party. He wore a black velvet coat lined with satin, purple trousers with a gold band running down the outside seam, a scarlet waistcoat, long lace ruffles falling down to the tips of his fingers, white gloves with several brilliant rings outside them, and long black ringlets rippling down upon his shoulders. It seemed impossible that such a Guy Fawkes could have been tolerated in any society. His audacity, which has proved more perennial than brass, was always the solid foundation of his character. She told him, however, that he made a fool of himself by appearing in such fantastic shape, and he afterwards modified his costume, but he was never to be put down. JOHN LOTHROP MOTLEY to his Wife, 13 June 1858: *Correspondence* (1889), i, 264.

The curse of London is its dirt. Also its lack of light. . . . My much ridiculed Jaegerism is an attempt at cleanliness and porousness: I want my body to breathe. I have long resigned myself to dust and dirt and squalor in external matters: if seven maids with seven mops swept my den for half a century they would make no impression on it; but I always have the window open night and day; I shun cotton and linen and all fibrous fabrics that collect odors, as far as my person is concerned. BERNARD SHAW to ELLEN TERRY, 31 December 1897: *Ellen Terry and Bernard Shaw: A Correspondence* (1931), 282.

I did take to the dance last night. Helen and I went as a country couple to a fancy dress affair. There were a lot of very nice males and females under 20 who made up for my grotesqueness. I had on an old Sussex pedlar's smock, black hat and red ribbon with a bunch of corn, knee-breeches, and grey stockings tied with black ribbons, and a red handkerchief as large as a sheet. Helen had a print dress bunched up behind to show a red petticoat and a lot of white stocking, and a sunbonnet on her head. We are now recovering on a most beautiful morning of sun above and solid mist filling up the valley in rolls like an inverted sky exactly. EDWARD THOMAS at Wick Green to MR. & MRS. MAC ARTHUR,

181

A la Mode

31 December 1911: *Life and Letters of Edward Thomas* (1939), 314.

It has cost me three guineas to-day for a periwig. I am undone! it was made by a Leicester lad, who married Mr. Worrall's daughter, where my mother lodged; so I thought it would be cheap, and especially since he lives in the city. JONATHAN SWIFT, 15 January 1711: *Journal to Stella* 1710–1713 (1924), 101.

MR. WELLS AND HIS TOP HATS. I have spent some time trying to trace the beginnings, the rise and fall of my successive top hats. They mark periods in human history as surely as do the ramshackle houses in which I spent the first half of my life and the incoherent phases of my upbringing and education. In the mind of the febrile psycho-analyst, these top hats might be made to show the most curious and significant phases in the upward struggle of the human intelligence. They were more voluntary and so more subtle in their fluctuating intimations than were turbans, fezes, pigtails and the like which outlasted whole generations. But that history of the rise and fall of the top hat has yet to be written. When I was born it had already passed its zenith; cricketers no longer played the game in top hats, though my father had begun in that fashion; but it still seemed the most natural thing in the world for me to take out my cousin on Sundays in this guise. Half the young men I met on that day sported similar glossy cylinders. In the City and West End, on a week-day, you rarely saw a man wearing anything else. The streets below repeated the rhythms of the clustering chimney-pots on the roofs above. I must have acquired my first specimen, when I acquired my morning coat and its tails, during the second year of my apprenticeship at Southsea. But was that the one I wore in London? I think it was and if so it went right on with me to 1891, when it died a natural death . . . in the presence of Mr. Frank Harris, the editor of the *Fortnightly Review*. After that I think I bought another to attend a funeral and a third seems to have marked a phase of social acquiescence before the War. I went to Bond Street picture shows, and the Academy, in the latter. It

ended as a charade property for my sons at Easton Glebe. Since
then I have had no more top hats. H. G. WELLS, *Experiment in
Autobiography* (1934), i, 284–5.

LADY MARY WORTLEY MONTAGU. Lady Mary Wortley is
arrived; I have seen her; I think her avarice, her dirt, and her
vivacity are all increased. Her dress, like her language, is a
galimatias of several countries; the ground-work rags, and the
embroidery nastiness. She needs no cap, no handkerchief, no
gown, no petticoat, no shoes. An old blacklaced hood represents
the first; the fur of a horseman's coat, which replaces the third,
serves for the second; a dimity petticoat is deputy, and officiates
for the fourth, and slippers act the part of the last. HORACE
WALPOLE at Arlington Street to GEORGE MONTAGU, 2 February 1762: *Letters* (1891), iii, 480–1.

XX

THE GENTLE ART

We should write as we speak; and that's a true familiar Rector which expresseth one's Mind, as if he were discoursing with the Party to whom he writes, in succinct and short Terms. James Howell, *Familiar Letters* (1645), 17.

I have been scribbling this morning, and I believe shall hardly fill this side to-day, but send it as it is; and it is good enough for naughty girls that won't write to a body, and to a good boy like Presto. I thought to have sent this to-night, but was kept by company, and would not; and, to say the truth, I had a little mind to expect one post more for a letter from MD. JONATHAN SWIFT, 19 September 1710: *Journal to Stella: 1710–1713* (Bohn Lib. 1924), 11.

You say such extravagant things of my letters, which are nothing but gossiping gazettes, that I cannot bear it. Then you have undone yourself with me, for you compare them to Madame Sévigné's; absolute treason! Do you know, there is scarce a book in the world I love so much as her letters. HORACE WALPOLE to SIR HORACE MANN, 12 September 1749: *Letters* (1891), ii, 181.

Methinks I am grown an uninteresting correspondent. Yet I know not how to help it. I never could *compose* letters; they were forced to write themselves, and live upon their daily bread. HORACE WALPOLE to SIR HORACE MANN, 7 May 1775: *Letters* (1891), vi, 208.

There is nothing could please me more than a letter filled with all the news of the country, but I fear you will think that too troublesome. You see I never cease writing 'till a whole sheet of paper is wrote out, I beg you will imitate me in this particular and give your letters good measure. You can tell me, what visits you receive or pay, who has been married or debauch'd, since my absence what fine girls you have starting up and beating of the vetterans of my acquaintance from future conquest. I suppose before I return I shall find all the blooming virgins I once left in Westmeath shrivelled into a parcel of hags with seven children a piece tearing down their petticoats. Most of the Bucks and Bloods whom I left hunting and drinking and swearing and getting bastards I find are dead. Poor devils they kick'd the world before them. I wonder what the devil they kick now? OLIVER GOLDSMITH to DANIEL HODSON, 31 August 1758: *Collected Letters* (1928), 53.

The rage of *finishing* may produce good essays and fine orations, but it makes frigid letters . . . to me the epistolary style is what it ought to be, when the writer, by a happy and becoming negligence, has the art of making you believe that he could write a great deal better if he would, but that he has too much judgment to use great exertions on small occasions—he will not draw Ulysses' bow to shoot at a pigeon. HANNAH MORE, 1786: *Memoirs* (1835), ii, 36.

Those mornings that I set apart for writing to you, my dearest cousin, are my holiday mornings. At those times I give myself dispensation from all poetical enjoyments, and as soon as I cease to converse with you, betake myself to a walk in the garden. You will observe therefore that my health cannot possibly suffer by such a procedure, but is rather likely to be benefitted; for finding it easy as well as pleasant to write when I write to you, I consequently spend less time at my desk than when Homer lies before me, and have more opportunity of taking exercise and air. Though you *seem* to be so, you are not *in fact* beforehand with me in what you say of my letters, for it has long been an agreed point between me and Mrs. Unwin that yours are the best in the world. You will say—'that is impossible, for I always write what comes uppermost, and never trouble myself either about method or expression.' And for that very reason, my dear, they are what they are, so good that they could not be better. As to expression, you have no need to study it; yours is sure to be such as it ought; and as to method, you know as well as I, that it is never more out of its place than in a letter. WILLIAM COWPER at Olney to LADY HESKETH, 20 March 1786: *Letters* (1912), ii, 14–15.

This is a letter of mere request, to beg remembrance from old and distant friends. Do pray write now and then, and make me up a good long letter of *small London chat*: you can scarcely think how welcome *living* intelligence is to those who have chiefly the *dead* to converse with, and I work hard at *old* stuff all morning, and sigh for some evening conversation about literature and politics, and the common occurrences of the day. MRS. PIOZZI (Thrale) to the REV. DANIEL LYSONS, 9 July 1796: *Autobiography* (1861), ii, 70.

I have now attained the true art of letter-writing, which we are always told is to express on paper exactly what one would say to the same person by word of mouth. I have been talking to you almost as fast as I could the whole of this letter. JANE AUSTEN to her sister CASSANDRA, 3 January 1801: *Letters* (1884), i, 253.

Partly from some constitutional infirmities, and partly from certain habits of mind, I do not write any letters unless upon business, not even to my dearest friends. Except during absence from my own family I have not written five letters of friendship during the last five years. WILLIAM WORDSWORTH at Grasmere, June 1902: *Early Letters of William and Dorothy Wordsworth* (1935), 283.

I am one of the most careless, negligent, ungrateful dogs in existence. I ought without doubt to have answered your long-looked-for and most valuable letter by the very first opportunity . . . I ought to say also that I tried twice to write to you: but the demons of dulness and disquietude shed their poppies and their gall upon me; twice I attempted, and *Cis patriae cecidere manus*. Upon the whole, I see well enough that I have made out but a very lame case for myself; therefore after all that I can say my only resource is to throw myself on the mercy of the judge, and to entreat him to hope that I shall never in future behave so badly. If bulk can supply other deficiencies you shall be satisfied; for I design to scribble nearly all the paper in the house. THOMAS CARLYLE at Edinburgh to JAMES JOHNSTONE in Nova Scotia, 5 March 1820: *Early Letters* (1886), 140–1.

I am afraid that we small fry of the press are about the worst letter-writers in the world. We always smell of the shop so confoundedly, and will be scribbling about literature or politics, or mayhap metaphysics, to the people who would rather hear news of their friends or economics of the wardrobe. HARTLEY COLERIDGE to his Mother, 16 May 1835: *Letters* (1936), 173–4.

In talking of letter-writing this evening, and referring to what Tucker has told of Jefferson's sacrifice of his time to correspondence, Taylor again mentioned the habits of Southey in this respect, and Wordsworth said that, for his own part, such was his horror of having his letters *preserved*, that in order to guard against it, he always took pains to make them as bad and dull as possible. THOMAS MOORE, 10 August 1837: *Memoirs* (1856), vii, 198.

Do you like writing to me? I hate writing in general, but these long letters to you are the comfort of my existence. I always have my portfolio carried on in my palanquin, which comes on early, because then, if I have anything to say to you before breakfast, I can say it, and I dare say it would be unwholesome to suppress a thought before breakfast. EMILY EDEN in India to her sister, 7 January 1838: *Up the Country*, 1866 (1937), 67.

Thank you for your letter; it was as pleasant as a quiet chat, as welcome as spring showers, as reviving as a friend's visit; in short, it was very like a page of *Cranford*. CHARLOTTE BRONTË to MRS. GASKELL, 5 July 1853: *Life* (1857), ii, 295.

I have got of late to be affected—'but why I know not,' as Hamlet says—with such a constant and chronic blue devilry, that I am ashamed to write to any one. Unfortunately, the disease with me takes the form of pure and unmitigated stupidity, so that it is not in the least interesting or romantic. *You* do not know what it is to re-echo daily poor Sir Andrew Aguecheek's pathetic complaint, 'Sometimes I have no more wit than a Christian or an ordinary man.' All this is intended, not as an apology for my silence, but an explanation thereof. I have been doing my best. I bought six months ago a memorandum-book, as big as a ledger, to take notes of my own conversation, in the manner recommended by the original autocrat who reigned over us, *consule Planco*, and I have been patiently hoping to catch myself saying or even thinking a good thing, in which case down it would have gone in black and white for your benefit. In vain I have placed myself in the attitude of Sterne's portraits, with my forefinger on the bump of ideality, in which attitude, he says, he believes he has often intercepted ideas which were intended for somebody else's brain. It is all no go. JOHN LOTHROP MOTLEY to OLIVER WENDELL HOLMES, 16 May 1858: *Correspondence* (1889), i, 222–3.

It is a great luxury to have a correspondent with whom one dares to be dull. J. R. GREEN to W. BOYD DAWKINS, 19 June 1863: *Letters* (1901), 128.

I have brought my paper and pencil and some books into a field, and find myself glad to say nothing to you—and that one's friend is there to say nothing to, is next best to his being there to say anything to. . . . So this scribble is only a form of silence which has to make a little inarticulate sound in order to be heard. EDWARD DOWDEN to MISS E. D. WEST, 16 June 1874: *Fragments from Old Letters* (1914), 97.

A letter which is not mainly about the writer of it lacks the prime flavour. The wine must smack a little of the cask. JAMES RUSSELL LOWELL to CHARLES ELIOT NORTON, 5 September 1871: *Letters* (1894), ii, 86.

The Gentle Art

The true use of a letter is to let one know that one is remembered and valued. JAMES RUSSELL LOWELL to MRS. LESLIE STEPHEN, 11 September 1889: *Letters* (1894), ii, 427.

I don't believe I ever wrote a literary letter—ever got discussing books or literary men or writers or artists of any sort in letters: the very idea of it makes me sick. I like letters to be personal—very personal—and then stop. WALT WHITMAN: *With Walt Whitman in Camden*, Horace Traubel (1908), i, 137.

You must tell me whether you have written any thing, or be writing. Things personal to yourself interest me most, and cannot be too trivial. Have you made any new acquaintance? Where's the mighty Coleridge? I have an idea that tis $\frac{1}{2}$ possible I may meet him and Wordsworth at Montpellier. THOMAS MANNING to CHARLES LAMB, 10 September 1802: *Letters* (1925), 82.

XXI

BOOKMANSHIP

Count thy Books in the Inventory, Jewels wherein a variety is the most excusable Prodigality, and right use (though but of a few) the least Husbandry. Richard Whitlock, *Zootomia* (1654), 247.

I would rather be a poor man in a garret with plenty of books than a king who did not love reading. T. B. Macaulay, 15 September 1842: *Life* (1876), ii, 180.

THE NOURISHMENT OF THE SOUL. In feeding your Soul with Science, you must first assume and suck in the matter into your apprehension, then must the memory retain and keep it in, afterwards by disputation, discourse, and meditation, it must be well concocted; then must it be agglutinated, and converted to nutriment. All this may be reduced to these two heads, *teneri fideliter*, and *uti faeliciter*, which are two of the happiest properties in a student. There is another act required to good concoction, call'd the act of Expulsion, which puts off all that is unsound and noxious; so in Study there must be an expulsive virtue to shun all that is erroneous, and there is no science but is full of such stuff, which by direction of Tutor, and choice of good Books, must be excerned. Do not confound yourself with multiplicity of Authors, two is enough upon any Science, provided they be plenary and orthodox; Philosophy should be your substantial food, Poetry your banqueting-stuff; Philosophy hath more of reality in it than any Knowledge, the Philosophers can fathom the deep, measure Mountains, reach the Stars with a staff, and bless Heaven with a girdle. JAMES HOWELL to his cousin MR. ST. GEON at Oxford, *Familiar Letters* (1654), 11.

Bookmanship

BOOKS IN IDLENESS. My life is like Harry the Fourth's supper of hens. *Poulet a la broche, Poulets en Ragoût, Poulet en Hachis, Poulets en Fricasées.* Reading here, Reading there; nothing but books but with different sauces. THOMAS GRAY to RICHARD WEST, 27 May 1742: *Letters* (1900), i, 103.

LADY MARY READS TO ESCAPE OLD AGE. The active scenes are over at my age. I indulge, with all the art I can, my taste for reading. If I would confine it to valuable books, they are almost as rare as valuable men. I must be content with what I can find. As I approach a second childhood, I endeavour to enter into the pleasures of it. Your youngest son is, perhaps, at this very moment riding on a poker with great delight, not at all regretting that it is not a gold one, and much less wishing it an Arabian horse, which he would not know how to manage. I am reading an idle tale, for expecting wit or truth in it, and am very glad it is not metaphysics to puzzle my judgment, or history to mislead my opinion. The methods may appear low to busy people; but, if he improves his strength, and I forget my infirmities, we attain very desirable ends. LADY MARY WORTLEY MONTAGU to her daughter the COUNTESS OF BUTE, 30 September 1757: *Letters* (1837), iii, 144.

THE FEW WHO UNDERSTAND. People read for amusement. If a book be capable of yielding amusement, it will naturally be read; for no man is an enemy to what gives him pleasure. Some books, indeed, being calculated for the intellects of a few, can please only a few; yet, if they produce this effect, they answer all the end the authors intended; and if those few be men of any note, which is generally the case, the herd of mankind will very willingly fall in with their judgment, and consent to admire what they do not understand. I question whether there are now in Europe two thousand, or even one thousand, persons who understand a word of *Newton's Principia*; yet there are in Europe many millions who extol Newton as a very great philosopher. Those are but a small number who have any sense of the beauties of *Milton*; yet everybody admires *Milton*, because it is the fashion.

Bookmanship

Of all the English poets of this age, Mr. Gray is most admired, and, I think, with justice; yet there are, comparatively speaking, but a few who know anything of his but his *Church-yard Elegy*, which is by no means the best of his works. JAMES BEATTIE to SIR WILLIAM FORBES, 4 May 1770: *Life* (1824), i, 150.

FOOLISH WRITERS FOR FOOLISH READERS. I am persuaded that foolish writers and readers are created for each other; and that Fortune provides readers as she does mates for ugly women. HORACE WALPOLE, 17 August 1773: *Letters* (1891), v, 494.

CHARLES LAMB LIKES OLD FAMILIAR PAGES. A book reads the better, which is our own, and has been so long known to us, that we know the topography of its blots, and dog's-ears, and can trace the dirt in it to having read it at tea with buttered muffins, or over a pipe, which I think is the maximum. CHARLES LAMB to S. T. COLERIDGE, 11 October 1802: *Letters* (1905), i, 250.

HANNAH MORE APPROVES IMPROVING BOOKS. We do not so much want books for good people, as books which will make bad ones better. HANNAH MORE, 10 September 1804: *Memoirs* (1835), iii, 215.

A WARNING FROM CARLYLE. There is nothing more injurious to the faculties than to keep poring over books continually without attempting to exhibit any of our own conceptions. THOMAS CARLYLE to JANE WELSH, 30 April 1822: *Early Letters* (1886), 208.

MACAULAY—THE COMPLETE BOOKMAN. Books are becoming everything to me. If I had at this moment my choice of life, I would bury myself in one of those immense libraries that we saw together at the universities, and never pass a waking hour without a book before me. T. B. MACAULAY to his sister MARGARET, 1834: *Life* (1876), i, 343.

FAMILIARITY BREEDS CONTENT. I have no pleasure from books which equals that of reading over for the hundredth time great productions which I almost know by heart. T. B. MACAULAY, 23 October 1838: *Ib.* (1876), ii, 18.

Bookmanship

ANTHONY TROLLOPE ASKS FOR MORE. That I can read and be happy while I am reading, is a great blessing. Could I remember, as some men do, what I read, I should have been able to call myself an educated man. But that power I never possessed. Something is always left,—something dim and inaccurate,—but still something sufficient to preserve the taste for more. ANTHONY TROLLOPE, *Autobiography*, 1883 (1923), 335.

MRS. BROWNING READS WITHOUT PRINCIPLE AND FEELS GUILTY. I read without principle. I have a sort of unity indeed, but it amalgamates instead of selecting,—do you understand. When I had to read the *Hebrew Bible*, from *Genesis* to *Malachi*, right through, and was never stopped by the Chaldee—and the Greek poets, and *Plato*, right through from end to end—I passed as thoroughly through the flood of all possible and impossible British and foreign novels and romances, with slices of metaphysics laid thick between the sorrows of the multitudinous Celestinas. It is only useful knowledge and the multiplication table I never tried hard at. And now—what now? Is this matter for exultation? Alas, no! Do I boast of my omnivorousness of reading, even apart from the romances? Certainly no!—never, except in joke. It's against my theories and ratiocinations, which take upon themselves to assert that we *all* generally err by *reading too much*, and out of proportion to what we think. I should be wiser, I am persuaded, if I had not read half as much—should have had stronger and better exercised faculties, and should stand higher in my own appreciation. The fact is, that the *ne plus ultra* of intellectual indolence is this reading of books. ELIZABETH BARRETT BROWNING to RICHARD HENGIST HORNE, 20 December 1843: *Letters of Elizabeth Barrett Browning to Richard Hengist Horne* (1877), ii, 151–2.

THOREAU READS TO LIVE. A truly good book teaches me better than to read it. I must soon lay it down, and commence living on its hint. . . . What I began by reading, I must finish by acting. H. D. THOREAU, *Journal* (1884), 407.

LOWELL'S POETIC BOTANIZING. I think one of the greatest

Bookmanship

pleasures is to come across a poem that one can honestly like; it is like finding a new flower. JAMES RUSSELL LOWELL to E. C. STEDMAN, 12 February 1866: *Letters* (1894), i, 399.

READING WITH PURPOSE. I suppose there never was a man who had had so much to do with books as I have, who owned so few. I never have purchased a book which I could do without, or which I did not mean to read through. THOMAS CARLYLE, 1869: *Letters* (1913), i, 336.

BOOKS AND FREEDOM. Some books leave us free and some books make us free. R. W. EMERSON, *Journals* (1913).

GROWTH OF LITERARY ACCEPTANCE. It takes twenty years to get a good book read. For each reader is struck with a new passage and at first only with the striking and superficial ones, and by this very attention to these the rest are slighted. But with time the graver and deeper thoughts are observed and pondered. New readers come from time to time,—their attention whetted by frequent and varied allusions to the book;—until at last every passage has found its reader and commentator. R. W. EMERSON, *Journals* (1913), x, 239–40.

MAGIC CASEMENTS. Another enjoyment of the year besides the hills and garden, is the bits of reading wholly unconnected with the world which yield a fresh pleasure that had almost died out of me. It is like looking up at branches of trees or clouds when one has been walking with a book in one's hand, they have a magical grace. So with bits of poetry and prose that startle me in the midst of my absorption. EDWARD DOWDEN, 19 August 1884: *Fragments of Old Letters* (1914), 160.

TENNYSON LIKES LONG BOOKS. I like those great *still* books. I wish there were a great novel in hundreds of volumes that I might go on and on. . . . ALFRED TENNYSON, 1890: *Memoir* (1897), ii, 372.

MASTER YOUR AUTHOR OR HE WILL MASTER YOU. In all reading undertaken for other than historical, critical or purely fancy-feeding and joy-giving purposes, one should merely skim and put by. Some little will always hold, enough to breed thought, not enough to stifle it; what one takes in mingles, instead of crushing down in a hard lump; the reader will be an original, not an echo. The more temptingly a writer lures the more swiftly one should flee him—except, always, for the poets, for the pure artists of poetry or prose. Every writer, who has other ends than to paint pictures and tell stories, is plotting against the freedom of every reader: the thing is to take from him not what he wants to force on you, but what you yourself need: if you don't cheat him he cheats you. STEPHEN McKENNA, 17 February 1907: *Journal and Letters* (1936), 98.

READING AND FRIENDSHIP. The pleasure of all reading is doubled when one lives with another who shares the same books. KATHERINE MANSFIELD, January 1922: *Letters* (1928), 362.

XXII

THE MAGIC PEN

The art of the pen . . . is to rouse the inward vision, instead of labouring with a Drop-scene brush, as if it were to the eye; because our flying minds cannot contain a protracted description. That is why the poets, who spring imagination with a word or a phrase, paint lasting pictures. The Shakespearian, the Dantesque, are in a line, two at most. George Meredith, 1885: *Diana of the Crossways* (Mickleham Ed. 1922), 170.

I write I neither know how nor why, and always make worse when I try to amend. HORACE WALPOLE to the REV. WILLIAM MASON, 11 May 1769: *Letters* (1891), v, 165.

Read over your compositions, and when you meet with a passage which you think is particularly fine, strike it out. DR. JOHNSON, 30 April 1773: *Boswell's Life* (1887), ii, 237.

I have written this Poem [*Jerusalem*] from immediate dictation, twelve or sometimes twenty or thirty lines at a time, without premeditation, and even against my will. The time it has taken in writing was thus rendered non-existent, and an immense Poem exists which seems to be the labour of a long life, all produced without labour or study. WILLIAM BLAKE to MR. BUTTS, 25 April 1803: *Life* (1863), ii, 192–3.

I could inform the dullest author how he might write an interesting book. Let him relate the events of his own life with honesty, not disguising the feelings that accompanied them. S. T. COLERIDGE to THOMAS POOLE, February 1797: *Letters* (1895), i, 4.

William went up into the orchard and finished the poem [*The Emigrant Mother*]. I went and sate with W. and walked backwards and forwards in the orchard till dinner time. He read me his poem. I read to him, and my Beloved slept. A sweet evening as it had been a sweet day, and I walked quietly along the side of Rydale lake with quiet thoughts—the hills and the lake were still—the owls had not begun to hoot, and the little birds had given over singing. I looked before me and saw a red light upon Silver How as if coming out of the vale below:

> There was a light of most strange birth,
> A light that came out of the earth,
> And spread along the dark hill-side.

Thus I was going on when I saw the shape of my Beloved in the road at a little distance. We turned back to see the light but it was fading—almost gone. The owls hooted when we sate on the wall at the foot of White Moss; the sky broke more and more, and we saw the moon now and then. John Green passed us with his cart; we sate on. When we came in sight of our own dear Grasmere, the vale looked fair and quiet in the moonshine, the Church was there and all the cottages. There were huge slow-travelling clouds in the sky, that threw large masses of shade upon some of the mountains. We walked backwards and for-wards, between home and Olliff's, till I was tired. William kindled, and began to write the poem. We carried cloaks into the orchard, and sate a while there. I left him, and he nearly finished the poem. I was tired to death, and went to bed before him. He came down to me, and read the poem to me in bed. DOROTHY WORDSWORTH at Grasmere, 17 March 1802: *Journals* (1924), 101–2.

Breakfasted in bed for the purpose of hastening the remainder of my *Cribb* work. It is singular the difference that bed makes, not only in the facility but the *fancy* of what I write. Whether it be the horizontal position (which Richerand, the French physiolo-gist, says is most favourable to thought), or more probably the removal of all those external objects that divert the attention, it is certain that the effect is always the same; and if I did not find that it relaxed me exceedingly, I should pass half my days in bed for the purpose of composition. THOMAS MOORE, 21 February 1819: (Diary) *Memoirs* (1853), ii, 270.

Sit down and write—something short—but write and write, though you could swear it was the most stupid stuff in nature, till you fairly get to the end. A week after it is finished it will look far better than you expected. The next you write will go on more smoothly and look better still. So likewise with the third and the fourth,—in regular progression,—till you wonder how such difficulties could ever stop you for a moment. Be not too careful for a subject; take the one you feel most interest in and understand best—some description of manners or passions—some picture of a kind of life you are familiar with, and which looks lovely in your eyes: and for a commencement, why should it give you pause? Take the precept of Horace,—*proripe in medias res*; rush forward and fear nothing. THOMAS CARLYLE to JANE WELSH, 25 December 1822: *Early Letters* (1886), 256.

When my sonnet was rejected [by *The Gem*] I exclaimed, 'Damn the age! I will write for antiquity.' CHARLES LAMB to BRYAN WALLER PROCTER, 22 January 1829: *Letters* (1905), ii, 797.

I was once told that the surest aid to the writing of a book was a piece of cobbler's wax on my chair. I certainly believe in the cobbler's wax much more than the inspiration. ANTHONY TROLLOPE, *Autobiography*, 1883 (1923), 111.

As I journeyed across France to Marseilles, and made then a terribly rough voyage to Alexandria, I wrote my allotted number of pages every day. On this occasion more than once I left my paper on the cabin table, rushing away to be sick in the privacy of my state room. It was February, and the weather was miserable; but still I did my work. *Labor omnia vincit improbus.* ANTHONY TROLLOPE *Ib.*, 108.

When authors write best, or, at least, when they write most fluently, an influence seems to waken in them, which becomes their master—which will have its own way—putting out of view all behests but its own, dictating certain words, and insisting on their being used, whether vehement or measured in their nature; new-moulding characters, giving unthought-of turns to incidents, rejecting carefully-elaborated old ideas, and suddenly creating and adopting new ones. CHARLOTTE BRONTË to G. H. LEWES, 12 January 1848: *Life* (1857), 53.

The theme is nothing, the life is everything. H. D. THOREAU, *Thoreau*, Channing (1902), 83.

A bad style is as bad as bad manners. A. H. CLOUGH, 21 February 1852: *Letters and Remains* (1865), 223.

During my whole life I have borne in mind the speech of a woman to Philip of Macedon: 'I appeal from Philip drunk to Philip sober.' After writing anything in the excitement of the moment, and being greatly pleased with it, I have always put it by for a day or two; and then carefully considering it in every possible light, I have altered it to the best of my judgment; thus appealing from myself drunk to myself sober. I was engaged on *The Pleasures of Memory* for nine years; on *Human Life* for nearly the same space of time; and *Italy* occupied me little less than sixteen years. SAMUEL ROGERS, *Table Talk* (1856), 19.

After a day of humiliation and stripes, if I can write it down, I am straightway relieved and can sleep well. After a day of joy, the beating heart is calmed again by the diary. If grace is given me by all the angels and I pray, if then I can catch one ejaculation of humility or hope and set it down in syllables, devotion is at an end. R. W. EMERSON, 21 October 1841: *Journals* (1911), vi, 94.

If one wait for the right time to come before writing, the right time never comes. JAMES RUSSELL LOWELL to CHARLES ELIOT. NORTON, 22 April 1883: *Letters* (1894), ii, 305.

Now there comes a barrel-organ to play just outside. It will inevitably make my head worse, and yet, for all that I enjoy it. An organ is always an assistance to me in doing any kind of mental work. GEORGE GISSING to his sister ELLEN, 9 August 1883: *Letters* (1926), 130-1.

The Magic Pen

I sit down religiously every morning, I sit down for eight hours every day—and the sitting down is all. In the course of that working day of 8 hours I write 3 sentences which I erase before leaving the table in despair. . . . Sometimes it takes all my resolution and power of self control to refrain from butting my head against the wall. I want to howl and foam at the mouth but I daren't do it for fear of waking that baby and alarming my wife. It's no joking matter. After such crises of despair I doze for hours still half conscious that there is that story I am unable to write. Then I wake up, try again—and at last go to bed completely done-up. So the days pass and nothing is done. At night I sleep. In the morning I get up with the horror of that powerlessness I must face through a day of vain efforts. JOSEPH CONRAD to EDWARD GARNETT, 29 March 1898: *Letters* (1928), 126–7.

If I *want* to write I write—and if I *don't* want to, I won't. D. H. LAWRENCE to ERNEST COLLINGS, 24 December 1912: *Letters* (1932), 86.

Most of my recent plays were written in the railway train between Hatfield and King's Cross. I write anywhere, on the top of omnibuses or wherever I may be; it is all the same to me. BERNARD SHAW, *Daily Mail*, 23 May 1928.

If you would hear the Muse you must prepare silent hours for her and not be disappointed if she breaks the appointment you have made with her. GEORGE MOORE, *Life*, Hone (1936), 361.

XXIII

HOW TO MAKE POETRY

> *Hobbs hints blue,—straight he turtle eats.*
> *Nobbs prints blue,—claret crowns his cup.*
> *Nokes outdares Stokes in azure feats,—*
> *Both gorge. Who fished the murex up?*
> *What porridge had John Keats?*
> Robert Browning, 'Popularity', *Dramatic Lyrics*.

> *And close your eyes with holy dread,*
> *For he on honey dew hath fed,*
> *And drank the milk of paradise.*
> S. T. Coleridge, *Kubla Khan*.

Was death invented that there might be poetry? If so, it is, after all, not so senseless an arrangement. WILLIAM CORY, 27 April 1873: *Letters and Journals* (1897), 348.

Prose = words in their best order;—poetry = the *best* words in the best order. S. T. COLERIDGE, 12 July 1827: *Table Talk* (1874), 48.

You have given me praise for having reflected faithfully in my Poems the feelings of human nature. I would fain hope that I have done so. But a great Poet ought to do more than this: he ought, to a certain degree, to rectify men's feelings, to give them new compositions of feeling, to render their feelings more sane, pure, and permanent, in short, more consonant to nature, to eternal nature, and the great moving spirit of things. He ought to travel before men occasionally as well as at their sides. WILLIAM WORDSWORTH to JOHN WILSON, 1802: *Early Letters of William and Dorothy Wordsworth* (1935), 295-6.

How to make Poetry

A poet ought not to pick nature's pocket: let him borrow, and so borrow as to repay by the very act of borrowing. Examine nature accurately, but write from recollection: and trust more to your imagination than to your memory. S. T. COLERIDGE, 22 September 1830: *Table Talk* (1874), 112–13.

Poetry should be a continuous and controlling mood, the mind should be steeped in poetical associations, and the diction nourished on the purest store of the Attic bee. JAMES RUSSELL LOWELL, 1877: *Letters* (1894), ii, 12.

I assure you I don't think I am at all a poet, but from loving verses, try to make some now and then. There are few but try in their lives, and most of us succeed alike. In short as naturalists account for insects in places where they can't tell how they got there, but cry the wind wafts their eggs about into all parts, and some perish, and some, meeting with proper juices, thrive; so nature, I believe, wafts about poetical eggs or seeds, and thence come poets, when the grain don't light upon a barren surface. HORACE WALPOLE to RICHARD WEST, 3 December 1736: *Supplement to the Letters of Horace Walpole* (1918), i, 8.

A young poet should be bound apprentice to *Pindar* for three years, whether his business be the ode or anything else. He will find nothing in the workshop which he expected to find, but quite enough of highly-wrought tools and well-seasoned materials. WALTER SAVAGE LANDOR to JOHN FORSTER, *Life* (1876), 497.

Popery almost destroys poetry. Englishmen who write good verse as Anglo-Catholics cease to write good verse as Roman Catholics. In our older literature there is no good Papist poet: there is a weak rhymer called Habington, a sort of Waller. WILLIAM CORY to REGINALD, VISCOUNT ESHER, 1874: *Ionicus* (1923), 64.

Poetry I take it, is as universally contagious as the small-pox; everyone catches it once in their life at least, and the sooner the better; for methinks an old rhymster makes as ridiculous a figure

How to make Poetry

as Socrates at fourscore. RICHARD WEST at Oxford to HORACE WALPOLE, 12 January 1736: *Letters of Horace Walpole* (1891), i, 11.

If poetry comes not as naturally as the leaves to a tree, it had better not come at all. JOHN KEATS to JOHN TAYLOR, 27 February 1818: *Works* (1895), 93.

I have *worked* at poetry—it has not been to me reverie, but art. As the physician and lawyer work at their several professions, so have I, and so do I, apply to mine. ELIZABETH BARRETT BROWNING, *Letters to R. H. Horne* (1877), ii, 119.

For a man to become a poet . . . he must be in love, or miserable. LORD BYRON, *Conversations*, Medwin (1824), 63.

XXIV

BUBBLES AND SQUEAKS

One age blows bubbles and the next breaks them. William Cowper, *Letters*, Anna Seward (1811), vi, 161.

Praise or blame has but a momentary effect on the man whose love of Beauty in the abstract makes him a severe critic of his own works. John Keats, *Letters* (1901), iv, 168.

How odious all authors are, and how doubly so to each other! Henry Edward Fox, Fourth Lord Holland, 3 January 1821: *Journal* (1923), 60.

SHAKESPEARE. Not a Pug in Barbary that has not a truer taste of things. THOMAS RYMER, *A Short View of Tragedy* (1693), 124.

SHAKESPEARE. A damned humbug. LORD BYRON to THOMAS MOORE 15 October 1819: *Memoirs of Thomas Moore* (1854), iii, 34.

MEASURE FOR MEASURE. A hateful work, although Shakespearian throughout. S. T. COLERIDGE, 24 June 1827: *Table Talk* (1874), 42.

BEN JONSON. I can't read *Ben Jonson*, especially his comedies. To me he appears to move in a wide sea of glue. ALFRED TENNYSON to FREDERICK LOCKER-LAMPSON, 1869: *Memoir*, (1897), 73.

MILTON. Who would remember him for his barbarous prose? HORACE WALPOLE, 14 November 1769: *Letters* (1891), v, 203.

TOM JONES. A dissolute book. Its run is over. SAMUEL RICHARDSON, 21 January 1750: *Correspondence* (1804), v, 275.

SWIFT. No one could be an ill-tempered man who wrote so much nonsense as Swift did. CHARLES JAMES FOX: *Table Talk*, Samuel Rogers (1856), 92.

THE BEGGAR'S OPERA. A mere pouring of bilge-water and oil of Vitriol on the deepest wounds of humanity. THOMAS CARLYLE, *Life of Lord Houghton*, Reid (1891), ii, 479.

DR. JOHNSON. I cannot imagine that Dr. Johnson's reputation will be very lasting. HORACE WALPOLE, *Walpoliana* (1800), 25.

LORD CHESTERFIELD'S LETTERS. They teach the morals of a whore, and the manners of a dancing master. SAMUEL JOHNSON, 1754: *Boswell's Life* (1887), i, 266.

THE DECLINE AND FALL OF THE ROMAN EMPIRE. Gibbons style is detestable, but his style is not the worst thing about him. His history has proved an effective bar to all real familiarity with the temper and habits of imperial Rome. S. T. COLERIDGE, 15 August 1833: *Table Talk* (1874), 273.

TRISTRAM SHANDY. The dregs of nonsense. HORACE WALPOLE to the REV. HENRY ZOUCH, 7 March 1761: *Letters* (1891), iii, 382.

A SENTIMENTAL JOURNEY. Poor and sickly stuff. S. T. COLERIDGE, 18 August 1833: *Table Talk* (1874), 280.

DAVID HUME. The most insolent despiser of truth and virtue that ever appeared in the world. JOHN WESLEY, 5 May 1772: *Journal* [n.d.], v, 458.

BOSWELL'S TOUR. The story of a mountebank and his zany. HORACE WALPOLE to H. G. CONWAY, 6 October 1785: *Letters*, (1891) ix, 25.

SHELLEY. Shelley is never a poet. R. W. EMERSON, 28 November 1839: *Journals*, (1914) v, 344.

BYRON. Byron is no poet. R. W. EMERSON, 1846: *Ib.*, vii, 163.

CHARLES DICKENS. His eye rests always on surfaces; he has no insight into character. R. W. EMERSON, 1839: *Ib.*

CHARLES DICKENS. A child of genius, but only a child, he never progresses, never improves, never studies, never restrains. DR. JOHN BROWN, 6 December 1855: *Letters* (1907), 107.

LANDOR. Has never learned . . . how to write simple and lucid English. S. T. COLERIDGE, 1 January 1834: *Table Talk* (1874), 300.

JOHN STUART MILL. An utterly shallow wretched segment of a human creature, incapable of understanding *Anything* in the ultimate conditions of it. JOHN RUSKIN, 12 September 1869: *Letters to Charles Eliot Norton* (1905), i, 245–6.

EDGAR ALLAN POE. An enthusiasm for Poe is the mark of a decidedly primitive stage of reflection. HENRY JAMES, *French Poets and Novelists* (1878), 60.

MACAULAY'S HISTORY OF ENGLAND. Full of low merits: it is like English manufactures of all kinds, neat, convenient, portable, saleable, made on purpose for Harpers to print a hundred thousand copies of. R. W. EMERSON, 1850: *Journals* (1911).

W. M. THACKERAY. A first rate journey-man though not a great artist. MATTHEW ARNOLD, 1853: *Letters to Arthur Hugh Clough* (1932), 132.

BULWER LYTTON. Essentially a man of tinsel; with versatile powers, but without genius. Very dead, he and his works, as soon as he dies. CHARLES ELIOT NORTON, 1873: *Letters* (1913), i, 461.

BULWER LYTTON. An impostor and an antinomian heretic. JAMES RUSSELL LOWELL to E. C. STEDMAN, 15 May 1866: *Letters* (1894), i, 408.

TYPEE. I am heartily sick of *Typee*. JAMES RUSSELL LOWELL to SYDNEY H. GAY, 1848: *Letters* (1894), i, 141.

GEORGE ELIOT. Her views of life, of God, of all that is deepest and truest in man, are low, miserable, hopeless, and she seems always wishing to drag her readers down to her dead level . . . she is unwholesome, and in a high sense unreal, and I trust that in fifty years she will be forgotten except by critics. DR. JOHN BROWN, 24 December 1872: *Letters* (1907), 213–14.

THE MILL ON THE FLOSS. That disgusting *Mill on the Floss.* JOHN RUSKIN, *Hortus Inclusus* (1887), 122.

JOHN RUSKIN. Ruskin has some vague truth for a backbone to his preposterous Priestly attitude and inebriate conceit as against adversaries. GEORGE MEREDITH to ——, 2 January 1870: *Letters* (1912), i, 201.

J. A. FROUDE. Anthony [Froude] has written a history of England with England left out. J. R. GREEN to E. A. FREEMAN, 3 February 1870: *Letters* (1901), 242.

WALT WHITMAN'S 'LEAVES OF GRASS'. One cannot leave it about for chance readers, and would be sorry to know that any woman had looked into it past the title page. CHARLES ELIOT NORTON to JAMES RUSSELL LOWELL, 23 September 1855: *Letters* (1913), i, 135.

MATTHEW ARNOLD. Never knew his business as a critic; he was a mere journalist, scrambling through by mother-wit. F. YORK POWELL to J. B. YEATS, 1901: *Life*, Elton (1906), i, 330.

RICHARD JEFFERIES. An ass. SAMUEL BUTLER, 24 February 1882: *Letters between Samuel Butler and Miss E. M. A. Savage* (1935), 273.

JOSEPH CONRAD. A completely worthless writer. GEORGE MOORE, *Life*, Hone (1936), 325.

RUDYARD KIPLING. He was never great. ARNOLD BENNETT, 25 October 1909: *Journals* (1932), 334.

GEORGE RUSSELL (A. E.). A bit of an ass. STEPHEN McKENNA, 17 November 1924: *Journals and Letters* (1936), 212.

Bubbles and Squeaks

PARADISE LOST. The triumph of classic vanity over his better judgment, often betrayed Milton into Pagan allusions . . . highly improper in a poem whose subject was of such consecrated sanctity. ANNA SEWARD, 19 October 1798: *Letters* (1811), v, 158.

DECLINE AND FALL OF THE ROMAN EMPIRE. I have seldom met with more affectation and less perspicuity. The instances of false English are many; and of false taste endless. I find little of the sober dignity of history; and the notes are as immodest . . . as they are profane. HANNAH MORE, 1788: *Memoirs* (1835), ii, 132.

PRIDE AND PREJUDICE. An accurate daguerreotype portrait of a commonplace face; a carefully-fenced, highly-cultivated garden, with neat borders and delicate flowers; but no glance of a bright vivid physiognomy, no open country, no fresh air, no blue hill, no bonny beck. I should hardly like to live with her ladies and gentlemen, in their elegant but confined houses. . . . CHARLOTTE BRONTË to G. H. LEWES, 12 January 1848: *Life*, Gaskell (1857), ii, 52–4.

UNCLE TOM'S CABIN. I read about a hundred pages, and found the book so painful, that I put it down, and certainly am not likely to take it up again. It is one-sided, exaggerated, false—with some cleverness, but of a very disagreeable kind. MISS MITFORD to the REV. WILLIAM HARNESS, 10 November 1852: *Life* (1810), iii, 245.

ROSSETTI. I dislike his face, and his manner, and his work, and I hate his poetry, and his friends. He is wrapped up in self-conceit and lives upon adulation. SAMUEL BUTLER to Miss E. M. A. SAVAGE, 23 September 1872: *Letters between Samuel Butler and Miss E. M. A. Savage*, 1871–1885 (1935), 32–3.

THACKERAY. Thackeray likes to dissect an ulcer or an aneurism; he has pleasure in putting his cruel knife or probe into quivering, living flesh. Thackeray would not like all the world to be good. CHARLOTTE BRONTË, 14 February 1852: *Life*, (1857) ii, 243.

EMERSON. He would have been a great writer and thinker, if Carlyle had not fallen in his way. Now he appears a mere copyist of the Scotchman. MISS MITFORD to CHARLES BONER, 7 April 1850: *Letters* (1925), 220–1.

FIELDING. The . . . grand agent in all his women, but his heroines, seems the *furor uterinus*; whose province, when insufficient for his purpose, he elegantly and ingeniously contrives to exasperate by cordials and philters! THOMAS GREEN, 11 February 1800: *Extracts from the Diary of a Lover of Literature* (1810), 199.

BIOGRAPHIA LITERARIA. Has . . . rather more absurdities than ever were collected together in a printed book before. MISS MITFORD to SIR WILLIAM ELFORD, 13 September 1817: *Life* (1870), ii, 11–12.

XXV

THE ART OF PRAISE

To commence author is to claim praise. Dr. Johnson, *The Rambler* (1751), 93.

Criticism is the art of praise. Richard Le Gallienne, *Retrospective Reviews* (1896), i, xv.

One quality I may safely arrogate to myself: I am not afraid to praise. Horace Walpole, *Walpoliana* (1800), 33.

This is a barbarous business of greatest this and supreme that that Swinburne and others practise. Gerard Manley Hopkins, 1880: *Further Letters* (1938), 99.

BACON'S ESSAYS. For reach of thought, variety and extent of view, sheer solid and powerful sense, and admirable sagacity, what works of man can be placed in competition with these wonderful effusions. THOMAS GREEN, 12 September 1798: *Extracts from the Diary of a Lover of Literature* (1810), 98–9.

THE COMPLEAT ANGLER. It breathes the very spirit of innocence, purity, and simplicity of heart. . . . It would sweeten a man's temper at any time to read it; it would Christianise every discordant angry passion. CHARLES LAMB to S. T. COLERIDGE, 28 October 1796: *Letters* (1905), i, 52.

HYDRIOTAPHIA. The last chapter . . . a piece of prose that has never been surpassed in our literature. W. SOMERSET MAUGHAM, *The Summing-Up* (1938), 35.

PARADISE LOST. The greatest achievement in the world of pure art that their (the English) race has produced. JOHN BAILEY, 21 December 1895: *Letters and Diaries* (1935), 54.

DRYDEN. Remember *Dryden*, and be blind to all his faults. THOMAS GRAY to JAMES BEATTIE, 2 October 1765: *Letters* (1900), iii, 95.

THE PILGRIM'S PROGRESS. One of the few books which may be read over repeatedly at different times, and each time with a new and different pleasure. I read it once as a theologian . . . once with devotional feelings—and once as a poet. I could not have believed beforehand that Calvinism could be painted in such exquisitely delightful colours. S. T. COLERIDGE, 31 May 1830: *Table Talk* (1874), 88–9.

POPE'S HOMER. By making the Iliad pass through your poetical crucible into an English form, without losing aught of its original beauty, you have drawn the golden current of Pactolus to Twickenham. LADY MARY WORTLEY MONTAGU to ALEXANDER POPE, 1 September 1717: *Letters* (1837), ii, 136.

AKENSIDE'S PLEASURES OF IMAGINATION. The most splendid metaphysical poem in any language. ANNA SEWARD, 7 February 1806: *Letters* (1811), vi, 247.

OSSIAN. Little inferior to either *Homer* or *Virgil*; in some respects superior to both. JOHN WESLEY, 15 May 1784: *Journal* [n.d.] vi, 507.

THE POETRY OF ISAAC WATTS. It is sufficient for Watts to have done better than others what no man has done well. DR. JOHNSON, *Lives of the English Poets* (1781), iv, 291.

SAMUEL RICHARDSON. An author . . . who has enlarged the knowledge of human nature, and taught the passions to move at the command of virtue. DR. JOHNSON, *The Rambler*, 14 March 1752.

SIR CHARLES GRANDISON. Joy to you, dear Sir, and joy to the world; you have done great things for it. And I will venture to affirm, that no one shall read you without either benefit, or—guilt. . . . When the pulpit falls, other expedients are necessary. I look on you as a peculiar instrument of Providence, adjusted to the peculiar exigency of the times; in which all would be *fine gentlemen*, and only are at a loss to know what that means. EDWARD YOUNG to SAMUEL RICHARDSON, 14 March 1754: *Correspondence of Samuel Richardson* (1804), v, 32–3.

HORACE WALPOLE. A Frenchman in manners and conduct, but he wrote pure English. There may have been rouge on his cheeks, but there was none in his writings. He wrote *red* when everybody else wrote and said *rouge*. WALTER SAVAGE LANDOR to A. DE N. WALKER, 1861: *Letters and Unpublished Writings* (1897), 123–4.

THOMAS GRAY. The only poet since Shakespeare entitled to the character of sublime. WILLIAM COWPER to JOSEPH HILL, 20 April 1777: *Letters* (1912), i, 28–9.

What he published during his life will establish his fame as long as our language lasts, and there is a man of genius left. HORACE WALPOLE to REV. WILLIAM COLE, 28 January 1772: *Letters* (1891), v, 371.

The two noblest lyric odes the world has produced, Gray's *Bard* and his *Eolian Lyre*. ANNA SEWARD, 6 May 1799: *Letters* (1811), v, 222.

MASON'S GRAY. The most entertaining book in the world. HORACE WALPOLE, 1775: *Letters* (1891), vi, 199.

STERNE. Sterne has published two little volumes, called *Sentimental Travels* [*sic*]. They are very pleasing, though too much dilated, and infinitely preferable to his tiresome *Tristram Shandy*, of which I never could get through three volumes. In these there is great good nature and strokes of delicacy. HORACE WALPOLE to GEORGE MONTAGU, 12 March 1768: *Letters* (1891), v, 91.

BOSWELL. Your *History* [*Account of Corsica*] was copied from books; your *Journal* [in Corsica] rose out of your own experience and observation. You express images which operated strongly upon yourself, and you have impressed them with great force upon your readers. I know not whether I could name any narrative by which curiosity is better excited or better gratified. DR. JOHNSON to JAMES BOSWELL, 9 September 1769: *Boswell's Life of Johnson* (1887), ii, 70.

THE DECLINE AND FALL. After the singular pleasure of reading you, Sir, the next satisfaction is to declare my admiration. I have read great part of your volume, and cannot decide to which of its various merits I give the preference, though I have no doubt of assigning my partiality to one virtue. . . . It is your amiable modesty. How can you know so much, judge so well, possess your subject, and your knowledge, and your power of judicious reflection so thoroughly, and yet command yourself and betray no dictatorial arrogance of decision? How unlike very ancient and very modern authors! You have, unexpectedly, given the world a classic history. The fame it must acquire will tend every day to acquit this panegyric of flattery. HORACE WALPOLE to EDWARD GIBBON, 14 February 1776: *Letters* (1891), vi, 307–8.

BOSWELL'S LIFE OF DR. JOHNSON. I think it would be, without exception, the most interesting book you ever read. JAMES BOSWELL to the REV. W. J. TEMPLE, 8 February 1790: *Letters of James Boswell to the Rev. W. J. Temple* (1857), 320.

The most entertaining book in the world. SIR WALTER SCOTT to JOHN WILSON CROKER, 30 January 1829: *The Croker Papers* (1884), ii, 28.

ERASMUS DARWIN'S 'BOTANIC GARDEN'. Darwin's splendid web of poetic fancy appears at length completely woven. It will shine to future ages, largely contributing to the lyric glories of a period, which has so pleasantly teemed with the rich fruits of Parnassus. ANNA SEWARD, 3 August 1792: *Letters* (1811), iii, 153.

SOUTHEY'S JOAN OF ARC. Nearer the *Paradise Lost* than any other epic attempt in our language. ANNA SEWARD, 2 January 1799: *Letters* (1811), v, 190.

The Art of Praise

JANE AUSTEN'S NOVELS. There are in the world no compositions which approach nearer to perfection. T. B. MACAULAY, 1 May 1851: *Life* (1876), ii, 293.

JOANNA BAILLIE. If you wish to speak of a real poet, Joanna Baillie is now the highest genius of our country. SIR WALTER SCOTT to JAMES BALLANTYNE, *Life* (1837–8), ii, 307.

GEORGE SAND. The greatest female genius the world ever saw. ELIZABETH BARRETT BROWNING to RICHARD HENGIST HORNE, 20 February 1841: *Letters* (1877), i, 243.

DON QUIXOTE. The best novel in the world. T. B. MACAULAY to his Sister, 14 October 1833: *Life* (1876), i, 296.

SCOTT. The author with the widest range since *Shakespeare*. ALFRED TENNYSON, 1890: *Memoir* (1897), ii, 372.

THE BRIDE OF LAMMERMOOR. No man since *Æschylus* could have written *The Bride of Lammermoor*. W. E. GLADSTONE, 1883: *Tennyson: a Memoir* (1897), ii, 281.

ESMOND. The greatest novel in the English language. ANTHONY TROLLOPE, *Autobiography* 1883 (1923), 170.

THE SCARLET LETTER. The most perfect American work of art. D. H. LAWRENCE, *Studies in Classic American Literature* (1924), 170.

AGNES GREY. The most perfect prose narrative in literature. GEORGE MOORE, *Life*, Hone (1936), 481.

UNCLE TOM'S CABIN. The most valuable addition that America has made to English literature. T. B. MACAULAY, 4 October 1852: *Life* (1876), ii, 321.

MOBY DICK. The greatest book of the sea ever written. D. H. LAWRENCE, *Studies in Classic American Literature* (1924), 160.

I am convinced that there are three things to rejoice at in this Age—*The Excursion*, Your Pictures, and Hazlitt's depth of Taste.

The Art of Praise

JOHN KEATS to BENJAMIN ROBERT HAYDON, 10 January 1818: *Letters* (1895), 64.

I think the *Oedipus Tyrannus*, the *Alchemist*, and *Tom Jones*, the three most perfect plots ever planned. S. T. COLERIDGE, 5 July 1834: *Table Talk* (1874), 332.

My breakfast party went off very well indeed, as far as talk was concerned. I had with me Landor, Milnes, and Serjeant Talfourd. A great deal of rattling on the part of Landor. He maintained *Blake* to be the greatest of poets; that *Milnes* is the greatest poet now living in England; and that Scott's *Marmion* is superior to all that *Byron* and *Wordsworth* have written and the description of the battle better than anything in *Homer*!!! HENRY CRABB ROBINSON, 20 May 1838: *Diary* (1872), ii, 205.

SCHOOL FOR SCANDAL. I am very shy of 'the Greatest Poem', the Greatest Picture, Symphony, &c., but one single thing I always was assured of: that *The School* was the best Comedy in the English Language. EDWARD FITZGERALD to W. F. POLLOCK, 1873: *Letters and Literary Remains* (1889), i, 357–8.

THOMAS CARLYLE. An imagination such as never rejoiced before the face of God, since Shakespeare. R. W. EMERSON, 1838: *Journals* (1911), iv, 405.

CHARLES DICKENS. No mortal man ever exerted so beneficial and extensive an influence over the human heart. WALTER SAVAGE LANDOR, 23 December 1843: *Letters* (1899), 127.

MOTLEY'S DUTCH REPUBLIC. The most exciting (and I believe the most veracious) piece of history in the world. JOHN BAILEY, 24 November 1894: *Letters and Diaries* (1935), 52.

AURORA LEIGH. The greatest poem in the English language, unsurpassed by anything but Shakespeare—*not* surpassed by Shakespeare's *sonnets*, and therefore the greatest poem in the language. JOHN RUSKIN to ROBERT BROWNING, 27 November 1856: *Letters* (1909), i, 247.

The Art of Praise

THE DEFENCE OF GUENEVERE AND OTHER POEMS. The most perfect first volume of poems ever published by any man. GEORGE MOORE, *Life*, Hone (1936), 360.

WASHINGTON IRVING. None of our present writers write such pure English; he reminds me of *Addison*, but he has more genius and a richer invention. Perhaps on the whole he is more like *Goldsmith*. WALTER SAVAGE LANDOR to MRS. GRAVES-SAWLE, 19 January 1863: *Letters* (1899), 229.

WALT WHITMAN. Read Whitman: he will never fail you, that is the test of divinity: *Jesus* and *Shelley* and *Whitman*, they are steadfast in faith, never wavering. LIONEL JOHNSON, 15 May 1885: *Some Winchester Letters of Lionel Johnson* (1919), 203.

TENNYSON. He has been the greatest artist in words we have had since Gray. JAMES RUSSELL LOWELL to CHARLES ELIOT NORTON, 4 December 1872: *Letters* (1894), ii, 98.

TENNYSON'S QUEEN MARY. When we were beginning to think that we were to have no more from you, you gave us the greatest of all your works [Queen Mary]. J. A. FROUDE to ALFRED TENNYSON, 7 May 1875: *Alfred, Lord Tennyson: A Memoir* (1897), 181.

OSCAR WILDE. The most Hellenic spirit of our age, the divinest wit of our age, the most eloquent of all who lived, the most inspired, the loveliest of all, the most devoted and religious worshipper of Beauty, the bravest, the greatest genius, the greatest lover—Oscar Wilde. JOHN COWPER POWYS, *Welsh Ambassadors*, Marlow (1936), 66.

THE MESSIAH, PILGRIM'S PROGRESS, and PARADISE LOST . . . the three greatest religious works produced in England. ALFRED TENNYSON, 1890: *Memoir* (1897), ii, 377.

ROBERT BRIDGES. I have no doubt at all that he is the poet living to-day whom the to-morrows of two or three centuries hence will still be interested in. JOHN BAILEY, *Letters and Diaries* (1935), 302.

The Art of Praise

DOUGHTY'S ARABIA DESERTA. Certainly the best prose written in the last two centuries. WILFRID SCAWEN BLUNT, *My Diaries* (1910), i, 273.

FARAWAY AND LONG AGO. The supreme record in all literature of a boy's life and experience. MORLEY ROBERTS, *W. H. Hudson: A Portrait* (1924), 18.

H. G. WELLS. I've got a curious book about the adventures of a young man and a girl on bicycles—it is called *The Wheels of Chance*. It's very funny. The young man is a draper's assistant who is described as weak and vulgar (only in the way he talks) and he turns out so nice. I don't see why he should be supposed to be vulgar because he is a draper's assistant. KATE GREENAWAY to JOHN RUSKIN, 3 March 1897: *Kate Greenaway*, Spielmann and Lazard (1908), 215.

PICKWICK PAPERS. So you never heard of the *Pickwick Papers*! Well! They publish a number once a month and print 25,000. The bookseller has made about 10,000l. by the speculation. It is fun—London life—but without anything unpleasant: a lady might read it *aloud*; and it is so graphic, so individual, and so true, that you could curtsey to all the people as you met them in the streets. I did not think there had been a place where English was spoken to which 'Boz' had not penetrated. All the boys and girls talk his fun—the boys in the streets; and yet they who are of the highest taste like it the most. Sir Benjamin Brodie takes it to read in his carriage between patient and patient; and Lord Denman studies *Pickwick* on the bench whilst the jury are deliberating. Do take some means to borrow the *Pickwick Papers*. It seems like not having heard of Hogarth, whom he resembles greatly, except that he takes a far more cheerful view, a Shakespearian view, of humanity. MISS MITFORD to MISS JEPHSON, 30 April 1837: *Letters* (1925), 192–3.

I am disconsolate that we have had the last number of *Pickwick*, the only bit of fun in India. It is one of the few books of which there has been a Calcutta reprint, lithographs and all. I have not read it through in numbers more than ten times, but now it is complete I think of studying it more correctly. EMILY EDEN at Simla to MRS. LISTER (Lady Theresa Lewis), 28 April 1838: *Miss Eden's Letters* (1919), 298.

WALT WHITMAN. I was calling on Madox Brown a fortnight ago, and he put into my hands your edition of *Walt Whitman's Poems.* . . . Since I have had it, I can read no other book; it holds me entirely spell-bound, and I go through it again and again with deepening delight and wonder. ANNE GILCHRIST to W. M. ROSSETTI, 22 June 1869: *Life* (1887), 177.

OUR VILLAGE. I can hardly feel that I am addressing an entire stranger in the author of *Our Village*, and yet I know it is right and proper, that I should apologize for the liberty I am taking. But really, after having accompanied you again, and again, as I have done, in 'violetting' and seeking for wood-sorrel: after having been with you to call upon Mrs. Allen in 'the dell', and becoming thoroughly acquainted with 'May and Lizzy', I cannot but hope, that you will kindly pardon my intrusion, and that my name may be sufficiently known to you to plead my cause. There are some writers whose works we cannot read without feeling as if we really *had* looked with them upon the scenes they bring before us, and as if such communion had almost given us a claim to something more than the mere intercourse between author and 'gentle reader'. Will you allow me to say that *your* writings have this effect upon me, and that you have taught me in making me know and love your *Village* so well, to wish for further knowledge, also, of *her* who has so vividly impressed its dingles and copses upon my imagination, and peopled them so cheerily with healthful and happy beings? MRS. HEMANS to MISS MITFORD, 6 June 1827: *Memorials* (1836), i, 151–2.

SAMUEL RICHARDSON. What a genius had Richardson! With every fault of style, of plot, of subject, which a writer could have —with the most wearying repetitions, the most distressing coarseness of painting—with characters the most abhorrent to our feelings, and scenes the most repugnant to our delicacy—he has yet contrived to enchain our every thought and passion: and this he has effected by his angelic heroine, and by her alone. MISS MITFORD to SIR WILLIAM ELFORD, 13 December 1812: *Life* (1870), i, 216.

XXVI

THE GOLDEN CALF

They may talk as they please about what they call pelf,
And how one ought never to think of one'self,
And how pleasures of thought surpass eating and drinking—
My pleasure of thought is the pleasure of thinking
How pleasant it is to have money, heigh ho!
How pleasant it is to have money.

Arthur Hugh Clough, *The Dipsychus.*

Gold is the chief ingredient in the composition of worldly happiness. Living in a cottage on love is certainly the worst diet and the worst habitation one can find out. ELIZABETH MONTAGU to the DUCHESS OF PORTLAND, 25 January 1740: *Letters* (1809), i, 82.

No man but a blockhead ever wrote, except for money. DR. JOHNSON, 1776: *Boswell's Life of Johnson* (1887), iii, 19.

He [Dr. Johnson] had less attention to profit from his labours than any man to whom literature has been a profession. JAMES BOSWELL, 1777: *Ib.*, iii, 110.

A man who thinks he has got anything to say should always write for money. There is always some air of priggishness in one who 'gives his advice gratis'. Modesty is preserved by the money-motive. Besides, the subtlest truths are like the remoter stars: you cannot see them unless you look a little on one side of them. You are likely to say your say the better for having your direct gaze fixed upon the five, ten, or twenty pound note which your prophecy is to bring you. COVENTRY PATMORE, *Memoirs and Correspondence* (1900), i, 261–2.

The Golden Calf

Dined with Sidney Colvin. He told me he once heard Tennyson read *The Revenge* in his deep chant—a sort of intoning with little variety of manner or expression, and he ended 'To be lost evermore in the main!' adding immediately in exactly the same voice and attitude without any pause 'And the scoundrels only gave me £300 for that! It was worth £500!' I don't like the story, but record it as first-hand and oddly characteristic of one side of Tennyson. If he had said it was worth £3,000 it would have been less absurd. JOHN BAILEY, 7 May 1925: *Letters and Diaries* (1935), 254.

I am very well—really so absurd a septuagenarian is seldom met with—and my stay at Whitby, where the weather grew to be almost weakly good-natured at last, did me good. A poem even got itself written there (which seems to me not altogether bad), and this intense activity of the brain has the same effect as exercise on my body, and somehow braced up the whole machine. My writing this was a lucky thing, for when I got back to London I found a letter from the New York *Ledger* enclosing a draft for 200L. for whatever I should choose to send. So I sent them what I had just written, pacifying my scruples with the thought that after all it was only my *name* they were paying for, and that they knew best what it was worth to them. JAMES RUSSELL LOWELL to MRS. EDWARD BURNETT, 23 September 1889: *Letters* (1894), ii, 430-1.

I ask myself one serious question what is it I want? What can I answer? My desires are as capricious as the big-bellied woman's who longd for a piece of her husband's nose. I have no certainty it is true; but why can't I do as some men of more merit who have liv'd upon more precarious terms? Scaron us'd jestingly to call himself the Lord Marquis of Quenault which was the name of the bookseller who employ'd him, and why may not I assert my privilege and quality on the same pretensions? . . . I know you have in Ireland a very indifferent Idea of a man who writes for bread, tho Swift and Steel did so in the earlier part of their lives. You Imagine, I suppose, that every author by profession lives in a garret, wears shabby clothes, and converses with the meanest company; but I assure you such a character is entirely chimerical. Nor do I believe there is one single writer, who has abilities to translate a french Novel, that does not keep better company wear finer cloaths and live more genteely than many who do pride themselves for nothing else in Ireland. OLIVER GOLDSMITH to DANIEL HODSON, 31 August 1758: *Collected Letters* (1928), 50–1.

I really think it is your bounden duty to look after your family interests. It is very unpoetical, and very un-Irish, and very un-romantic to attend to worldly cares, but if not attended to they at last become too strong for the most poetical head and the most ardent heart. J. W. CROKER to TOM MOORE, 13 November 1813: *The Croker Papers* (1884), i, 52.

Moore is a very worthy man, but not a little improvident. His excellent wife contrives to maintain the whole family on a guinea a-week; and he, when in London, thinks nothing of throwing away that sum weekly on hackney-coaches and gloves. I said to him, 'You must have made ten thousand pounds by your musical publications.' He replied, 'More than that.' In short, he has received for his various works nearly thirty thousand pounds. SAMUEL ROGERS, *Table Talk* (1856), 282.

Literature is a thriving trade. Moxon has just brought me the account of my fifth (popular) edition of *Faust*, of which he has sold 1500 copies. I find myself £6. 2. 7 out of pocket. ABRAHAM HAYWARD to SIR G. C. LEWIS, 8 February 1840: *Letters* (1886), i, 246.

The literary market is very bad. Shilling romances, and other books as cheap, and all good, for they are translations, many of them, from the best French writers, have quite knocked up the good old profession, which, established on a discreet foundation of puffing, permitted a fair profit to publisher and scribe. LORD BEACONSFIELD to his Sister, 16 April 1857: *Correspondence with His Sister* 1832–1852 (1886), 258.

The Golden Calf

If indeed a man writes his books badly, or paints his pictures badly, because he can make his money faster in that fashion than by doing them well, and at the same time proclaims them to be the best he can do,—if in fact he sells shoddy for broadcloth,—he is dishonest, as is any other fraudulent dealer. ANTHONY TROLLOPE, *Autobiography*, 1883 (1923), 98–9.

I must tell you a good manœuvre of the Biblipole's. He proposes to give me fifty guineas if I will amplify the Wellington article a little, annex to it a full account of the late battle, and let him publish it within three weeks in one volume, like the *Life of Nelson* as a *Life of Wellington*, and with my name. Now he knows very well that if he had *primâ facie* proposed to give me £150 for a *Life of Wellington*, I should not have listened to any such proposal. I might with good reason have considered it as a derogatory offer. But because, through my principle of doing things of this kind as well as I can without any reference to price or quantity, he got from me a fair *Life of Nelson* instead of a mere expansion of a paper in his review, and thereby (though he paid me £200 instead of £100, which was the original offer for one volume), got from me for £200 what I certainly would not have sold to him for £500, had the thing been a straightforward business from the beginning—because he has dealt so thrivingly in one instance, he wanted to trepan me into this kind of bargain. ROBERT SOUTHEY to GROSVENOR C. BEDFORD, 28 June 1815: *Letters* (1856), ii, 13.

After breakfast I went down to the British Museum. I had been immersed half-an-hour in my MSS., when happening to turn my head round I found seated next to me Thackeray with a file of old newspapers before him writing the ninth number of the *Virginians*. . . . I can conceive nothing more harassing in the literary way than his way of living from hand to mouth. I mean in regard to the way in which he furnishes food for the printer's devil. Here he is just finishing the number which must appear in a few days . . . whether ill or well, stupid or fertile, he must produce the same amount of fun, pathos, or sentiment. . . . I should think it would wear his life out. JOHN LOTHROP MOTLEY to his Wife, 27 June 1858: *Correspondence* (1889), i, 279–80.

Keep to your bank, and the bank will keep you. Trust not to the public; you may hang, starve, drown yourself for anything that worthy personage cares. I bless every star, that Providence, not seeing good to make me independent, has seen it next good to settle upon me the stable foundation of Leadenhall. Sit down, good B. B., in the banking-office; what! is there not from six to eleven, P.M. six days in the week, and is there not all Sunday. Fie, what a superfluity of man's time, if you could think so! Enough for relaxation, mirth, converse, poetry, good thoughts, quiet thoughts. Oh, the corroding, torturing, tormenting thoughts that disturb the brain of the unlucky wight, who must draw upon it for daily sustenance! Henceforth I retract all my fond complaints of mercantile employment; look upon them as lovers' quarrels. I was but half in earnest. Welcome dead timber of the desk, that gives me life. A little grumbling is a wholesome medicine for the spleen, but in my inner heart do I approve and embrace this close, but unharassing way of life. I am quite serious. CHARLES LAMB to BERNARD BARTON, 9 January 1823: *Letters* (1905), ii, 594.

He [William Blake] spoke of his horror of money—of his having turned pale when money was offered him. HENRY CRABB ROBINSON, 18 February 1826: *Diary* (1872), ii, 16.

It is a foolish Thing, that one cannot either live as one pleases, or where or with whom one pleases, without Money. Swift somewhere says, that Money is Liberty; and I fear Money is Friendship too and Society, and almost every external Blessing. It is a great, tho' ill-natured Comfort, to see most of those who have it in Plenty, without Pleasure, without Liberty, and without Friends. THOMAS GRAY to DR. WARTON, 11 December 1746: *Letters* (1900), i, 150.

The *Courier* of this evening accuses me of having 'received and pocketed' large sums for my works. I have never yet received,

The Golden Calf

nor wish to receive, a farthing for any. Mr. Murray offered a thousand for *The Giaour* and *Bride of Abydos*, which I said was too much, and that if he could afford it at the end of six months, I would then direct how it might be disposed of; but neither then, nor at any other period, have I ever availed myself of the profits on my account. For the republication of the Satire I refused four hundred guineas; and for the previous editions I never asked nor received a *sou*, nor for any writing whatever. LORD BYRON to R. C. DALLAS, 17 February 1814: *Letters and Journals* (1899), iii, 1.

Oh money, money, how blindly thou hast been worshipped, and how stupidly abused! Thou art health and liberty, and strength; and he that has thee may rattle his pockets at the foul fiend. CHARLES LAMB to S. T. COLERIDGE, 7 June 1809: *Letters* (1905), i, 401.

I am not fond of money, or anxious about it. But, though every day makes me less and less eager for wealth, every day shows me more and more strongly how necessary a competence is to a man who desires to be either great or useful. . . . For I must live: I can live only by my pen: and it is absolutely impossible for any man to write enough to procure him a decent subsistence, and at the same time to take an active part in politics. I have not during this session been able to send a single line to the *Edinburgh Review*; and if I had been out of office, I should have been able to do very little. Edward Bulwer has just given up the *New Monthly Magazine* on the ground that he cannot conduct it and attend to his Parliamentary duties. Cobbett has been compelled to neglect his *Register* so much that its sale has fallen almost to nothing. Now, in order to live like a gentleman, it would be necessary for me to write, not as I have done hitherto, but regularly, and even daily. I have never made more than two hundred a year by my pen. I could not support myself in comfort on less than five hundred; and I shall in all probability have many others to support. T. B. MACAULAY to his sister HANNAH, 17 August 1833: *Life* (1876), i, 323–4.

The Golden Calf

CLARISSA has almost killed me. You know how my business engages me. You know by what snatches of time I write, that I may not neglect that, and that I may preserve that independency which is the comfort of my life. I never sought out of myself for patrons. My own industry, and God's providence, have been my whole reliance. SAMUEL RICHARDSON to MR. DEFREVAL, 21 January 1750: *Correspondence* (1804), v, 273.

Ballantyne called on me this morning. *Venit illa superma dies.* My extremity is come. Cadell has received letters from London which all but positively announce the failure of Hurst and Robinson, so that Constable & Co. must follow, and I must go with poor James Ballantyne for company. I suppose it will involve my all. But if they leave me £500, I can still make it £1000 or £2000 a year. And if they take my salaries of £1300 and £300, they cannot but give me something out of them. I have been rash in anticipating funds to buy land, but then I made from £5000 to £10,000 year, and land was my temptation. I think nobody can lose a penny—that is one comfort. Men will think pride has had a fall. Let them indulge their own pride in thinking that my fall makes them higher, or seems so at least. I have the satisfaction to recollect that my prosperity has been of advantage to many, and that some at least will forgive my transient wealth on account of the innocence of my intentions, and my real wish to do good to the poor. This news will make sad hearts at Darnick, and in the cottages of Abbotsford, which I do not nourish the least hope of preserving. It has been my Delilah, and so I have often termed it; and now the recollection of the extensive woods I planted, and the walks I have formed, from which strangers must derive both the pleasure and profit, will excite feelings likely to sober my gayest moments. I have half resolved never to see the place again. How could I tread my hall with such a diminished crest? How live a poor indebted man where I was once the wealthy the honoured? My children are provided; thank God for that. I was to have gone there on Saturday in joy and prosperity to receive my friends. My dogs will wait for me in vain. It is foolish

The Golden Calf

—but the thoughts of parting from these dumb creatures have moved me more than any of the painful reflections I have put down. Poor things, I must get them kind masters; there may be yet those who loving me may love my dog because it has been mine. I must end this, or I shall lose the tone of mind with which men should meet distress.

I find my dogs' feet on my knees. I hear them whining and seeking me everywhere—this is nonsense, but it is what they would do could they know how things are. Poor Will Laidlaw! poor Tom Purdie! this will be news to ring your heart, and many a poor fellow's besides to whom my prosperity was daily bread. SIR WALTER SCOTT, 18 December 1825: *Journal* (1890), i, 52–3.

I have had visits from all the monied people, offering their purses —and those who are creditors sending their managers and creditors to assure me of their joining in and adopting any measures I may propose. I am glad of this for their sake, and for my own —for although I shall not desire to steer, yet I am the only person that can *cann*, as Lieutenant Hatchway says, to any good purpose. A very odd anonymous offer I had of £30,000 which I rejected, as I did every other. Unless I die, I shall beat up against this foul weather. A penny I will not borrow from anyone. Since my creditors are content to be patient, I have the means of righting them perfectly, and the confidence to employ them. I would have given a good deal to have avoided the *coup d'éclat*; but that having taken place, I would not give sixpence for any other results. I fear you will think I am writing in the heat of excited resistance to bad fortune. My dear Lockhart, I am as calm and temperate as you ever saw me, and working at *Woodstock* like a very tiger. I am grieved for Lady Scott and Anne, who cannot conceive adversity can have the better of them, even for a moment. If it teaches a little of the frugality which I never had the heart to enforce when money was plenty, and it seemed cruel to interrupt the enjoyment of it in the way they liked best, it will be well. SIR WALTER SCOTT at Edinburgh to J. G. LOCKHART, 20 January 1826: *Life* (1837–8), 218.

Instead of marvelling, with Johnson, how anything but profit should incite men to literary labour, I am rather surprised that mere emolument should induce them to labour so well. THOMAS GREEN, 14 September 1796: *Extracts from the Diary of a Lover of Literature* (1810).

I guess that I shall clear between two and three hundred pounds by my authorship; with that sum I intend, so far as I may be said to have any intention, to return to my old acquaintance, the plough, and, if I can meet with a lease by which I can live, to commence Farmer.—I do not intend to give up Poetry; being bred to labour, secures me independence, and the Muses are my chief, sometimes have been my only enjoyment.—If my practice second my resolution, I shall have principally at heart the serious business of life; but while following my plough, or building up my shocks, I shall cast a leisure glance to that dear, that only feature of my character which gave me the notice of Caledonia, and the patronage of a Wallace. ROBERT BURNS at Edinburgh to MRS. DUNLOP, 22 March 1787: *Letters* (1931), i, 81.

His [Edward Lear's] whole life seems to have been an artistic *Wanderjahr*, and perhaps it is owing to this that he has preserved such perfect freshness of feeling, his humour and gaiety, his love of children and nonsense. He is delighted just now with the sale of his Christmas book, some 3000 copies have gone, but his profits are only some £60. Still he is happy, and every day he comes in he chats and tells me of some new idea for a picture, or of some change in a picture we have seen. Surely nothing is so perfect, so self-sufficing as the artist-life. J. R. GREEN at San Remo to MISS VON GLEHN, 10 March 1871: *Letters* (1901), 290–1.

The struggle of life gets harder as one goes on, instead of being lightened. It would be a strange sensation to look forward with easy confidence for a year or two. GEORGE GISSING to his brother ALGERNON, 12 July 1893: *Letters* (1926), 334.

A sufficient income is indispensable to the practice of **virtue;** and the man who will let any unselfish consideration **stand between** him and its attainment is a weakling, a dupe and a predestined slave. BERNARD SHAW, *The Irrational Knot*, Pref. (1905), xix.

Net earnings received during 1913. *Books* £6,924. 18s. 1d. *Plays* £8,524. 19s. 0d. Total £15,449. 17s. 1d. The gross sum (before paying agents' fees) was £17,166. 10s. 1d. In addition, interest on investments, £405. 11s. 3d. All this handsomely beats last year's record. ARNOLD BENNETT, *Journals* (1932), ii, 76.

It is a fine world and I wish I knew how to make £200 a year in it. EDWARD THOMAS to GORDON BOTTOMLEY, 16 June 1915: *Life and Letters* (1939), 328.

XXVII

SAY IT WITH BOOKS

The best part of every author is in general to be found in his book. Dr. Johnson, *Biographia*, Anna Seward (1799), 600.

By this messenger, on this good day, I commend the enclosed *Holy Hymns* and *Sonnets* (which for the matter, not the workmanship, have yet escaped the fire) to your judgment, and to your protection too, if you think them worthy of it; and I have appointed this enclosed *Sonnet* to usher them to your happy hand. John Donne at Mitcham to the Lady Magdalen Herbert. 11 July 1607: 'George Herbert', *Lives*, Izaak Walton (1675), 268–9.

Comes Mr. Creed, who brought me some books from Holland with him, well bound and good books, which I thought he did intend to give me, but I found that I must pay him. Samuel Pepys, 5 October 1660: *Diary* (1893), i, 255.

The Stanzas [*Elegy in a Country Churchyard*] which I now enclose to you have had the misfortune, by Mr. Walpole's fault, to be made still more public, for which they certainly were never meant; but it is too late to complain. They have been so applauded, it is quite a shame to repeat it. I mean not to be modest; but I mean it is a shame for those who have said such superlative Things about them, that I cannot repeat them. I should have been glad that you and two or three more People had liked them, which would have satisfied my ambition on this head amply. Thomas Gray to Dr. Warton, 17 December 1750: *Correspondence* (1935), i, 335.

Say it with Books

I have received the *Castle of Otranto*, and return you my thanks for it. It engages our attention here, makes some of us cry a little, and all in general afraid to go to bed o' nights. THOMAS GRAY at Cambridge to HORACE WALPOLE, 30 December 1764: *Ib.* ii, 855.

I want to send you something from the Strawberry press; tell me how I shall convey it; it is nothing less than the most curious book that ever set its foot into the world. I expect to hear you scream hither: if you don't I shall be disappointed, for I have kept it as a most profound secret from you, till I was ready to surprise you with it; I knew your impatience, and would not let you have it piecemeal. It is the Life of the great philosopher, Lord Herbert, written by himself. . . . I found it a year ago at Lady Hertford's, to whom Lady Powis had lent it. I took it up, and soon threw it down again, as the dullest thing I ever saw. She persuaded me to take it home. My Lady Waldegrave was here in all her grief; Gray and I read it to amuse her. We could not get on for laughing and screaming. I begged to have it to print: Lord Powis, sensible of the extravagance, refused—I insisted—he persisted. I told my Lady Hertford, it was no matter, I would print it, I was determined. I sat down and wrote a flattering dedication to Lord Powis, which I knew he would swallow: he did, and gave up his ancestor. But this was not enough; I was resolved the world should not think I admired it seriously, though there are really fine passages in it, and good sense too: I drew up an equivocal preface, in which you will discover my opinion, and sent it with the dedication. The Earl gulped down the one under the palliative of the other, and here you will have it all. Pray take notice of the pedigree, of which I am exceedingly proud; observe how I have clearly arranged so involved a descent; one may boast of one's heraldry. I shall send you, too, Lady Temple's Poems. Pray keep both under lock and key, for there are but two hundred copies of Lord Herbert, and but one hundred of the Poems suffered to be printed. HORACE WALPOLE at Strawberry Hill to GEORGE MONTAGU, 16 July 1764: *Letters* (1891), iv, 252-3.

Say it with Books

I beg your acceptance of my *Account of Corsica*, to which you have a better claim than you perhaps imagine, as I dare say you have forgotten what you said to me at Paris when I had the honour of giving you a few anecdotes of what I had just come from seeing among the brave islanders. In short, Sir, your telling me that I ought to publish something in order to show the Corsicans in a proper light, was my first incitement to undertake the work which has now made its appearance. JAMES BOSWELL to HORACE WALPOLE, 28 February 1768, *Letters* (1925), i, 146–7.

Many years ago, when I used to read in the library of your College, I promised to recompense the College for that permission by adding to their books a Baskerville *Virgil*. I have now sent it, and desire you to reposit it on the shelves in my name. DR. JOHNSON to THOMAS WARTON, Trinity College, Cambridge 31 May 1769: *Boswell's Life of Johnson* (1887), ii, 67.

I send you *Table Talk*. It is a medley of many things, some that may be useful, and some that, for aught I know, may be very diverting. I am merry that I may decoy people into my company, and grave that they may be the better for it. Now and then I put on the garb of a philosopher, and take the opportunity that disguise procures me, to drop a word in favour of religion. In short, there is some froth, and here and there a bit of sweet-meat, which seems to entitle it justly to the name of a certain dish the ladies call a trifle. WILLIAM COWPER to the REV. JOHN NEWTON, 18 February 1781: *Letters* (1912), i, 102–3.

I have ten thousand apologies to make, for not having long ago returned you my best thanks for the very agreeable present you made me of the three last volumes of your *History*. I cannot express to you the pleasure it gives me to find, that by the universal assent of every man of taste and learning, whom I either know or correspond with, it sets you at the very head of the whole literary tribe at present existing in Europe. ADAM SMITH to EDWARD GIBBON, 10 December 1788: *The Autobiography and Correspondence of Edward Gibbon* (1869), 345.

Say it with Books

Lord Oxford has presented me with Bishop Wilson's edition of the *Bible*, in three vols. quarto, superbly bound in morocco, (Oh! that he would himself study this blessed book), to which in a most flattering inscription . . . he attributes my having done far more good than is true. Alas! when I receive these undue compliments, I am ready to answer with my old friend Johnson—'Sir, I am a miserable sinner.' HANNAH MORE to her Sister, 1795: *Memoirs* (1835), ii, 435.

This comes to entreat your obliging acceptance of a certain square volume called *The Lady of the Lake*. I am now enabled to send her to my friends as the Romans of yore used to lend their wives, and greatly it is to my own relief; for never was man more bored of his wife (and that's a bold word) than I am of the said Lady. I hope, however, you will find her agreeable company for an evening or two—and I don't think you will be disposed greatly to abuse me for using your cover for another copy to be left at Hatchard's for Canning, who did me the honour to wish to see it as soon as possible. SIR WALTER SCOTT to JOHN WILSON CROKER, 3 May 1810: *The Croker Papers* (1884).

May I request your Lordship to accept a copy of the thing (i.e. *Childe Harold*, Cantos 1 and 2) which accompanies this note? . . . If I were not perfectly convinced that any thing I may have formerly uttered in the boyish rashness of my misplaced resentment had made as little impression as it deserved to make, I should hardly have the confidence—perhaps your Lordship may give it a stronger and more appropriate appellation—to send you a quarto of the same scribbler. But your Lordship, I am sorry to observe, is troubled with the gout; if my book can produce a *laugh* against itself or the author, it will be of some service. If it can set you to *sleep*, the benefit will be yet greater; and as some facetious personage observed half a century ago, that 'poetry is a mere drug', I offer you mine as a humble assistant to the *eau médicinale*. LORD BYRON to LORD HOLLAND, 5 March 1812: *Letters and Journals* (1898), ii, 106.

Say it with Books

Thanks for the books you have given me and for all the books you mean to give me. I will bind up the *Political Sonnets* and *Ode* according to your suggestion. I have not bound the poems yet. I wait till people have done borrowing them. I think I shall get a chain, and chain them to my shelves, More Bodleiano, and people may come and read them at chain's length. For of those who borrow, some read slow, some mean to read but don't read, and some neither read nor mean to read, but borrow to leave you an opinion of their sagacity. I must do my money-borrowing friends the justice to say that there is nothing of this caprice or wantonness of alienation in them. When they borrow my money they never fail to make use of it. CHARLES LAMB to WILLIAM WORDSWORTH, 9 April 1816: *Letters* (1905), i, 484.

I send you the elegy [*Adonais*] on poor Keats—and I wish it were better worth your acceptance. You will see, by the preface, that it was written before I could obtain any particular account of his last moments; all that I still know was communicated to me by a friend who had derived his information from Colonel Finch; I have ventured to express, as I felt, the respect and admiration which *your* conduct towards him demands. P. B. SHELLEY at Pisa to JOSEPH SEVERN, 29 November 1821: *Letters* (1915), ii, 922.

One day, in the snowy winter of 1852, I met Thackeray sturdily ploughing his way down Beacon Street [Boston, Mass.] with a copy of *Henry Esmond* (the English edition then just issued) under his arm. Seeing me some way off, he held aloft the volumes and began to shout in great glee. When I came up to him he cried out, 'Here is the *very* best I can do, and I am carrying it to Prescott as a reward of merit for having given me my first dinner in America. I stand by this book, and am willing to leave it, when I go, as my card.' JAMES T. FIELDS, *Yesterdays with Authors* (1872), 17.

Upon my return from a little excursion to the country, I found your splendid work [*Bibliographical Tour*], which I think one of the most handsome that ever came from the British Press—and return you my best thanks for placing it in my possession as a mark of your regard. You have contrived to strew flowers over a path which, in other hands, would have proved a very dull one; and all *Bibliomanes* must remember you long, as he who first united their antiquarian details with good-humoured raillery and cheerfulness. I am planning a room at Abbotsford to be built next year for my books, and I will take care that your valued gift holds a place upon my future shelves, as much honoured as its worth deserves, and for that purpose an ingenious artist of Edinburgh has promised to give your Tour an envelope worthy of the contents. You see from all this, that I have no idea of suffering these splendid volumes to travel any farther in quest of the nameless and unknown Author of Waverley. As I have met with some inconvenience in consequence of public opinion having *inaccurately* identified me with this gentleman, I think I am fairly enabled to indemnify myself by *intercepting this valuable testimony of your regard*. SIR WALTER SCOTT to THOMAS FROGNALL DIBDIN, 13 June 1821: *Dibdin: Literary Reminiscences* (1836), ii, 675.

I have to thank you and Moxon for a delightful Vol: your last, I hope not, of *Elia*. I have read it all, except some of the popular fallacies which I reserve not to get through my Cake all at once. The Book has much pleased the whole of my family, viz. my Wife, Daughter, Miss Hutchinson, and my poor dear Sister, on her sick bed . . . I am not sure but I like Old China and The Wedding as well as any of the Essays.—I read Love me and love my Dog to my poor Sister this morning, while I was rubbing her legs at the same time.—She was much pleased. . . . WILLIAM WORDSWORTH to CHARLES LAMB, 17 May 1833: *Letters of William and Dorothy Wordsworth, The Later Years* (1939), ii, 656–7.

Poor Teufelsdröckh!—Creature of mischance, miscalculation, and thousand-fold obstruction! Here nevertheless he is [in *Sartor Resartus*], as you see; has struggled across the Stygian marshes, and now, as a stitched pamphlet 'for Friends', cannot be burnt or lost before his time. I send you one copy for your own behoof; three others you yourself can perhaps find fit readers for; as you spoke in the plural number, I thought there might be three; more would rather surprise me. From the British side of the water I have met simply *not* one intelligent response. THOMAS CARLYLE to RALPH WALDO EMERSON, 12 August 1834: *Correspondence of Carlyle and Emerson 1834–1872* (1883), i, 20.

About a month ago there went a copy of a Book called *French Revolution*, with your address on it. . . . I wish you a happy reading of it therefore; it is the only copy of my sending that has crossed the water Ill printed, (there are many errors, one or two gross ones), ill written, ill thought! But in fine it *is* off my hands: that is a fact worth all others. As to its reception here or elsewhere, I anticipate nothing or little. Gabble, gabble, the astonishment of the dull public brain is likely to be considerable, and its ejaculations unedifying. We will let it go its way. Beat this thing, I say always, under thy dull hoofs, O dull Public! trample it and tumble it into all sinks and kennels; if thou canst kill it, kill it in God's name: if thou canst not kill it, why then thou wilt not. THOMAS CARLYLE to RALPH WALDO EMERSON, 1 June 1837: *Ib.*, i, 124.

My Friend, I *thank* you for this Volume [*Essays*] of yours; not for the copy alone which you sent to me, but for writing and printing such a Book. *Euge!* say I, from afar. The voice of one crying in the desert:—it is once more the voice of a *man*. Ah me! I feel as if in the wide world there were still but this one voice that responded intelligently to my own; as if the rest were all hearsays, melodious or unmelodious echoes; as if this alone were true and alive. My blessing on you, good Ralph Waldo! I read the Book all yesterday. . . . It has rebuked me, it has aroused and comforted me. Objections of all kind I might make, how many objections to superficies and detail, to a dialect of thought and speech as yet imperfect enough, a hundred-fold too narrow for the Infinitude it strives to speak: but what were all that, It *is* an Infinitude, the real vision and belief of one, seen face to face, a 'voice of the heart of Nature' is here once more. This is the one fact for me, which absorbs all others whatsoever. Persist, persist; you have much to say and do. THOMAS CARLYLE TO RALPH WALDO EMERSON, 8 May 1841: *Ib.*, i, 325.

For the love I bear you as a man whose writings enlist my whole heart and nature in admiration of their Truth and Beauty, set these books upon your shelves; believing that you have no more earnest and sincere homage than mine. CHARLES DICKENS with a copy of his *Works* to ALFRED TENNYSON, 10 March 1843: *Tennyson: a Memoir* (1897), i, 219.

It is now a great many weeks that I have been your debtor for a book which in various senses was very welcome to me. *Alton Locke* arrived in Annandale, by post, from my wife, early in September, and was swiftly read by me, under the bright sunshine, by the sound of rushing brooks and other rural accompaniments. I believe the book is still doing duty in those parts; for I had to leave it behind me on loan, to satisfy the public demand. Forgive me, that I have not, even by a word, thanked you for this favour. THOMAS CARLYLE TO CHARLES KINGSLEY, 31 October 1850: *Charles Kingsley* (1877), i, 244.

I am not blind to the worth of the wonderful gift of *Leaves of Grass*. I find it the most extraordinary piece of wit and wisdom that America has yet contributed. I am very happy in reading it, as great power makes us happy. It meets the demand I am always making of what seemed the sterile and stringy nature, as if too much handiwork, or too much lymph in the temperament, were making our western wits fat and mean. I give you joy of your free and brave thought. I have great joy in it. I find incomparable things said incomparably well, as they must be. I find the courage of treatment that so delights us, and which large perception only can inspire. I greet you at the beginning of a great career, which yet must have had a long preground somewhere, for such a start. I rubbed my eyes a little, to see if this sunbeam were no illusion; but the solid sense of the book is a sober certainty. It has the best merits, namely, of fortifying and encouraging. I did not know until I last night saw the book advertised in a newspaper that I could trust the name as real and available for a post office. I wish to see my benefactor, and have felt much like striking my tasks and visiting New York to pay you my respects. R. W. EMERSON to WALT WHITMAN, 21 July 1855.

I am taking the opportunity to send you the last book I have written [*Grandmother's Story*]. I doubt whether you will care to read it; I doubt whether you will like it, if you do. I wish that, if it reaches you in safety, you could sit down at once and acknowledge its receipt. You may add, if you choose, that you 'hope in the near future to have the pleasure of reading it',—the 'near future' standing for the Greek Kalends. This I say in all sincerity. A volume like this carries dismay with it, when the recipient supposes he is expected to reach it from title to Finis, and it is only as a friendly token that I send it. OLIVER WENDELL HOLMES to MR. IRELAND, 15 January 1885: *Life* (1896), ii, 292–3.

I am grateful for the gift of the little book [*The Spirit of Place*]. I knew the contents, and I read them again with the first freshness, the delight in the delicacy of the touch that can be so firm. It is the style of a queenly lady walking without her robes. GEORGE MEREDITH to ALICE MEYNELL, 20 January 1899: *Letters* (1912), ii, 500–1.

XXVIII

PLAGUE OF PLAGIARY

They knew 'e stole; 'e knew they knowed.
They didn't tell, nor make a fuss,
But winked at 'Omer down the road,
An' e' winked back—the same as us!
Rudyard Kipling, *The Seven Seas* (1899), 162.

A mutual commerce makes poetry flourish; but then poets, like merchants, should repay with something of their own what they take from others; not, like pirates, make prize of all they meet. ALEXANDER POPE to W. WALSH, 2 July 1706: *Works* (1753), vii, 45.

I think none but Pikes and Poets prey upon their kind. WILLIAM WARBURTON to DAVID GARRICK, 22 April 1762: *A Bookman's Budget*, (1917), Austin Dobson, 159.

All things which come to much, whether they be books, buildings, pictures, music, or living beings, are suggested by others of their own kind. It is always the most successful, like Handel and Shakespeare, who owe most to their forerunners, in spite of the modifications with which their works descend. SAMUEL BUTLER, *Alps and Sanctuaries* (1881), 87–8.

With the riches of El Dorado lying about him, he [Coleridge] would condescend to filch a handful of gold from any man whose purse he fancied, and in fact reproduced in a new form, applying itself to intellectual wealth, that maniacal propensity which is sometimes well known to attack enormous proprietors and millionaires for acts of petty larceny. THOMAS DE QUINCEY, *Works* (1889), ii, 146–7.

Plague of Plagiary

Hume wrote, and the French imitated him, and we the French, and the French us; and so philosophisms fly to and fro, in series of imitated imitations—shadows of shadows of shadows of a farthing-candle placed between two looking-glasses. S. T. COLERIDGE to ROBERT SOUTHEY, 15 October 1799: *Letters* (1895), i, 307.

I am taxed with being a plagiarist, when I am least conscious of being one; but I am not very scrupulous, I own, when I have a good idea, how I came into possession of it. LORD BYRON, *Conversations*, Medwin (1824), 140.

We are still expecting the Works of Lord Chesterfield and Lord Lyttelton—on my part with no manner of impatience; one was an ape of the French, the other of the Greeks, and I like neither secondhand pertness nor solemnity. HORACE WALPOLE to the REV. WILLIAM MASON, 14 February 1774: *Letters* (1891), vi, 59.

Wordsworth says Ben Jonson was a great plagiarist from the ancients. HENRY CRABB ROBINSON, 20 January 1839: *Diary* (1872), ii, 214.

I do not put Southey on a level with Sterne, who could hardly be acquitted of dishonest plagiary—(tho' he could hardly expect to steal undetected from so common a book as Burton's *Anatomy of Melancholy*—and the very humour, and originality of Walter Shandy is to talk out of books) but in managing the mixture of monodram and story polylogue, in passing by chromatic slides and graduated toning from the purely humorous to the humorous pathetic—(not jerking, like Byron, from morbid woe—to mirthless laughter) I cannot help thinking the libertine parson greatly superiour to the virtuous layman. HARTLEY COLERIDGE, 1847: *Letters* (1936), 295.

Plagiarists are always suspicious of being stolen from,—as pickpockets are observed commonly to walk with their hands in their breeches' pockets. S. T. COLERIDGE, 4 January 1823: *Table Talk* (1874), 11.

EPILOGUE

And when like her, O Saki, you shall pass
Among the guests star-scattered in the grass
And in thy joyous errand reach the spot
Where I made one turn down an empty glass!
　　　Edward FitzGerald, *Omar Khayyam* (1859).

It is a good thing when these authors die for then one gets their works
and is done with them. Lord Melbourne; Lord David Cecil, *The*
Young Melbourne (1939), 253.

LAURENCE STERNE. The celebrated writer Sterne, after being
long the idol of this town, died in a mean lodging without a single
friend who felt interest in his fate, except Becket, his bookseller,
who was the only person that attended his interment. He was
buried in a graveyard near Tyburn, belonging to the parish of
Marylebone, and the corpse being marked by some of the *resurrection men* (as they are called), was taken up soon afterward and
carried to an anatomy professor of Cambridge. A gentleman who
was present at the dissection told me, he recognized Sterne's face
the moment he saw the body. EDMOND MALONE, Prior (1860),
373–4.

DR. JOHNSON. I trust, I shall not be accused of affectation, when
I declare, that I find myself unable to express all that I felt upon
the loss of such a 'Guide, Philosopher, and Friend'. I shall,
therefore, not say one word of my own, but adopt those of an
eminent friend, which he uttered with an abrupt felicity, superior
to all studied compositions:—'He has made a chasm, which not
only nothing can fill up, but which nothing has a tendency to fill

up.—Johnson is dead. Let us go to the next best:—there is nobody;—no man can be said to put you in mind of Johnson.' JAMES BOSWELL, *Life of Johnson* (1887), iv, 420–1.

JAMES BOSWELL. I have now the painful task of informing you that my dear brother expired this morning at two o'clock: we have both lost a kind, affectionate friend, and I shall never have such another. T. D. BOSWELL to REV. W. J. TEMPLE, 19 May 1795: *Letters of James Boswell to the Rev. W. J. Temple* (1857), 357.

OLIVER GOLDSMITH. The republic of Parnassus has lost a member; Dr. Goldsmith is dead of a purple fever, and I think might have been saved if he had continued James's powder, which had had much effect, but his physician interposed. His numerous friends neglected him shamefully at last, as if they had no business with him when it was too serious to laugh. He had lately written Epitaphs for them all, some of which hurt, and perhaps made them not sorry that his own was the first necessary. The poor soul had sometimes parts, though never common sense. HORACE WALPOLE at Strawberry Hill to the REV. WILLIAM MASON, 7 April 1774: *Letters* (1891), vi, 72.

SIR WALTER SCOTT. Poor Scott is gone; and I can not be sorry for it. A powerful mind in ruins is the most heart-breaking thing which it is possible to conceive. T. B. MACAULAY to his sister HANNAH, 25 September 1832: *Life* (1876), i, 275.

CHARLES LAMB. Have newspapers or letters recorded the death of Charles Lamb? 'There's a great spirit gone' a prophet's mantle not soon to be caught not lightly worn again. He wrought as effectually in restoring a larger and braver spirit of feeling and of criticism in England as Wordsworth himself. He should have an Epitaph over him like 'O rare Ben Jonson'. W. B. DONNE to R. C. TRENCH, February 1835: *W. B. Donne and his Friends* (1905), 18.

EDWARD GIBBON. Heard of the death of Mr. Gibbon the historian the calumniator of the despised Nazarene, the derider of

Epilogue

Christianity. Awful dispensation! He too was my acquaintance. Lord, I bless thee, considering how much infidel acquaintance I have had, that my soul never came into their secret. How many souls have his writings polluted. Lord, preserve others from their contagion. HANNAH MORE, 19 January 1794: *Memoirs* (1835), ii, 412.

JOHN KEATS. Is it true, what Shelley writes me, that poor John Keats died at Rome of the *Quarterly Review*? I am very sorry for it . . . I know, by experience, that a savage review is Hemlock to a sucking author; and the one on me (which produced the *English Bards, etc.*) knocked me down—but I got up again. Instead of bursting a blood-vessel, I drank three bottles of claret, and began an answer, finding that there was nothing in the Article for which I could lawfully knock Jeffrey on the head, in an honourable way. However, I would not be the person who wrote the homicidal article, for all the honour and glory in the World, though I by no means approve of the School of Scribbling which it treats upon. LORD BYRON to JOHN MURRAY, 26 April 1821: *Letters and Journals* (1901), v, 269–70.

SHELLEY. We have been burning the bodies of Shelley and Williams on the sea-shore, to render them fit for removal and regular interment. You can have no idea what an extraordinary effect such a funeral pile has, on a desolate shore, with mountains in the background and the sea before, and the singular appearance the salt and frankincense gave to the flame. All of Shelley was consumed, except his heart, which would not take the flame, and is now preserved in spirits of wine. . . . It was not a Bible that was found in Shelley's pocket, but John Keats' poems. However, it would not have been strange, for he was a great admirer of Scripture as a composition. LORD BYRON at Pisa to THOMAS MOORE, 27 August 1822: *Ib.*, vi, 108–10.

THOMAS CARLYLE. The death of Carlyle is no sorrow to me. It is, I believe, not an end—but a beginning of his real life. Nay, perhaps also of mine. My remorse, every day he lived, for having

Epilogue

not enough loved him in the days gone by, is not greater now, but less, in the hope that he knows what I am feeling about him at this—and all other—moments. JOHN RUSKIN to MARY GLADSTONE, 15 February 1881: *Letters to M. G. and H. G.* (1903), 65–6.

ROBERT BROWNING. Yesterday I was at Browning's funeral. I thought in the Abbey of what Juvenal walking with Umbritius says of the old fountain, 'Quanto prestantius esset numen aquae etc.', but I applied it to the grave. Sweeter the green grass turf than Abbey pavements. But the noble poet was deeply with his fellows, and it may be appropriate that he should lie among them, in hearing of the roar. GEORGE MEREDITH to FREDERICK GREENWOOD, 1 January 1890: *Letters* (1912), ii, 433.

CHARLES DICKENS. The morning of the funeral was very fine. Eleanor and I left 91, Victoria Street at twenty minutes past nine. As we reached the entrance to Dean's Yard, and as St. Stephen's clock chimed the half-hour, a hearse and mourning coaches swept round the Broad Sanctuary; they seemed to bring with them an unusual stillness; then, as they drove under the archway into Dean's Yard, the great bell began to toll. There was hardly a creature in the street or in the Abbey, that 'Temple of Silence and Reconciliation', and no one but ourselves knew whose funeral had passed, or for whom the big bell was tolling. Later in the day we saw the coffin in the grave, covered with flowers, and then there was an immense crowd of excited and sympathetic mourners. FREDERICK LOCKER-LAMPSON, *My Confidences* (1896), 328.

SWINBURNE. The death of Swinburne makes me feel very lonely. It is now three or four years ago since I stood by the empty space reserved for him amongst his ancestors, the naval branch of the family, in Bonchurch churchyard. The great rocks towered above, the deep blue sea murmured far below. It was a lovely, calm summer day. He had great faults, but there was something in him which made me deny faults. Never again will Nature be voiced as she was by him. I can imagine her mourning in solitude that she has lost the interpreter of her thoughts to man. WILLIAM HALE WHITE (Mark Rutherford), 18 April 1909: *The Groombridge Diary* (1925), 157–8.

TENNYSON. At Tennyson's funeral in Westminster Abbey. The music was sweet and impressive, but as a funeral the scene was less penetrating than a plain country interment would have been. Lunched afterwards at the National Liberal Club with E. Gosse, Austin Dobson, Theodore Watts, and William Watson. THOMAS HARDY, 12 October 1892: *Later Years of Hardy* (1930), 13.

BIBLIOGRAPHY

Books from which Quotations have been made

Letters of Matthew Arnold. G. W. E. Russell (1895).

Letters of Matthew Arnold to Arthur Hugh Clough. Howard Foster Lowry (1932).

Brief Lives, chiefly of Contemporaries, set down by John Aubrey, between the Years 1669 and 1696. Andrew Clark (1898).

The Scandal and Credulities of John Aubrey. John Collier (1931).

Northanger Abbey. Jane Austen (1818).

Memoir of Jane Austen. J. E. Austen Leigh (1871).

Letters of Jane Austen. Lord Brabourne (1884).

Lord Beaconsfield's Correspondence with his Sister, 1832–1852. (1886.)

Letters and Diaries. John Bailey. Edited by his Wife (1935).

Life and Writings of James Beattie. Sir William Forbes (1824).

The Journals of Arnold Bennett. Sir Newman Flower (1932).

Arnold Bennett: a Portrait done at Home together with 170 Letters from A. B. Dorothy Cheston Bennett (1935).

Arnold Bennett's Letters to his Nephew. R. Bennett (1935).

Life of William Blake with Selections from his Poems and other Writings. Alexander Gilchrist (1863).

My Diaries, being a Personal Narrative of Events, 1888–1914. Wilfrid Scawen Blunt, with a Foreword by Lady Gregory (1910).

Letters of James Boswell to the Rev. W. J. Temple (1857).

Letters of James Boswell. Chauncy Brewster Tinker (1925).

Boswelliana, The Common-place Book of James Boswell (1874).

Boswell's Life of Johnson including Boswell's Journal of a Tour in the Hebrides and Johnson's Diary of a Journey into North Wales. George Birkbeck Hill, D.C.L. (1887).

Bibliography

Gastronomy as a Fine Art. A Translation of the 'Physiologie du Goût' of Brillat-Savarin. By R. E. Anderson, M.A. (1876).

Mrs. Brookfield and her Circle. Charles and Frances Brookfield (1905).

Life of Charlotte Brontë. Mrs. Gaskell (1856).

Letters of Dr. John Brown. John Brown and D. W. Forrest, D.D. (1907).

Letters of Thomas Edward Brown. Sidney T. Irwin (1900).

Letters of Elizabeth Barrett Browning to Richard Hengist Horne. Mayer (1877).

Letters of Elizabeth Barrett Browning. Frederick G. Kenyon (1897).

Men and Women. Robert Browning (1855).

Memorials of Edward Burne-Jones. G. B.-J. (1904).

Early Diaries of Frances Burney, 1768–1778. Annie Raine Ellis (1913).

Letters of Robert Burns. J. De Lancey Ferguson (1931).

The Anatomy of Melancholy. Robert Burton (1638).

Alps and Sanctuaries of Piedmont and Canton Ticino. Samuel Butler (1881).

Letters between Samuel Butler and Miss E. M. A. Savage, 1871–1885. Geoffrey Keynes and Brian Hill (1935).

Journal of the Conversation of Lord Byron noted during a Residence with his Lordship at Pisa in the Years 1821 and 1822. Thomas Medwin (1824).

Letters and Journals of Lord Byron. Rowland E. Prothero (1898–1901).

Jane Welsh Carlyle: Letters to Her Family, 1839–1863. Leonard Huxley (1924).

New Letters and Memorials of Jane Welsh Carlyle. Sir James Crichton Browne (1903).

Letters and Memorials of Jane Welsh Carlyle prepared for publication by Thomas Carlyle. James Anthony Froude (1883).

Reminiscences of Thomas Carlyle. Edited by James Anthony Froude (1881).

Early Letters of Thomas Carlyle. Charles Eliot Norton (1886).

Bibliography

Correspondence of Thomas Carlyle and Ralph Waldo Emerson. Charles Eliot Norton (1883).

New Letters of Thomas Carlyle. Alexander Carlyle (1904).

Autobiography. G. K. Chesterton (1937).

Letters and Remains of Arthur Hugh Clough. (1865.)

Rural Rides. William Cobbett, Edited by Edward Thomas (1912).

'*Kubla Khan*'. S. T. Coleridge, *Poems* (1894).

Specimens of the Table Talk of Samuel Taylor Coleridge. H. N. Coleridge (1874).

Letters of Samuel Taylor Coleridge. Ernest Hartley Coleridge (1895).

Letters of Hartley Coleridge. G. E. and E. L. Griggs (1936).

Letters from Conrad: 1895 to 1924. Edward Garnett (1928).

Extracts from the Letters and Journals of William Cory, author of '*Ionica*'. Francis Warre Cornish (1897).

Ionicus. Reginald, Viscount Esher (1923).

The Task. William Cowper (1785).

Letters of William Cowper. J. G. Frazer (1912).

The Croker Papers: Correspondence and Diaries of John Wilson Croker, LL.D., F.R.S. Louis J. Jennings (1884).

The Beautiful Teetotaller. T. W. H. Crosland (1905).

Literary Reminiscences. Thomas Frognall Dibdin (1836).

Letters of Charles Dickens. By his Sister-in-law and his eldest Daughter (1880).

Goldsworthy Lowes Dickinson. E. M. Forster (1934).

Disraeli, Benjamin. See under Beaconsfield.

A Bookman's Budget. Austin Dobson (1917).

William Bodham Donne and his Friends. By Catherine B. Johnson (1905).

Fragments from Old Letters. E. D. [Edward Dowden] to E. D. W. 1869–1892. (1914).

Up the Country: Letters written to her Sister from the Upper Provinces of India. Emily Eden (1866). Thompson (1937).

Bibliography

Miss Eden's Letters. Violet Dickinson (1919).

Journals of Ralph Waldo Emerson. Edward Waldo Emerson and Waldo Emerson Forbes (1914).

Original Letters of Eminent Literary Men of the Sixteenth, Seventeenth and Eighteenth Centuries. Sir Henry Ellis (1843).

Diary of John Evelyn. Austin Dobson (1906).

Juliana Horatia Ewing and Her Books. Horatia K. F. Eden (1896).

Florence Farr, Bernard Shaw and W. B. Yeats. Clifford Bax (1941).

Yesterdays with Authors. James T. Fields (1872).

Omar Khayyam. Edward FitzGerald (1859).

Letters and Literary Remains of Edward FitzGerald. William Aldis Wright (1889).

Some New Letters of Edward FitzGerald, by F. R. Barton, C.M.G., with a Foreword by Viscount Grey of Fallodon, K.G. (1923).

A FitzGerald Friendship; being hitherto Unpublished Letters from Edward FitzGerald to William Bodham Donne. Mrs. Catharine Bodham Johnson and Neilson Campbell Hannay, B.D., Ph.D. (1930).

Memories of Old Friends. Caroline Fox. H. N. Pym (1882).

Autobiography and Correspondence of Edward Gibbon. A. Murray (1869).

Retrospective Reviews. Richard le Gallienne (1896).

Travels in England. Richard le Gallienne (1900).

Life and Letters of John Gay. Lewis Melville (1921).

Anne Gilchrist: her Life and Writings. Herbert Harlakenden Gilchrist with a Prefatory Notice by William Michael Rossetti (1887).

Letters of George Gissing to Members of His Family. Algernon and Ellen Gissing (1926).

Collected Letters of Oliver Goldsmith. Katharine C. Balderston (1928).

The Letters of Thomas Gray. Duncan C. Tovey (1900).

Bibliography

Correspondence of Thomas Gray. Paget Toynbee and Leonard Whibley (1935).

Extracts from the Diary of a Lover of Literature. [Thomas Green.] (1810).

Letters of John Richard Green. Leslie Stephen (1901).

Kate Greenaway. M. H. Spielmann and E. S. Lazard (1905).

The Greville Memoirs: A Journal of the Reigns of King George IV and King William IV. Charles C. F. Greville. Edited by Henry Reeve (1875).

The Greville Memoirs: A Journal of the Reign of Queen Victoria from 1837 to 1852. Charles C. F. Greville. Edited by Henry Reeve (1885).

Later Years of Thomas Hardy. Florence Emily Hardy (1930).

Reminiscences of a Student's Life. Jane Ellen Harrison (1925).

Passages from the American Notebooks of Nathaniel Hawthorne (1868).

Pages from the Notebooks of Nathaniel Hawthorne. Moncure D. Conway (1869).

Life of Benjamin Robert Haydon from His Autobiography and Journals. Tom Taylor (1853).

A Selection from the Correspondence of Abraham Hayward, Q.C. Henry E. Carlisle (1886).

The Spirit of the Age. William Hazlitt (1825). *Complete Works.* P. P. Howe (1932).

Reliquae Hearnianae. Philip Bliss (1869).

Memorials of Mrs. Hemans with Illustration of her Literary Character from her Private Correspondence. Henry F. Chorley (1836).

Letters of George Birkbeck Hill. Arranged by his Daughter, Lucy Crump (1906).

George Herbert's Remains. (1848.)

The Autocrat of the Breakfast Table. Oliver Wendell Holmes (1858).

Life and Letters of Oliver Wendell Holmes. J. T. Morse (1896).

Gerard Manley Hopkins. G. F. Lahey, S.J. (1930).

Further Letters of Gerard Manley Hopkins. C. C. Abbott (1938).

Bibliography

A.E.H. Laurence Housman (1937).

Epistolae Ho-Elianae: Familiar Letters. James Howell (1737).

W. H. Hudson: a Portrait. Morley Roberts (1924).

Table Talk. Leigh Hunt (1851).

The Sketch Book. Washington Irving (1859).

Romance and Reality: Essays and Studies. Holbrook Jackson (1911).

French Poets and Novelists. Henry James (1878).

Partial Portraits. Henry James (1888).

The Rambler. Samuel Johnson (1751).

Lives of the English Poets. Samuel Johnson (1781).

Some Winchester Letters. Lionel Johnson (1919).

Timber or Discoveries Made upon Men and Matter: as they have Flowed out of his Daily Readings. Ben Jonson (1641).

The Letters of John Keats. H. Buxton Forman (1895).

Charles Kingsley: Letters and Memories. By His Wife (1877).

The Seven Seas. Rudyard Kipling (1899).

The Letters of Charles Lamb. E. V. Lucas (1905).

Miscellaneous Prose of Charles and Mary Lamb. E. V. Lucas (1912).

Walter Savage Landor—a Biography. John Forster (1876).

Letters and other Unpublished Writings of Walter Savage Landor. Stephen Wheeler (1897).

Letters of Walter Savage Landor: Private and Public Letters. Stephen Wheeler (1899).

Studies in Classic American Literature. D. H. Lawrence (1924).

The Letters of D. H. Lawrence. Aldous Huxley (1932).

Letters of Edward Lear. Lady Strachey (1907).

My Confidences: an Autobiographical Sketch addressed to my Descendants. Frederick Locker-Lampson. Edited by Augustine Birrell (1896).

Letters of James Russell Lowell. Charles Eliot Norton (1894).

Journals and Letters of Stephen MacKenna. E. R. Dodds (1936).

Life and Letters of Lord Macaulay. George Otto Trevelyan, M.P. (1876).

Life of Edmond Malone. Sir James Prior (1860).

Bibliography

Letters of Thomas Manning to Charles Lamb. G. A. Anderson (1925).

Letters of Katherine Mansfield. J. Middleton Murry (1928).

Harriet Martineau's Autobiography. Maria Weston Chapman (1877).

The Summing-Up. W. Somerset Maugham (1938).

The Young Melbourne. Lord David Cecil (1939).

Diana of the Crossways. George Meredith (1885).

Letters of George Meredith Collected and Edited by His Son. (1912.)

Monographs Personal and Social. Richard Monckton Milnes, Lord Houghton (1873).

The Life, Letters, and Friendships of Richard Monckton Milnes, First Lord Houghton. By T. Wemyss Reid (1891).

The Life of Mary Russell Mitford related in a Selection from her Letters to her Friends. A. G. L'Estrange (1870).

Letters of Mary Russell Mitford. R. Brimley Johnson (1925).

Letters and Works of Lady Mary Wortley Montagu. Lord Wharncliffe (1837).

Letters of Mrs. Elizabeth Montagu. Matthew Montagu (1809–13).

The Life of George Moore. Joseph Hone (1936).

Memoir of Mrs. Hannah More. William Roberts (1834).

Memoirs, Journals and Correspondence of Thomas Moore. Lord John Russell (1853–6).

Correspondence of John Lothrop Motley, D.C.L. George William Curtis (1889).

Letters of Charles Eliot Norton, with Biographical Comment by His Daughter and M. A. De Wolfe Howe (1913).

Memoirs and Correspondence of Coventry Patmore. Basil Champneys (1900).

Portrait of My Family. Derek Patmore (1935).

Modern Men and Manners. Hesketh Pearson (1921).

The Diary of Samuel Pepys, M.A., F.R.S. Edited with Additions by Henry B. Wheatley, F.S.A. (1893).

Autobiography, Letters and Literary Remains of Mrs. Piozzi (Thrale). Abraham Haywood (1861).

Bibliography

The Works of Alexander Pope, Esq. William Warburton (1753).

Anecdotes, Observations, and Characters, of Books and Men. Collected from the Conversation of Mr. Pope, and other Eminent Persons of his Time. By the Rev. Joseph Spence. Samuel Weller Singer (1858).

Frederick York Powell—a Life. Oliver Elton (1906).

Welsh Ambassadors: Powys Lives and Letters. Louis Marlow (1936).

Works of Thomas de Quincey. David Masson (1889).

Letters of Sir Walter Raleigh: 1879–1922. Lady Raleigh (1926).

Correspondence of Samuel Richardson to which is Prefaced a Biographical Account of that Author and Observations on his Writings. Anna Laetitia Barbauld (1804).

Self-Portrait taken from the Letters and Journals of Charles Ricketts, R.A. Collected and compiled by T. Sturge Moore. Edited by Cecil Lewis (1939).

Recollections of the Table Talk of Samuel Rogers to which is added Porsoniana (1856).

Diary, Reminiscences, and Correspondence of Henry Crabb Robinson. Thomas Sadler, Ph.D. (1872).

The Crown of Wild Olive. John Ruskin (1866).

Hortus Inclusus. John Ruskin (1887).

Letters to M. G. and H. G. John Ruskin. With a Preface by the Right Hon. G. Wyndham (1903).

Letters of John Ruskin to Charles Eliot Norton. C. E. Norton (1905).

Letters of John Ruskin. E. T. Cook and Alexander Wedderburn (1909).

Life of John Ruskin. E. T. Cook (1911).

Last Pages from a Journal with other Papers. Mark Rutherford. Edited by his Wife (1915).

Letters to Three Friends. William Hale White (Mark Rutherford) (1924).

A Short View of Tragedy. Thomas Rymer (1693).

Life of Sir Walter Scott. J. G. Lockhart (1837–8).

Bibliography

The Journal of Sir Walter Scott from the Original Manuscript at Abbotsford. (1891).

Familiar Letters of Sir Walter Scott. (1894).

Letters of Anna Seward. (1811).

Biographica. Anna Seward (1799).

The Irrational Knot. Bernard Shaw (1905).

Man and Superman. Bernard Shaw (1903).

Bernard Shaw. Frank Harris (1931).

Ellen Terry and Bernard Shaw: A Correspondence. Christopher St. John (1931).

Life of Shelley. Thomas Jefferson Hogg. (1858).

Letters of Percy Bysshe Shelley. Roger Ingpen (1915).

Letters, Verses and Other Writings. Edith Sichell (1918).

Penny Foolish: A Book of Tirades and Panegyrics. Sir Osbert Sitwell (1935).

Memoir of Sydney Smith. Lord Holland (1855).

Anecdotes . . . from the Conversation of Mr. Pope and other eminent persons of his times. By the Rev. Joseph Spence. S. W. Singer (1858).

Selections from the Letters of Robert Southey. J. W. Warter (1956).

Life of John Sterling. Thomas Carlyle (1851).

Correspondence between John Sterling and Ralph Waldo Emerson. Edward Waldo Emerson (1897).

Letters of Robert Louis Stevenson to his Family and Friends. Sidney Colvin (1901).

Journal to Stella, A.D. 1710–1713. Jonathan Swift. Frederick Ryland (Bohn Ed. 1924).

Correspondence of Jonathan Swift. F. Ecrington Ball (1913).

John Addington Symonds: a Biography. Horatio F. Brown (1894).

Letters of Algernon Charles Swinburne. Thomas Hake and Arthur Compton-Rickett (1918).

Letters of Lady Louisa Stuart to Miss Louisa Clinton. Hon. James A. Home (1903).

Records of Tennyson, Ruskin and Browning. Anne Ritchie (1892).

Essays by Sir William Temple. J. A. Nicklin (n.d.).

Alfred, Lord Tennyson: a Memoir. Hallam, Lord Tennyson (1897).

Life and Letters of Edward Thomas. John Moore (1939).

Bibliography

Summer: from the Journal of Henry D. Thoreau. H. G. O. Blake (1884).

Cape Cod. Henry David Thoreau (1893).

Essays and Other Writings of Henry Thoreau. Will H. Dircks (Scott Library Ed.).

Thoreau: the Poet-Naturalist. William Ellery Channing. F. B. Sanborn (1902).

Records of Shelley, Byron and the Author. Edward John Trelawney (1878).

Trollope: a Commentary. Michael Sadleir (1927).

Autobiography, Anthony Trollope, 1883. Michael Sadleir (1923).

Walpoliana. (1800.)

Letters of Horace Walpole, Fourth Earl of Orford. Peter Cunningham (1891).

Supplement to the Letters of Horace Walpole, Fourth Earl of Orford. Paget Toynbee, M.A., D.Litt. (1918).

Experiment in Autobiography. H. G. Wells (1934).

The Journal of the Rev. John Wesley, A.M. Nehemiah Curnock [n.d.].

The Lives of Dr. John Donne, Sir Henry Wotton, Mr. Richard Hooker and Mr. George Herbert. Izaak Walton (1675).

Zootomia, or Observations on the Present Manners of the English. Richard Whitlock (1654).

Specimen Days and Collect. Walt Whitman (1882).

In re Walt Whitman. Edited by His Literary Executors, Horace L. Traubel, Richard Maurice Bucke, Thomas B. Harned (1893).

With Walt Whitman in Camden. Horace Traubel (1908).

Aubrey de Vere: a Memoir. Wilfrid Ward (1904).

Experiment in Autobiography. H. G. Wells (1934).

The Groombridge Diary. Dorothy Hale White (1925).

Journals of Dorothy Wordsworth. William Knight (1897).

Early Letters of William and Dorothy Wordsworth, 1787–1805. E. de Selincourt (1935).

Life and Letters of George Wyndham. J. W. MacKail and Guy Wyndham [n.d.].

INDEX OF AUTHORS

Quoted from or referred to in the text

Index of Authors

Burne-Jones, Georgiana, Lady, 32

Burney, Fanny, 21, 22, 174–5

Burns, Robert, 15, 105, 126, 135, 159, 228

Burton, Robert, 71, 240

Butler, Samuel, 42, 43, 157, 207–8, 239

Byron, Lord, 16, 48, 71, 77, 79, 105, 106, 108, 113, 123, 125, 129, 154, 160–1, 164–5, 170–2, 203–5, 215, 225, 233, 240, 243

Caesar, Julius, 14, 46

Carlyle, Jane Welsh, 43, 51, 59, 78–9, 87, 93, 94, 113, 150, 154, 172, 192, 198

Carlyle, Thomas, 16, 24, 27, 40, 42, 43, 50, 51, 59, 60–1, 78–9, 83, 86, 93, 94, 99, 100, 122, 148–9, 150, 154, 165, 172, 178–9, 186–7, 192, 194, 198, 205, 215, 235–7, 243

Cecil, Lord David, 241

Cervantes, Miguel, 214

Chaucer, Geoffrey, 69

Chesterfield, Lord, 205, 240

Chesterton, G. K., 32, 156

Cicero, 14, 20, 117

Clifford, Mrs. W. K., 108

Clough, A. H., 51, 132, 161, 199, 220

Cobbett, William, 17

Coleridge, Hartley, 179, 187, 240

Coleridge, H. N., 105

Coleridge, S. T., 23, 26, 125, 142, 144, 165, 170, 196, 201–2, 204–5, 210–11, 215, 225, 239–40

Colvin, Sir Sidney, 221

Congreve, William, 73, 157–8

Conrad, Joseph, 200, 207

Corelli, Marie, 151

Cory, William, 64, 126, 155, 201–2

Cowper, William, 98, 134–5, 157, 185–6, 204, 212

Crabbe, George, 53

Craik, G. L., 93

Croker, J. W., 90, 213, 222, 233

Crosland, T. W. H., 162

Darwin, Erasmus, 213

Davidson, John, 162

Davies, W. H., 151

Davy, Sir Humphry, 17

Dickens, Charles, 30, 87, 141, 143, 206, 215, 217–18, 237, 244

Dickinson, G. Lowes, 56, 87

Diogenes, 50

Disraeli, Benjamin, 180, 222

Dobson, Austin, 245

Donne, John, 230

Donne, W. B., 50, 174, 242

Doughty, Charles, 217

Dowden, Edward, 188, 194

Dryden, John, 80, 211

Eden, Emily, 79, 117–18, 187, 217–18

Edgeworth, Maria, 114

Eliot, George, 26, 112, 207

Ellis, T. F., 62, 138

Emerson, R. W., 27, 28, 40, 51, 87, 89, 100, 130, 132, 165, 194, 199, 205–6, 209, 215, 235–8

Esher, Reginald, Viscount, 202

Evelyn, John, 45

Ewing, Joanna Horatia, 55, 113

258

Index of Authors

Index of Authors

Index of Authors

Index of Authors

Index of Authors

Index of Authors